2433A: Microsoft® Visual Basic® Scripting Edition and Microsoft Windows® Script Host Essentials

Microsoft®

Course Number: 2433A
Part Number: X10-24588
Released: 05/2001

END-USER LICENSE AGREEMENT FOR MICROSOFT OFFICIAL CURRICULUM COURSEWARE –STUDENT EDITION

PLEASE READ THIS END-USER LICENSE AGREEMENT ("EULA") CAREFULLY. BY USING THE MATERIALS AND/OR USING OR INSTALLING THE SOFTWARE THAT ACCOMPANIES THIS EULA (COLLECTIVELY, THE "LICENSED CONTENT"), YOU AGREE TO THE TERMS OF THIS EULA. IF YOU DO NOT AGREE, DO NOT USE THE LICENSED CONTENT.

1.　　　**GENERAL.** This EULA is a legal agreement between you (either an individual or a single entity) and Microsoft Corporation ("Microsoft"). This EULA governs the Licensed Content, which includes computer software (including online and electronic documentation), training materials, and any other associated media and printed materials. This EULA applies to updates, supplements, add-on components, and Internet-based services components of the Licensed Content that Microsoft may provide or make available to you unless Microsoft provides other terms with the update, supplement, add-on component, or Internet-based services component. Microsoft reserves the right to discontinue any Internet-based services provided to you or made available to you through the use of the Licensed Content. This EULA also governs any product support services relating to the Licensed Content except as may be included in another agreement between you and Microsoft. An amendment or addendum to this EULA may accompany the Licensed Content.

2.　　　**GENERAL GRANT OF LICENSE.** Microsoft grants you the following rights, conditioned on your compliance with all the terms and conditions of this EULA. Microsoft grants you a limited, non-exclusive, royalty-free license to install and use the Licensed Content solely in conjunction with your participation as a student in an Authorized Training Session (as defined below). You may install and use one copy of the software on a single computer, device, workstation, terminal, or other digital electronic or analog device ("Device"). You may make a second copy of the software and install it on a portable Device for the exclusive use of the person who is the primary user of the first copy of the software. A license for the software may not be shared for use by multiple end users. An "Authorized Training Session" means a training session conducted at a Microsoft Certified Technical Education Center, an IT Academy, via a Microsoft Certified Partner, or such other entity as Microsoft may designate from time to time in writing, by a Microsoft Certified Trainer (for more information on these entities, please visit www.microsoft.com). WITHOUT LIMITING THE FOREGOING, COPYING OR REPRODUCTION OF THE LICENSED CONTENT TO ANY SERVER OR LOCATION FOR FURTHER REPRODUCTION OR REDISTRIBUTION IS EXPRESSLY PROHIBITED.

3.　　　**DESCRIPTION OF OTHER RIGHTS AND LICENSE LIMITATIONS**

　　　3.1　　*Use of Documentation and Printed Training Materials.*

　　　　　3.1.1　　The documents and related graphics included in the Licensed Content may include technical inaccuracies or typographical errors. Changes are periodically made to the content. Microsoft may make improvements and/or changes in any of the components of the Licensed Content at any time without notice. The names of companies, products, people, characters and/or data mentioned in the Licensed Content may be fictitious and are in no way intended to represent any real individual, company, product or event, unless otherwise noted.

　　　　　3.1.2　　Microsoft grants you the right to reproduce portions of documents (such as student workbooks, white papers, press releases, datasheets and FAQs) (the "Documents") provided with the Licensed Content. You may not print any book (either electronic or print version) in its entirety. If you choose to reproduce Documents, you agree that: (a) use of such printed Documents will be solely in conjunction with your personal training use; (b) the Documents will not republished or posted on any network computer or broadcast in any media; (c) any reproduction will include either the Document's original copyright notice or a copyright notice to Microsoft's benefit substantially in the format provided below; and (d) to comply with all terms and conditions of this EULA. In addition, no modifications may made to any Document.

　　　　　Form of Notice:

　　　　　© 2001. Reprinted with permission by Microsoft Corporation. All rights reserved.

　　　　　Microsoft and Windows are either registered trademarks or trademarks of Microsoft Corporation in the US and/or other countries. Other product and company names mentioned herein may be the trademarks of their respective owners.

　　　3.2　　*Use of Media Elements.* The Licensed Content may include certain photographs, clip art, animations, sounds, music, and video clips (together "Media Elements"). You may not modify these Media Elements.

　　　3.3　　*Use of Sample Code.* In the event that the Licensed Content includes sample code in source or object format ("Sample Code"), Microsoft grants you a limited, non-exclusive, royalty-free license to use, copy and modify the Sample Code; if you elect to exercise the foregoing rights, you agree to comply with all other terms and conditions of this EULA, including without limitation Sections 3.4, 3.5, and 6.

　　　3.4　　*Permitted Modifications.* In the event that you exercise any rights provided under this EULA to create modifications of the Licensed Content, you agree that any such modifications: (a) will not be used for providing training where a fee is charged in public or private classes; (b) indemnify, hold harmless, and defend Microsoft from and against any claims or lawsuits, including attorneys' fees, which arise from or result from your use of any modified version of the Licensed Content; and (c) not to transfer or assign any rights to any modified version of the Licensed Content to any third party without the express written permission of Microsoft.

3.5   *Reproduction/Redistribution Licensed Content.* Except as expressly provided in this EULA, you may not reproduce or distribute the Licensed Content or any portion thereof (including any permitted modifications) to any third parties without the express written permission of Microsoft.

4.   **RESERVATION OF RIGHTS AND OWNERSHIP.** Microsoft reserves all rights not expressly granted to you in this EULA. The Licensed Content is protected by copyright and other intellectual property laws and treaties. Microsoft or its suppliers own the title, copyright, and other intellectual property rights in the Licensed Content. You may not remove or obscure any copyright, trademark or patent notices that appear on the Licensed Content, or any components thereof, as delivered to you. **The Licensed Content is licensed, not sold.**

5.   **LIMITATIONS ON REVERSE ENGINEERING, DECOMPILATION, AND DISASSEMBLY.** You may not reverse engineer, decompile, or disassemble the Software or Media Elements, except and only to the extent that such activity is expressly permitted by applicable law notwithstanding this limitation.

6.   **LIMITATIONS ON SALE, RENTAL, ETC. AND CERTAIN ASSIGNMENTS.** You may not provide commercial hosting services with, sell, rent, lease, lend, sublicense, or assign copies of the Licensed Content, or any portion thereof (including any permitted modifications thereof) on a stand-alone basis or as part of any collection, product or service.

7.   **CONSENT TO USE OF DATA.** You agree that Microsoft and its affiliates may collect and use technical information gathered as part of the product support services provided to you, if any, related to the Licensed Content. Microsoft may use this information solely to improve our products or to provide customized services or technologies to you and will not disclose this information in a form that personally identifies you.

8.   **LINKS TO THIRD PARTY SITES.** You may link to third party sites through the use of the Licensed Content. The third party sites are not under the control of Microsoft, and Microsoft is not responsible for the contents of any third party sites, any links contained in third party sites, or any changes or updates to third party sites. Microsoft is not responsible for webcasting or any other form of transmission received from any third party sites. Microsoft is providing these links to third party sites to you only as a convenience, and the inclusion of any link does not imply an endorsement by Microsoft of the third party site.

9.   **ADDITIONAL LICENSED CONTENT/SERVICES.** This EULA applies to updates, supplements, add-on components, or Internet-based services components, of the Licensed Content that Microsoft may provide to you or make available to you after the date you obtain your initial copy of the Licensed Content, unless we provide other terms along with the update, supplement, add-on component, or Internet-based services component. Microsoft reserves the right to discontinue any Internet-based services provided to you or made available to you through the use of the Licensed Content.

10.   **U.S. GOVERNMENT LICENSE RIGHTS.** All software provided to the U.S. Government pursuant to solicitations issued on or after December 1, 1995 is provided with the commercial license rights and restrictions described elsewhere herein. All software provided to the U.S. Government pursuant to solicitations issued prior to December 1, 1995 is provided with "Restricted Rights" as provided for in FAR, 48 CFR 52.227-14 (JUNE 1987) or DFAR, 48 CFR 252.227-7013 (OCT 1988), as applicable.

11.   **EXPORT RESTRICTIONS.** You acknowledge that the Licensed Content is subject to U.S. export jurisdiction. You agree to comply with all applicable international and national laws that apply to the Licensed Content, including the U.S. Export Administration Regulations, as well as end-user, end-use, and destination restrictions issued by U.S. and other governments. For additional information see <http://www.microsoft.com/exporting/>.

12.   **TRANSFER.** The initial user of the Licensed Content may make a one-time permanent transfer of this EULA and Licensed Content to another end user, provided the initial user retains no copies of the Licensed Content. The transfer may not be an indirect transfer, such as a consignment. Prior to the transfer, the end user receiving the Licensed Content must agree to all the EULA terms.

13.   **"NOT FOR RESALE" LICENSED CONTENT.** Licensed Content identified as "Not For Resale" or "NFR," may not be sold or otherwise transferred for value, or used for any purpose other than demonstration, test or evaluation.

14.   **TERMINATION.** Without prejudice to any other rights, Microsoft may terminate this EULA if you fail to comply with the terms and conditions of this EULA. In such event, you must destroy all copies of the Licensed Content and all of its component parts.

15.   <u>**DISCLAIMER OF WARRANTIES.**</u> **TO THE MAXIMUM EXTENT PERMITTED BY APPLICABLE LAW, MICROSOFT AND ITS SUPPLIERS PROVIDE THE LICENSED CONTENT AND SUPPORT SERVICES (IF ANY)** *AS IS AND WITH ALL FAULTS,* **AND MICROSOFT AND ITS SUPPLIERS HEREBY DISCLAIM ALL OTHER WARRANTIES AND CONDITIONS, WHETHER EXPRESS, IMPLIED OR STATUTORY, INCLUDING, BUT NOT LIMITED TO, ANY (IF ANY) IMPLIED WARRANTIES, DUTIES OR CONDITIONS OF MERCHANTABILITY, OF FITNESS FOR A PARTICULAR PURPOSE, OF RELIABILITY OR AVAILABILITY, OF ACCURACY OR COMPLETENESS OF RESPONSES, OF RESULTS, OF WORKMANLIKE EFFORT, OF LACK OF VIRUSES, AND OF LACK OF NEGLIGENCE, ALL WITH REGARD TO THE LICENSED CONTENT, AND THE PROVISION OF OR FAILURE TO PROVIDE SUPPORT OR OTHER SERVICES, INFORMATION, SOFTWARE, AND RELATED CONTENT THROUGH THE LICENSED CONTENT, OR OTHERWISE ARISING OUT OF THE USE OF THE LICENSED CONTENT. ALSO, THERE IS NO WARRANTY OR CONDITION OF TITLE, QUIET ENJOYMENT, QUIET POSSESSION, CORRESPONDENCE TO DESCRIPTION OR NON-INFRINGEMENT WITH REGARD TO THE LICENSED CONTENT. THE ENTIRE RISK AS TO THE QUALITY, OR ARISING OUT OF THE USE OR PERFORMANCE OF THE LICENSED CONTENT, AND ANY SUPPORT SERVICES, REMAINS WITH YOU.**

16.   <u>**EXCLUSION OF INCIDENTAL, CONSEQUENTIAL AND CERTAIN OTHER DAMAGES.**</u> **TO THE MAXIMUM EXTENT PERMITTED BY APPLICABLE LAW, IN NO EVENT SHALL MICROSOFT OR ITS SUPPLIERS BE LIABLE FOR ANY SPECIAL, INCIDENTAL, PUNITIVE, INDIRECT, OR CONSEQUENTIAL DAMAGES WHATSOEVER (INCLUDING, BUT NOT**

LIMITED TO, DAMAGES FOR LOSS OF PROFITS OR CONFIDENTIAL OR OTHER INFORMATION, FOR BUSINESS INTERRUPTION, FOR PERSONAL INJURY, FOR LOSS OF PRIVACY, FOR FAILURE TO MEET ANY DUTY INCLUDING OF GOOD FAITH OR OF REASONABLE CARE, FOR NEGLIGENCE, AND FOR ANY OTHER PECUNIARY OR OTHER LOSS WHATSOEVER) ARISING OUT OF OR IN ANY WAY RELATED TO THE USE OF OR INABILITY TO USE THE LICENSED CONTENT, THE PROVISION OF OR FAILURE TO PROVIDE SUPPORT OR OTHER SERVICES, INFORMATION, SOFTWARE, AND RELATED CONTENT THROUGH THE LICENSED CONTENT, OR OTHERWISE ARISING OUT OF THE USE OF THE LICENSED CONTENT, OR OTHERWISE UNDER OR IN CONNECTION WITH ANY PROVISION OF THIS EULA, EVEN IN THE EVENT OF THE FAULT, TORT (INCLUDING NEGLIGENCE), MISREPRESENTATION, STRICT LIABILITY, BREACH OF CONTRACT OR BREACH OF WARRANTY OF MICROSOFT OR ANY SUPPLIER, AND EVEN IF MICROSOFT OR ANY SUPPLIER HAS BEEN ADVISED OF THE POSSIBILITY OF SUCH DAMAGES. BECAUSE SOME STATES/JURISDICTIONS DO NOT ALLOW THE EXCLUSION OR LIMITATION OF LIABILITY FOR CONSEQUENTIAL OR INCIDENTAL DAMAGES, THE ABOVE LIMITATION MAY NOT APPLY TO YOU.

17. <u>LIMITATION OF LIABILITY AND REMEDIES.</u> NOTWITHSTANDING ANY DAMAGES THAT YOU MIGHT INCUR FOR ANY REASON WHATSOEVER (INCLUDING, WITHOUT LIMITATION, ALL DAMAGES REFERENCED HEREIN AND ALL DIRECT OR GENERAL DAMAGES IN CONTRACT OR ANYTHING ELSE), THE ENTIRE LIABILITY OF MICROSOFT AND ANY OF ITS SUPPLIERS UNDER ANY PROVISION OF THIS EULA AND YOUR EXCLUSIVE REMEDY HEREUNDER SHALL BE LIMITED TO THE GREATER OF THE ACTUAL DAMAGES YOU INCUR IN REASONABLE RELIANCE ON THE LICENSED CONTENT UP TO THE AMOUNT ACTUALLY PAID BY YOU FOR THE LICENSED CONTENT OR US$5.00. THE FOREGOING LIMITATIONS, EXCLUSIONS AND DISCLAIMERS SHALL APPLY TO THE MAXIMUM EXTENT PERMITTED BY APPLICABLE LAW, EVEN IF ANY REMEDY FAILS ITS ESSENTIAL PURPOSE.

18. **APPLICABLE LAW.** If you acquired this Licensed Content in the United States, this EULA is governed by the laws of the State of Washington. If you acquired this Licensed Content in Canada, unless expressly prohibited by local law, this EULA is governed by the laws in force in the Province of Ontario, Canada; and, in respect of any dispute which may arise hereunder, you consent to the jurisdiction of the federal and provincial courts sitting in Toronto, Ontario. If you acquired this Licensed Content in the European Union, Iceland, Norway, or Switzerland, then local law applies. If you acquired this Licensed Content in any other country, then local law may apply.

19. **ENTIRE AGREEMENT; SEVERABILITY.** This EULA (including any addendum or amendment to this EULA which is included with the Licensed Content) are the entire agreement between you and Microsoft relating to the Licensed Content and the support services (if any) and they supersede all prior or contemporaneous oral or written communications, proposals and representations with respect to the Licensed Content or any other subject matter covered by this EULA. To the extent the terms of any Microsoft policies or programs for support services conflict with the terms of this EULA, the terms of this EULA shall control. If any provision of this EULA is held to be void, invalid, unenforceable or illegal, the other provisions shall continue in full force and effect.

Should you have any questions concerning this EULA, or if you desire to contact Microsoft for any reason, please use the address information enclosed in this Licensed Content to contact the Microsoft subsidiary serving your country or visit Microsoft on the World Wide Web at http://www.microsoft.com.

Si vous avez acquis votre Contenu Sous Licence Microsoft au CANADA :

DÉNI DE GARANTIES. Dans la mesure maximale permise par les lois applicables, le Contenu Sous Licence et les services de soutien technique (le cas échéant) sont fournis *TELS QUELS ET AVEC TOUS LES DÉFAUTS* par Microsoft et ses fournisseurs, lesquels par les présentes dénient toutes autres garanties et conditions expresses, implicites ou en vertu de la loi, notamment, mais sans limitation, (le cas échéant) les garanties, devoirs ou conditions implicites de qualité marchande, d'adaptation à une fin usage particulière, de fiabilité ou de disponibilité, d'exactitude ou d'exhaustivité des réponses, des résultats, des efforts déployés selon les règles de l'art, d'absence de virus et d'absence de négligence, le tout à l'égard du Contenu Sous Licence et de la prestation des services de soutien technique ou de l'omission de la 'une telle prestation des services de soutien technique ou à l'égard de la fourniture ou de l'omission de la fourniture de tous autres services, renseignements, Contenus Sous Licence, et contenu qui s'y rapporte grâce au Contenu Sous Licence ou provenant autrement de l'utilisation du Contenu Sous Licence. PAR AILLEURS, IL N'Y A AUCUNE GARANTIE OU CONDITION QUANT AU TITRE DE PROPRIÉTÉ, À LA JOUISSANCE OU LA POSSESSION PAISIBLE, À LA CONCORDANCE À UNE DESCRIPTION NI QUANT À UNE ABSENCE DE CONTREFAÇON CONCERNANT LE CONTENU SOUS LICENCE.

<u>EXCLUSION DES DOMMAGES ACCESSOIRES, INDIRECTS ET DE CERTAINS AUTRES DOMMAGES.</u> DANS LA MESURE MAXIMALE PERMISE PAR LES LOIS APPLICABLES, EN AUCUN CAS MICROSOFT OU SES FOURNISSEURS NE SERONT RESPONSABLES DES DOMMAGES SPÉCIAUX, CONSÉCUTIFS, ACCESSOIRES OU INDIRECTS DE QUELQUE NATURE QUE CE SOIT (NOTAMMENT, LES DOMMAGES À L'ÉGARD DU MANQUE À GAGNER OU DE LA DIVULGATION DE RENSEIGNEMENTS CONFIDENTIELS OU AUTRES, DE LA PERTE D'EXPLOITATION, DE BLESSURES CORPORELLES, DE LA VIOLATION DE LA VIE PRIVÉE, DE L'OMISSION DE REMPLIR TOUT DEVOIR, Y COMPRIS D'AGIR DE BONNE FOI OU D'EXERCER UN SOIN RAISONNABLE, DE LA NÉGLIGENCE ET DE TOUTE AUTRE PERTE PÉCUNIAIRE OU AUTRE PERTE

DE QUELQUE NATURE QUE CE SOIT) SE RAPPORTANT DE QUELQUE MANIÈRE QUE CE SOIT À L'UTILISATION DU CONTENU SOUS LICENCE OU À L'INCAPACITÉ DE S'EN SERVIR, À LA PRESTATION OU À L'OMISSION DE LA 'UNE TELLE PRESTATION DE SERVICES DE SOUTIEN TECHNIQUE OU À LA FOURNITURE OU À L'OMISSION DE LA FOURNITURE DE TOUS AUTRES SERVICES, RENSEIGNEMENTS, CONTENUS SOUS LICENCE, ET CONTENU QUI S'Y RAPPORTE GRÂCE AU CONTENU SOUS LICENCE OU PROVENANT AUTREMENT DE L'UTILISATION DU CONTENU SOUS LICENCE OU AUTREMENT AUX TERMES DE TOUTE DISPOSITION DE LA U PRÉSENTE CONVENTION EULA OU RELATIVEMENT À UNE TELLE DISPOSITION, MÊME EN CAS DE FAUTE, DE DÉLIT CIVIL (Y COMPRIS LA NÉGLIGENCE), DE RESPONSABILITÉ STRICTE, DE VIOLATION DE CONTRAT OU DE VIOLATION DE GARANTIE DE MICROSOFT OU DE TOUT FOURNISSEUR ET MÊME SI MICROSOFT OU TOUT FOURNISSEUR A ÉTÉ AVISÉ DE LA POSSIBILITÉ DE TELS DOMMAGES.

LIMITATION DE RESPONSABILITÉ ET RECOURS.   MALGRÉ LES DOMMAGES QUE VOUS PUISSIEZ SUBIR POUR QUELQUE MOTIF QUE CE SOIT (NOTAMMENT, MAIS SANS LIMITATION, TOUS LES DOMMAGES SUSMENTIONNÉS ET TOUS LES DOMMAGES DIRECTS OU GÉNÉRAUX OU AUTRES), LA SEULE RESPONSABILITÉ 'OBLIGATION INTÉGRALE DE MICROSOFT ET DE L'UN OU L'AUTRE DE SES FOURNISSEURS AUX TERMES DE TOUTE DISPOSITION DEU LA PRÉSENTE CONVENTION EULA ET VOTRE RECOURS EXCLUSIF À L'ÉGARD DE TOUT CE QUI PRÉCÈDE SE LIMITE AU PLUS ÉLEVÉ ENTRE LES MONTANTS SUIVANTS : LE MONTANT QUE VOUS AVEZ RÉELLEMENT PAYÉ POUR LE CONTENU SOUS LICENCE OU 5,00 $US. LES LIMITES, EXCLUSIONS ET DÉNIS QUI PRÉCÈDENT (Y COMPRIS LES CLAUSES CI-DESSUS), S'APPLIQUENT DANS LA MESURE MAXIMALE PERMISE PAR LES LOIS APPLICABLES, MÊME SI TOUT RECOURS N'ATTEINT PAS SON BUT ESSENTIEL.

À moins que cela ne soit prohibé par le droit local applicable, la présente Convention est régie par les lois de la province d'Ontario, Canada. Vous consentez Chacune des parties à la présente reconnaît irrévocablement à la compétence des tribunaux fédéraux et provinciaux siégeant à Toronto, dans de la province d'Ontario et consent à instituer tout litige qui pourrait découler de la présente auprès des tribunaux situés dans le district judiciaire de York, province d'Ontario.

Au cas où vous auriez des questions concernant cette licence ou que vous désiriez vous mettre en rapport avec Microsoft pour quelque raison que ce soit, veuillez utiliser l'information contenue dans le Contenu Sous Licence pour contacter la filiale de succursale Microsoft desservant votre pays, dont l'adresse est fournie dans ce produit, ou visitez écrivez à : Microsoft sur le World Wide Web à http://www.microsoft.com

Contents

About This Course

This section provides you with a brief description of the course, audience, suggested prerequisites, and course objectives.

Description

This three-day instructor-led course provides students with the knowledge and experience to develop their own administrative scripts with Microsoft® Visual Basic® Scripting Edition (VBScript). The course focuses on writing scripts for commonly encountered administrative tasks. The course also expands upon these concepts so that they embrace more general programming issues.

Audience

This course is intended for Microsoft Windows® 2000 systems administrators who want to learn how to develop administrative scripts for their enterprise networks.

In addition, anyone who wants an introduction to the VBScript programming language will benefit from this course.

Student Prerequisites

This course requires that students meet the following prerequisites. The students must have:

- Practical experience using and administering Windows 2000.
- Practical experience using and administering Active Directory™ directory service.
- Practical experience using and administering system security.
- Practical experience using and administering services.
- Practical experience using systems management information.
- Awareness of the potential uses of logon scripts.

In addition, it is desirable that students have had some exposure to writing batch files.

Course Objectives

After completing this course, students will be able to:

- Describe Windows Script Host (WSH) and associated scripting technologies.
- Use objects in code written in Visual Basic Scripting Edition.
- Master the essentials of the VBScript language.
- Master debugging and error handling with VBScript.
- Use VBScript to interact with Active Directory Services Interface (ADSI).
- Develop logon, logoff, startup, and shutdown scripts.
- Develop scripts that perform common administrative tasks.
- Identify ways to use VBScript in other scenarios.

Student Materials Compact Disc Contents

The Student Materials compact disc contains the following files and folders:

- *Autorun.exe.* When the CD is inserted into the CD-ROM drive, or when you double-click the autorun.exe file, this file opens the CD and allows you to browse the Student Materials CD or install Internet Explorer.

- *Default.htm.* This file opens the Student Materials Web page. It provides you with resources pertaining to this course, including additional reading, review and lab answers, lab files, multimedia presentations, and course-related Web sites.

- *Readme.txt.* This file contains a description of the compact disc contents and setup instructions in ASCII format (non-Microsoft Word document).

- *2433A_ms.doc.* This file is the Manual Classroom Setup Guide. It contains the steps for manually installing the classroom computers.

- *Democode.* This folder contains demonstration code. If there is no demonstration code, the Democode folder does not appear.

- *Fonts.* This folder contains fonts that are required to view the Microsoft PowerPoint presentation and Web-based materials.

- *Ie5.* This folder contains Microsoft Internet Explorer 5.5.

- *Labs.* This folder contains files that are used in the hands-on labs. These files may be used to prepare the student computers for the hands-on labs.

- *Menu.* This folder contains elements for autorun.exe.

- *Mplayer.* This folder contains files that are required to install Microsoft Windows Media™ Player.

- *Practices.* This folder contains files that are used in the hands-on practices. If there are no practices, the Practices folder does not appear.

- *PrimalSCRIPT.* This folder contains files that are required to install PrimalSCRIPT.

- *Setup.* This folder contains additional files that may be required for lab setup. If no additional files are required, the Setup folder does not appear.

- *Webfiles.* This folder contains the files that are required to view the Student Materials Web page.

- *Wordview.* This folder contains the Word Viewer that is used to view any Word document (.doc) files that are included on the compact disc.

Document Conventions

The following conventions are used in course materials to distinguish elements of the text.

Convention	Use
◆	Indicates an introductory page. This symbol appears next to a topic heading when additional information on the topic is covered on the page or pages that follow it.
bold	Represents commands, command options, and syntax that must be typed exactly as shown. It also indicates commands on menus and buttons, dialog box titles and options, and icon and menu names.
italic	In syntax statements or descriptive text, indicates argument names or placeholders for variable information. Italic is also used for introducing new terms, for book titles, and for emphasis in the text.
Title Capitals	Indicate domain names, user names, computer names, directory names, and folder and file names, except when specifically referring to case-sensitive names. Unless otherwise indicated, you can use lowercase letters when you type a directory name or file name in a dialog box or at a command prompt.
ALL CAPITALS	Indicate the names of keys, key sequences, and key combinations—for example, ALT+SPACEBAR.
monospace	Represents code samples or examples of screen text.
[ ]	In syntax statements, enclose optional items. For example, [*filename*] in command syntax indicates that you can choose to type a file name with the command. Type only the information within the brackets, not the brackets themselves.
{ }	In syntax statements, enclose required items. Type only the information within the braces, not the braces themselves.
|	In syntax statements, separates an either/or choice.
▶	Indicates a procedure with sequential steps.
...	In syntax statements, specifies that the preceding item may be repeated.
. . .	Represents an omitted portion of a code sample.

msdn training

Introduction

Contents

Microsoft®

Introduction

- **Name**
- **Company Affiliation**
- **Title/Function**
- **Job Responsibility**
- **Scripting and Programming Experience**
- **Microsoft Windows 2000 Experience**
- **Expectations for the Course**

Course Materials

- **Name Card**
- **Student Workbook**
- **Student Materials Compact Disc**
- **Course Evaluation**

The following materials are included with your kit:

- *Name card.* Write your name on both sides of the name card.

- *Student workbook.* The student workbook contains the material covered in class, in addition to the hands-on lab exercises.

- *Student Materials compact disc.* The Student Materials compact disc contains the Web page that provides you with links to resources pertaining to this course, including additional readings, review and lab answers, lab files, multimedia presentations, and course-related Web sites.

Note To open the Web page, insert the Student Materials compact disc into the CD-ROM drive, and then in the root directory of the compact disc, double-click **Autorun.exe** or **Default.htm**.

- *Course evaluation.* To provide feedback on the instructor, course, and software product, send e-mail to mstrain@microsoft.com. Be sure to type **Course 2433A** in the subject line. Your comments will help us improve future courses.

To provide additional comments or inquire about the Microsoft Certified Professional program, send e-mail to mcp@msprograms.com.

Prerequisites

- Course 1560, *Updating Support Skills from Microsoft Windows NT 4.0 to Windows 2000*, or equivalent knowledge

- Experience with a Batch Language Is an Advantage

- No Programming Experience Is Assumed

This course requires that you meet the following prerequisites:

- Attended course 1560, *Updating Support Skills from Microsoft® Windows® NT® 4.0 to Microsoft Windows 2000* or have equivalent knowledge.

- A good understanding of Windows 2000 and knowledge of its features.

  This course covers the implementation of some of these features that use Microsoft Visual Basic® Scripting Edition (VBScript). There is no time available to explain how the features of Windows 2000 work.

- Experience with a Batch language, such as the Microsoft MS-DOS® Command Language, is an advantage.

No previous programming experience is required.

Course Outline

- **Module 1: Overview of Windows Scripting Technologies**
- **Module 2: Working with Objects**
- **Module 3: Script Logic**
- **Module 4: Error Handling and Debugging**
- **Module 5: Understanding ADSI**
- **Module 6: Creating Logon Scripts**
- **Module 7: Administrative Scripts**
- **Module 8: Beyond the Basics**

Module 1, "Overview of Windows Scripting Technologies," introduces Windows Script Technologies (WST) and explains what components make up WST. This module covers information on configuring your script's execution and the Windows Script Hose (WSH) environment. This module also compares how scripting differs from batch files, and provides guidance on which of the two main scripting languages (VBScript and Microsoft JScript®) you should choose to perform certain tasks.

Module 2, "Working with Objects," explains the object terminology and how scripts use objects. This module introduces reference tools to help you work with various object models. Finally, this module introduces some of the object models that are often used in scripting.

Module 3, "Script Logic," explains the logic and format used in scripting. The module outlines the recommended scripting format and template. The module introduces the principles and terminology of Visual Basic Scripting Edition and identifies the logic of various statements, conditions, and loops.

Module 4, "Error Handling and Debugging," describes the run-time error-handling techniques that you can use with the Visual Basic Scripting Edition. You will learn how to use the **Err** object and how to set run-time error traps. Additionally, the module introduces debugging concepts and tools that enable you to quickly and easily find logic errors in your code.

Module 5, "Understanding ADSI," focuses exclusively on how Active Directory™ Services Interface (ADSI) is used to find, create, and modify objects in the Active Directory directory service.

Module 6, "Creating Logon Scripts," focuses on how Windows 2000 can implement logon, logoff, startup, and shutdown scripts. It also covers how you can use batch files to support legacy clients on the network. Finally, this module covers some of the script management issues involved in supporting a logon script in an enterprise network.

Module 7, "Administrative Scripts," focuses on several common tasks that an administrator is likely to use script for. These include modifying the registry and using **FileSystemObject** to manage files and folders on a computer's hard disk drive.

Module 8, "Beyond the Basics," provides an insight into how you can use Windows Script with other components to enhance other areas of operations. The module details how you can use technologies such as Windows Script Files (WSF), Windows Management Instrumentation (WMI), and Active Server Pages (ASP) to enhance scripts. In addition, the module identifies reference material that will aid your future learning.

Expectations

- **What This Course Provides:**
  - A detailed introduction to Windows Script Technologies
  - A detailed introduction to writing code in VBScript
  - Examples of working scripts
  - Reference materials
- **What This Course Does Not Provide:**
  - A description of all script functionality

This course provides a complete introduction to Windows Script Technologies (WST) and the Visual Basic Scripting Edition programming language. However, it is important to understand what the course will and will not provide.

What This Course Provides

This course provides you with a detailed introduction to all of the components that make up the WST available in Windows today. It does this by providing working examples of basic concepts and techniques that you must understand to develop administrative scripts. This course includes reference material that you can use when working with script in the future. The aim of this course is to provide you with a basic level of experience with WST. After the course, you will be able to understand, develop, troubleshoot, and debug code written in VBScript and related technologies.

What This Course Does Not Provide

This course does not cover all of the object models, objects, methods, and properties that are available in VBScript. This sort of information is best obtained from a good online reference such as Microsoft MSDN®. It is also important to understand that this course does not give you the skills to become a programmer. You can achieve these skills and fulfill those requirements by working with Visual Basic or Microsoft Visual C++® on a regular basis.

Microsoft Certified Professional Program

The Microsoft Certified Professional program includes the following certifications:

- Microsoft Certified Systems Engineer + Internet (MCSE + Internet)
- Microsoft Certified Systems Engineer (MCSE)
- Microsoft Certified Database Administrator (MCDBA)
- Microsoft Certified Solution Developer (MCSD)
- Microsoft Certified Professional + Site Building (MCP + Site Building)
- Microsoft Certified Professional + Internet (MCP + Internet)
- Microsoft Certified Professional (MCP)
- Microsoft Certified Trainer (MCT)

For More Information   See the "Certification" section of the Web page provided on the compact disc or the Microsoft Training and Certification Web site at http://www.microsoft.com/trainingandservices/

You can also send e-mail to mcp@msprograms.com if you have specific certification questions.

Exam Preparation Guides

To help prepare for the MCP exams, you can use the preparation guides that are available for each exam. Each Exam Preparation Guide contains exam-specific information, such as a list of the topics on which you will be tested. These guides are available on the Microsoft Certified Professional Web site at http://www.microsoft.com/trainingandservices/

Important   MSDN Training curriculum helps you to prepare for Microsoft Certified Professional (MCP) exams. However, no one-to-one correlation exists between MSDN Training courses and MCP exams. Passing MCP exams requires real-world experience with the products—MSDN Training courses help get you started.

Facilities

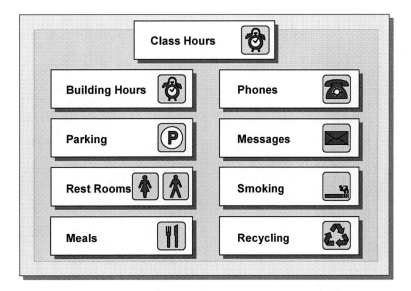

msdn training

Module 1: Overview of Windows Scripting Technologies

Contents

Microsoft

Overview

- ■ **Introducing WSH**
- ■ **Running Scripts**
- ■ **Working with Scripts**
- ■ **Comparing VBScript and Visual Basic**

To use Microsoft® Windows® Script Technologies (WST), you must understand some basic concepts, such as how Windows Script Host (WSH) functions and what types of scripts can be run by using WSH.

In this module, you will learn about WSH and how to work with script files.

At the end of this module, you will be able to:

- ■ Describe the various technologies associated with running Windows Scripts.
- ■ Run scripts.
- ■ Work with scripts.
- ■ Describe the major differences between Microsoft Visual Basic® and Visual Basic Scripting Edition (VBScript).

◆ Introducing WSH

- ■ **The WSH Environment**
- ■ **Features of WSH**
- ■ **Types of Script Files**

In this section, you will learn about the WSH environment. You will also learn about the features of WSH.

WSH is not a single file—it is a set of components that you can use to run scripts. These components are present whether you use the Windows Script Host environment or other script environments, such as Microsoft Windows 2000 Internet Information Services (IIS).

Script files can be run in the WSH environment, whether the script is written in Visual Basic Scripting Edition or Microsoft JScript®.

WSH is supported on all of the Windows 32-bit operating systems, such as Microsoft Windows 95, Microsoft Windows 98, Microsoft Windows Millennium Edition (Me), Microsoft Windows NT® version 4.0, and Windows 2000. WSH version 1.0 shipped with Windows 98 (Version 1.0). You can download version 2.0 of WSH, and you can install it on any of these operating systems.

The WSH Environment

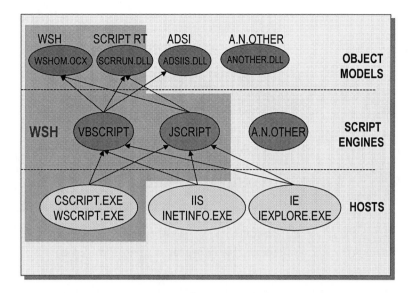

WSH has several components. These components work together to provide the operating system with the ability to run and interoperate with scripts.

Hosts

Hosts are the programs that run your scripts. Before WSH was developed, Internet Information Services (IIS) and Microsoft Internet Explorer were the only hosts available from Microsoft. As a result, scripting was restricted to the Web. However, with the addition of CScript.exe and WScript.exe, you can now run scripts outside of the Web environment. These hosts accept scripts and determine which script engine you need to parse, interpret, and execute those scripts.

Script Engines

The WSH environment natively supports two scripting languages: Visual Basic Scripting Edition and JScript.

After the scripting host determines the language used in your scripts, it loads the appropriate script engine and passes your script to it for execution. WSH includes two different script engines, one for VBScript and one for JScript, to run scripts that you write in these languages.

Object Models

Script programming usually makes extensive use of objects. Objects represent packaged functionality that you can reuse in your scripts. They provide a concept known as black-box reuse. You use objects in your scripts to perform many tasks. The advantage of using objects is that they perform complex tasks without requiring you to understand how to implement the code they contain.

Related objects are defined in structures called object models. The object models are defined by type libraries contained in dynamic link libraries (DLL) or ActiveX Control (OCX) files.

When you install WSH, you install the hosts, two native script engines and two object models, the Windows Script Host, and the Script Run-time object models.

Note   For more information about objects and specific object models, see Module 2, "Working With Objects," in Course 2433A, *Microsoft Visual Basic Scripting Edition and Microsoft Windows Script Host Essentials*.

Extensibility

This WSH environment is extensible. You can install additional script engines to use new script languages. You can also install new type libraries to gain access to additional object models.

Features of WSH

- **Small Memory Footprint**
- **Language-Independent**
  - You can extend it to other script engines
- **Script Reuse**
- **Command-Line Reference**

WSH is ideal for non-interactive scripting needs, such as batch, logon, and administrative scripting.

In addition to non-interactive processing, WSH scripts can involve some degree of user interaction, such as confirming prompts and entering variable information.

Small Memory Footprint

The low system overhead of running scripts with WSH makes it ideal for your administrative scripts.

Language-Independent

Although WSH natively supports the Visual Basic Scripting Edition and JScript languages, you can extend the environment so that it can run scripts written in other languages, such as PerlScript.

Script Reuse

By using WSH, you can save your scripts as operating system files. The content of your script files is plain text. Therefore, you can write and save your script files by using a simple text editor such as Notepad. After you save the script files, you can run your scripts many times; you do not need to rewrite code every time you want to run a certain set of actions. This is a useful feature if you have scripts that must be run on a regular basis.

Command-Line Reference

Prior to WSH, the only native script language that the Windows operating system supported was the command language supported though Cmd.exe.

Administrators often construct batch files (.bat) that contain multiple commands. These commands are still supported and are an important part of the administrator's toolset.

In addition, specially written command utilities, such as those provided in the Windows 2000 Resource Kit, can be the most efficient way to get a task done. You will explore some of these command-line utilities and learn how they can be integrated with Visual Basic Scripting Edition throughout this course.

A full command-line reference is provided in Windows 2000 Help.

Types of Script Files

- **Script Files**
  - .vbs and .vbe
  - .js and .jse
- **Script Control Files**
  - .wsh
- **XML Script Files**
  - .wsf
  - .wsc

Working in the WSH environment involves using many file types. WSH identifies the type of file by its file extension. It is essential to understand the role each of these file types can play within the WSH environment.

The following table describes the common file types used in the WSH environment

File suffix	Role
.vbs and .vbe	Script file written in VBScript.
.js and .jse	Script file written in JScript.
.wsh	Script control file. This type of file controls the execution of a script.
.wsf	Windows script file written by using Extensible Markup Language (XML) format.
.wsc	Script Component file. This type of file represents a COM component written in script.

Script Files

The .vbs and .vbe files are script files written in the Visual Basic Scripting Edition language. A .vbe file is an encoded version of the script.

Similarly, the .js and .jse files are scripts written in JScript. A .jse file is an encoded version of the script.

Note For more information about .vbe files, see Module 6, "Creating Logon Scripts," in Course 2433A, *Microsoft Visual Basic Scripting Edition and Microsoft Windows Script Host Essentials*.

Script Control Files

For each individual script that you run, you can record specific settings by using a control file. These files have a .wsh file extension. A .wsh file is a text file that uses a format similar to the format of .ini files. It is created automatically when you set the properties for a supported script file in Windows Explorer.

To create a .wsh file for your script, perform the following steps:

1. Open Windows Explorer.
2. Right-click the script file.
3. On the context menu, click **Properties**.
4. On the Properties page, select the settings you want for the script, and then click **OK** or **Apply**.

This creates a .wsh file with the same name as the script file and in the same folder as the script file.

Note   The .wsh file works in a similar way that shortcuts (.lnk) or .pif files work in Windows. It is a pointer to the file that you want to execute. It also configures the environment settings that the script will inherit.

The following is an example of a simple .wsh file:

Example

```
[ScriptFile]
Path=C:\Scripting\Reference Scripts\SHOWVAR.VBS
[Options]
Timeout=20
DisplayLogo=0
```

In the above example, the **Path** setting identifies the script file that this .wsh file executes. The **Timeout** setting sets a maximum script execution time of 20 seconds. The **DisplayLogo** setting is set to 0, which means that a run-time logo will not be displayed.

XML Script Files

The WSH environment supports two different XML-based script files.

Windows Script Files

A .wsf file is a specific type of script file that uses Extensible Markup Language (XML) to enhance the features available to script.

Note   For more information about the features available to a .wsf file, see Module 8, "Beyond the Basics," in Course 2433A, *Microsoft Visual Basic Scripting Edition and Microsoft Windows Script Host Essentials*.

Windows Script Component Files

A .wsc file is also implemented in XML. It registers the contents of the script file as a Component Object Model (COM) component. This technology was formally known as Scriptlets and is often used to extend the functionally of Web servers. The XML format that is required to register your code as a COM component is very strict and beyond the scope of this course.

◆ Running Scripts

■ **Running Scripts with Wscript.exe**

■ **Running Scripts with Cscript.exe**

■ **Script Language Engines**

The execution of scripts is controlled by the environment that they are run in. This section examines the two hosts available to WSH: WScript.exe and CScript.exe.

While you can use both hosts to run your scripts, there are differences between the two. These differences may affect which host you choose to run your scripts. This section describes the similarities and differences of these two environments.

Running Scripts with WScript.exe

> ■ **Running Scripts from Windows**
>
> - Double-click files or icons
>
> - Use the Windows Run command
>
> - Use a file drag and drop operation
>
> - Create WSH file
>
> ■ **WScript Is the Default Host**

One of the hosts you can use to run your scripts is WScript.exe.

Running Scripts from Windows

You can run scripts by using WScript.exe in the following ways:

■ Double-click the script files in Windows Explorer.

By default, double-clicking any script file will cause WScript.exe to run the script.

■ Use the Windows **Run** command.

If you use the **Run** command from the **Start** menu, WScript.exe runs the script.

■ Drag the script file onto WScript.exe.

You can drag a script file onto WScript.exe, or you can create a shortcut to it.

■ Create a WSH file.

You can create a WSH file that can then be used to run the script file.

WScript.exe Is the Default Host

All of the previous methods of using WScript.exe to run your scripts are presented on the assumption that WScript.exe is the default script host. If you change the default to CScript.exe, all of the previous methods will run the scripts in CScript.exe.

Caution Visual Basic Scripting Edition–based viruses can be a major problem if this behavior is not fully understood by the user. For more information about the steps that you can take to prevent these viruses, see Module 6, "Creating Logon Scripts," in Course 2433A, *Microsoft Visual Basic Scripting Edition and Microsoft Windows Script Host Essentials*.

Running Scripts with CScript.exe

- **Running Scripts with CScript.exe**
  - Use the Run dialog box or command prompt
  - Drag and drop the file
- **CScript Parameters**
  - // modifies host settings
  - / passes data to the script itself
- **Changing the Default Script Host**
  - //h:CScript or //h:WScript

CScript.exe is the command-line version of WScript.exe. Similar to WScript.exe, it supports script execution by using the Windows **Run** command or by using the drag and drop operation. However, CScript is not the default script host. If you want to use CScript to run your scripts, then you either must explicitly call it or set it as the default script host.

Running Scripts with CScript.exe

To use CScript.exe explicitly, you can type a command line at the command prompt or in the **Run** dialog by using the following syntax:

Syntax

```
CScript [host options...][script name][options and parameters]
```

The terms are defined as follows:

- Host options

  These options enable or disable various WSH features. For example:

Example

```
CScript //nologo myscript.vbs
```

This example stops the WSH from displaying its logo when it runs the Myscript.vbs script.

- Script name

  This is the name of the script file, complete with extension and any necessary path information. For example:

Example

```
CScript C:\Scripts\Qbackup.vbs
```

This example runs the script file Qbackup.vbs in the C:\Scripts folder.

- Script options and parameters

  These are parameters, or arguments, that are to be passed to the script itself. For example:

Example

```
CScript myscript.vbs /C:
```

This example passes the value *C:* as an argument to the Myscript.vbs script. The script can then use the parameter to display some information about drive C.

Be aware of the difference between using a single forward slash and a double forward slash to pass parameters at the command line. The former indicates data that is to be passed into the script, and the latter is used as a setting for the CScript environment.

CScript Parameters

Each parameter is optional. If you simply type **CScript** at the command prompt, the CScript syntax and the valid host parameters are displayed.

CScript.exe supports the host parameters listed in the following table.

Parameter	Description
//?	Shows command usage.
//I	Interactive mode. Displays the user prompts and script errors. This is the default.
//B	Batch mode. Suppresses command-line display of user prompts and script errors. This is the opposite of //I.
//T:*nn*	Enables time-out option. This is the maximum number of seconds the script can run before it is forcibly terminated by WSH, as specified by *nn*. The default is unlimited.
//LOGO	Displays a banner. This is the default setting.
//NOLOGO	This switch prevents the banner from appearing at run time.
//H:CScript	Registers CScript.exe as the default host for running scripts.
//H:WScript	Registers WScript.exe as the default host for running scripts.
//S	Saves the current command-line options for this user.
//E:*engine*	Executes the script with the specified scripting engine. This enables script to be run even if it has a different file extension.
//D	Turns on the debugger.
//X	Launches the script in the debugger.
//JOB:<*JobID*>	Runs the specified JobID from the .wsf file (where *JobID* is…).
//U	Enables you to use Unicode for redirected input/output (I/O) from the console.

Often used

Note The host parameters described in the previous table are not case sensitive.

Changing the Default Script Host

Changing the default host for a user is done using the command-line options of WSH; for example:

Example

```
CScript.exe //H:cscript
```

This changes the default host to CScript.exe for the duration of the users logon session.

If you were to add the //S option to this command, the setting is saved for the current user and is the default every time the user logs on to the computer in the future.

Note   These settings are stored in the registry at the following location:

HKEY_CURRENT_USER\Software\Microsoft\Windows Scripting Host\Settings

---

Script Language Engines

- ■ **Choosing a Script Language**
- ■ **VBScript**
  - No programming experience, or familiarity with Visual Basic or Visual Basic for Applications
- ■ **Microsoft JScript**
  - Familiarity with C, Visual C++, or Java

Two different languages are natively supported by WSH: Visual Basic Scripting Edition and JScript.

Choosing a Scripting Language

Although both languages have similar capabilities, you might find that your background makes learning one of the languages easier than learning the other language.

VBScript

If you are new to programming, then VBScript will be easier to learn. VBScript will also be easier to learn if you have a background in programming using Visual Basic or Visual Basic for Applications.

Microsoft JScript

If you have a background in C, Microsoft Visual C++®, or Java, then Microsoft JScript is more appropriate. You will find that it has more familiar programming constructs than VBScript.

With each update of the scripting engines, Microsoft is bringing the feature sets of the languages closer together. Also, with the addition of XML support in WSH version 2.0, you can use the language that is best suited to a particular task, even within the same script. You can develop scripts that have a mix of languages contained within them. One section can be written in VBScript, and another section can be written in JScript, all within the same script file.

Note   There are a few areas in which one scripting languages is more powerful than the other. For example, JScript has very powerful error handling routines, whereas Visual Basic Scripting Edition has excellent run-time expression evaluation. Detailed comparison of the two languages is outside the scope of this course.

For more information about the differences between VBScript and JScript, see http://msdn.microsoft.com/scripting/default.htm

◆ Working with Scripts

- **Writing Scripts**
- **Debugging Scripts**
- **Troubleshooting**

To create scripts, you must have the following: a development tool to write the script and a host to run the script in. There are a number of development tools available. The simplest one is Notepad. However, while you can carry out all of your scripting work by using Notepad, it does not have any specific functionality that makes scripting easy.

This section describes the process of writing scripts.

Writing Scripts

- **WSH 2.0**
  - Part of Windows 2000 and Windows ME
  - Download for Windows NT 4.0, Windows 95, and Windows 98
- **Development Tools**
  - Notepad
  - Third-party IDEs
  - Visual InterDev or Visual Basic for Applications
- **Reference Documentation**

Before you can successfully write and then run your scripts, you must make sure that the following two basic requirements are met:

- WSH must be present on the computer that you intend to run the script on.
- You must have a suitable script-creation environment for the development of your scripts.

WSH 2.0

WSH 2.0 ships with the following versions of Windows:

- Windows Millenium Edition (Me)
- Windows 2000 Professional
- Windows 2000 Server
- Windows 2000 Advanced Server
- Windows 2000 Datacenter Server

WSH version 1.0 is integrated into Windows 98. Both Windows 95 and Windows NT version 4.0 were released before WSH, so they must be upgraded to support WSH 2.0. You can download an upgrade for Windows 95 and Windows 98 and a service pack for Windows NT 4.0. WSH 2.0 includes:

- Visual Basic Scripting Edition and JScript version 5.1
- Windows Script Runtime version 5.1

Note Updates to the script engines also ship with Internet Explorer updates. For example, version 5.5 of the script engines ships with version 5.5 of Internet Explorer. Check the documentation of future updates of Internet Explorer to find which script engine version they contain.

Development Tools

Currently, WSH is shipped without a dedicated development tool for scripting. However, you can obtain tools that enable you to develop scripts on your Windows platform.

The most basic development tool is Notepad.exe. Using Notepad as your scripting development tool has the following advantages:

- It is installed on all Windows machines by default.

- It supports cut and paste and other text-editing operations.

- It has low memory and processor requirements.

Using Notepad does not impose any specific limitations on the code that you develop. However, this tool provides no specific scripting functionality, such as object browsing or integrated debugging.

There are other development tools available from third parties that are far more powerful than Notepad. There are also the Integrated Development Environments (IDEs) of Microsoft Visual InterDev® and Visual Basic for Applications. These programs offer features that include the Object Browser and mature, integrated debugging tools. However, these tools are not designed exclusively for Visual Basic Scripting Edition. As a result, there are compatibility and programmatic issues that you need to understand before you can use these tools to develop scripts.

Reference Documentation

It is a good idea to install the Visual Basic Scripting Edition and Windows Script Host online reference documentation. These provide an invaluable guide to the objects, methods, and properties that are available in VBScript and WSH, as well as many examples. The VBScript documentation also provides a reference to the VBScript language syntax.

You can install the WSH documentation by downloading and running Wshdoc.exe from:
http://msdn.microsoft.com/scripting/windowshost/wshdoc.exe

You can install the VBScript documentation and samples by downloading and running Vbsdoc.exe from:
http://msdn.microsoft.com/scripting/VBScript/download/vbsdoc.exe

Debugging Scripts

- **Script Errors**
  - Syntax errors
  - Run-time errors
  - Logic errors
- **Microsoft Script Debugger**
  - Installing Microsoft Script Debugger
  - Features of Microsoft Script Debugger

Even the most experienced programmer will encounter bugs and errors in their code. Your scripts will also be vulnerable to errors. Finding and fixing errors is an essential day-to-day task that you must master to develop robust, useful scripts.

Script Errors

Errors in your script can be categorized into three groups:

- Syntax errors.

  This type of error results when you have not followed all of the rules of the language. For example, omitting a quotation mark where one is required will generate a syntax error. Syntax errors are picked up as the script is compiled and executed. For this reason they are sometimes called compilation errors.

  Compilation is the process of turning the code that you write into a set of instructions that the processor can execute. Syntax errors will prevent your code from running. You will receive a message box that indicates the type of syntax error that has occurred.

- Run-time errors.

  A run-time error occurs when your code, although syntactically correct, attempts to perform an action that is not possible at the time it is attempted. For example, a run-time error occurs if your script attempts to open a file that does not exist or attempts to save a file to the floppy drive when no disk is present. Run-time errors cause your script to stop unexpectedly. You will receive a message box that indicates the type of action that was attempted but was not possible.

- Logic errors.

  A logic error occurs when a script runs without syntax or run-time errors, but the results are unexpected or unintended. For example, a script might prompt the user for a password. The script is supposed to prevent the user from proceeding without a valid password, but it allows the user to process without a password. This could be due to a logic error in the script.

  Logic errors are typically the most difficult ones to fix, because they are the most difficult ones to identify. Logic errors usually results in bugs in your script.

  Microsoft Script Debugger can be used to run your code line-by-line to see why the script does not run the script the way it was intended. This is the most efficient approach to finding and fixing logic errors.

Microsoft Script Debugger

Included with Windows 2000 is version 1.0 of the Microsoft Script Debugger tool. This tool is designed to help you find problems or bugs with the execution of scripts.

Installing Microsoft Script Debugger

You can use **Add/Remove Programs** in **Control Panel** to install the script debugger. It is listed under **Windows Components**. Installing the debugger in this manner installs the debugger itself and a comprehensive help file into the *systemroot*\Help\debug\Sdbug.htm folder (where *systemroot* is the folder that contains the Windows 2000 system files).

An update to this debugger is available from the Windows Script Web site, which fixes some of the known issues with version 1.0. This version is called 1.0a and can be obtained from:
http://msdn.microsoft.com/scripting/debugger/downloads/10a/x86/Scd10en.exe

Features of Microsoft Script Debugger

Some of the features of the Microsoft Script Debugger include the ability to run script commands directly, set breakpoints in your code, and view a list of procedures whose execution is pending.

Note   The script debugger documentation is written with the focus on Internet scripts rather than WSH. While this can be confusing for an administrator who has no Internet Explorer script experience, the majority of the information it provides can be applied to WSH scripting.

To see how to use the features of Microsoft Script Debugger, see Module 4, "Error Handling and Debugging," in Course 2433A, *Microsoft Visual Basic Scripting Edition and Microsoft Windows Script Host Essentials*.

Troubleshooting

> - **WScript.Echo Method**
>   - Generates a message box in WScript
>   - Outputs to the command line in CScript
> - **The Debugger Launches Without a Loaded Script**
>   - From the command-prompt, check which line caused the failure
>   - Log off and log back on to reset the debugger
> - **Visual Studio Installation**
>   - Overrides Microsoft Script Debugger

When you are working with scripts, you must be aware of some basic troubleshooting information.

WScript.Echo Method

The following statement behaves differently in WScript and CScript:

Example

```
WScript.Echo "This is a message"
```

With WScript.exe, this method results in a message box that interrupts the execution of the script until the user clicks **OK**.

With CScript.exe, this method outputs the text directly to the command line and then continues executing the script. No user interaction is required.

The Debugger Launches Without a Loaded Script

If the debugger launches without a loaded script, it is usually due to a syntax error in your script. If this is the case, you can switch to the command prompt where an error message will be displayed. The error message will highlight the line and character at which the error was found.

If this fails to help, and the script window is still missing, log off and log back on to clear the problem.

Visual Studio Installation

If you install Microsoft Visual Studio® version 6.0 after the Windows Script Debugger, the behavior of WSH is modified because Visual Studio handles all script errors. Every time a script error is encountered, a message box appears containing the following message:

There was an unexpected error. Would you like to debug the application?

If you click **Yes** in the message box, Visual InterDev starts instead of the Microsoft Script Debugger. If this is not the desired behavior, then you can reset the default debugger in one of two ways:

- Remove and reinstall the debugger.

- Modify the registry entry for the default debugger directly.
  The registry key for the default debugger is:

  HKEY_CLASSES_ROOT\CLSID\
  {834128A2-51F4-11D0-8F20-00805F2CD064}\LocalServer32

  For the script debugger, this entry should contain C:\Program Files\Microsoft Script Debugger\msscrdbg.exe. For Visual InterDev, it should contain C:\Program Files\Microsoft Script Debugger\mdm.exe.

Caution   Modifying the registry can result in your machine being unable to start. Always ensure you have a system backup before changing any registry values.

Comparing VBScript and Visual Basic

- **VBScript Is an Interpreted Language**
  - Not compiled into an executable
- **Syntax Differences**
  - Code must be in procedures in Visual Basic
  - The only data type is variant
  - No Debug.Print
  - Cannot access type library references directly
  - Constants have to be explicitly declared

Visual Basic Scripting Edition is a subset of the Visual Basic for Applications language that is used in Microsoft Office and the Visual Basic development system. If you are already familiar with the Visual Basic language, then you will find writing scripts with VBScript easy. However, you should be aware that there are some differences between the two languages. Some of the differences are described below.

VBScript Is an Interpreted Language

Visual Basic Scripting Edition is an interpreted language. This means that it is processed and parsed for syntax correctness at run time and not prepackaged as an executable file before it is run. Script written in VBScript is slower to execute than script written in Visual Basic.

Syntax Differences

Unlike Visual Basic, Visual Basic Scripting Edition does not require that the main body of the script be enclosed in a **Sub ()** or **Function ()** procedure.

VBScript has only one data type, called a **Variant**, which is used to contain many different kinds of data. For example, it contains strings, integers, and so on. You cannot declare an explicit data type in VBScript.

There is no support in VBScript for the **Debug.Print** statement used in Visual Basic. The WSH equivalent is **WScript.Echo**.

One limitation of VBScript is its lack of native support for referencing type library information. This is most apparent with constants. If you wish to use a constant name to reference a value, you must explicitly declare it at the start of the script.

Note   With the XML support in WSH 2.0, you can overcome this limitation. For more information, see Module 8, "Beyond the Basics," in Course 2433A, *Microsoft Visual Basic Scripting Edition and Microsoft Windows Script Host Essentials*.

This is not a definitive list of the differences between the languages. It simply illustrates that there are some important differences that will affect the ability to reuse code examples from one language in the code to another language.

Lab 1: Configuring and Using WSH

Objectives

After completing this lab, you will be able to:

- Run scripts.
- Configure a WSH file for your scripts.
- Manage the WSH environment on a computer.
- Edit scripts by using an IDE.

Prerequisites

Before working on this lab, you must have:

- An understanding of the Windows 2000 graphical user interface (GUI).
- The ability to work with Windows Explorer.

Scenario

You are the administrator of a corporate network. You want to run scripts written in Visual Basic Scripting Edition by using WSH technologies. You must control and configure the script host that you will use to run your scripts. In addition, you want to install the documentation for WSH and VBScript. Finally, you want to review and edit scripts by using an IDE.

Estimated time to complete this lab: 45 minutes

Exercise 1
Configuring WSH

In this exercise, you will examine and configure the various settings for the WSH environment.

▶ **To list the script settings for the CScript.exe host**

1. Log on to your computer as **Administrator** with a password of **password**.

2. On the **Start** menu, click **Run...**

3. In the **Run** dialog box, type **cmd** and then click **OK**.

4. In the command prompt window, type **CScript** and then press ENTER.

   The list of switches for the CScript host is listed.

5. Review the list of switches.

   You can use the //H:CScript switch to change the default host for your scripts to CScript.exe.

▶ **To run a script file**

1. At the command prompt, change to the Lab01 starter folder by typing: **cd *install_folder*\Labs\Lab01\Starter** (*install_folder* is C:\Program Files\MSDNTrain\2433A by default).

2. Type **Scr1.vbs** and then press ENTER.

   The script file runs. The WScript host launches the script.

3. Type **CScript.exe Scr1.vbs** and then press ENTER.

   The CScript host launches the script.

▶ **To change the default script host**

1. At the command prompt, type **CScript.exe //H:Cscript** and then press ENTER.

   You are notified that the default host has been set to CScript.exe.

2. Type **Scr1.vbs** and then press ENTER.

   The CScript host launches the script.

▶ **To create a WSH file for Scr1.vbs**

1. Using Windows Explorer, go to the *install_folder*\Labs\Lab01\Starter folder (*install_folder* is C:\ Program Files\MSDNTrain\2433A by default).

2. Click **Scr1.vbs**.

3. On the **File** menu, click **Properties**.

4. In the Properties dialog, click the **Script** tab.

5. Select the **Stop script after specified number of seconds** check box, and then click **OK**.

   A new file named Scr1.wsh is created in the same folder as the .vbs file.

▶ **To open the WSH file for Scr1.vbs**

1. Click **Start**, point to **Programs**, point to **Accessories**, and then click **Notepad**.

2. In Notepad, on the **File** menu, click **Open**.

3. In the **Open** dialog box, navigate to the *install_folder*\Labs\Lab01\Starter folder.

4. In the **Files of type** list, click **All Files**.

5. In the open dialog, click **Scr1.wsh**, and then click **Open**.

▶ **To modify the WSH file for Scr1.vbs**

1. Locate the line that reads **Timeout=10**.

2. Modify this line so that it reads **Timeout=5**.

3. On the **File** menu, click **Save**.

4. Close Notepad.

5. In the command prompt window, type **WScript Scr1.wsh** and then press ENTER.

6. Wait for five seconds. Do not click **OK** or press ENTER in the message box. Wait for the script to be forcibly shut down by the host.

Exercise 2
Installing the WSH and VBScript documentation

In this exercise, you will install and review the WSH and Visual Basic Scripting Edition documentation.

▶ **To install the WSH documentation**

1. Using Windows Explorer, go to the *install_folder*\Labs\Lab01\Starter folder.

2. Double-click **wshdoc.exe**.

3. In the **Where would you like to install Windows Script Host 2.0 documentation?** dialog box, click **OK** to accept the default location.

4. You might be prompted that the folder does not exist and asked whether you want to create it. If you receive this message, click **Yes**.

   The WSH documentation is installed.

▶ **To install the VBScript documentation**

1. Using Windows Explorer, go to the i*nstall_folder*\Labs\Lab01\Starter folder.

2. Double-click **vbsdoc.exe**.

3. In the **Where would you like to install VBScript V5.5 documentation?** dialog box, click **OK to accept the default location.**

4. You might be prompted that the folder does not exist and asked whether you want to create it. If you receive this message, click **Yes**.

   The VBScript documentation is installed.

▶ **To review the WSH documentation**

1. Click **Start**, point to **Programs**, point to **Microsoft Windows Script**, and then click **Windows Script Host 2.0 Documentation**.

2. In the WSH documentation window, click the **Index** tab.

3. In the **Type in the keyword to find** box, type **Echo**

4. Click **Display**.

5. Review the information provided about the **Echo** method.

6. Close the WSH documentation window.

▶ **To review the VBScript documentation**

1. Click **Start**, point to **Programs**, point to **Microsoft Windows Script**, and then click **VBScript V5.5 Documentation**.

2. In the VBScript documentation window, under **Contents**, expand **User's Guide**.

3. Click **What Is VBScript?**

4. Review the information provided.

5. Close the VBScript documentation window.

Exercise 3
Using an IDE to Edit Script Files

In this exercise, you will use the PrimalSCRIPT IDE.

▶ **To open a script file in Primal Script**

1. Click **Start**, point to **Programs**, point to **SAPIEN Technologies, Inc.**, and then click **PrimalSCRIPT 2.0**.

2. In the **PrimalSCRIPT 2.0** dialog box, click **OK**.

3. In the **Tips and Tricks** dialog box, clear the **Show tips at each startup of PrimalSCRIPT** check box, and then click **OK**.

4. On the **File** menu, click **Open**.

5. In the **Open** dialog box, browse to the *install_folder*\Labs\Lab01\Starter folder.

6. Click **Scr1.vbs**, and then click **Open**.

7. Review the contents of the file.

▶ **To use the auto-complete features of the IDE**

1. Click at the end of line 5, and then press ENTER.

2. Type **WScript**

   Notice that the command you have just typed is gray. This indicates that the IDE recognizes the word that you have typed.

3. Type a single period.

   Notice that a list of the available valid terms is displayed. These are the members of the **WScript** object.

4. In the list, double-click **Echo**.

   The IDE auto-complete feature enters the word into your script.

5. Type a space.

   Note that some on-screen help is provided by the IDE.

6. Type **"Welcome to the VBScript and WSH course!"** (including the quotation marks).

▶ **To save and run the script**

1. On the **File** menu, click **Save**.

2. On the **Script** menu, click **Run Script**.

3. Click **OK** in each of the message boxes that you receive.

4. On the **File** menu, click **Exit**.

Review

- **Introducing WSH**
- **Running Scripts**
- **Working with Scripts**
- **Comparing VBScript and Visual Basic**

1. What are the script host executable files?

2. Which host is the default host?

3. Which script engine will be invoked with the Myscript.jse file?

4. What is the Visual Basic Scripting Edition equivalent of the **Debug.Print** command in Visual Basic?

msdn training

Module 2: Working with Objects

Contents

Microsoft

Overview

- **Object Terminology**
- **Creating and Using Objects**
- **Understanding Object Models**
- **Common Object Models**

Understanding objects is fundamental to the script writing process. This module describes what an object is, and how you can use them in scripts.

At the end of this module, you will be able to:

- Understand how scripts use objects.
- Understand object terminology.
- Use an object browser.
- Understand how scripts interact with the Component Object Model (COM).
- Explain the use of various object models.

◆ Object Terminology

- **Understanding Object Terminology**
- **Methods and Properties**
- **Understanding Instantiation Terminology**

Using objects in your scripts gives you many advantages, such as efficiency, reliability, and reuse of existing functionality. Before you can use objects in your scripts, you must understand the terms and concepts applicable to programming with objects.

This section describes the terminology used when programming with objects. It also includes an analogy that helps to summarize the key concepts introduced in this section.

Understanding Object Terminology

- ■ **Objects**
  - ● Packaged functionality
- ■ **Compiled Objects**

You will encounter some terminology as you start to use objects in your scripts. Each term has a distinct meaning. You will come across these terms frequently. Each term, and how they relate to each other, is described below.

Objects

Objects are packaged pieces of functionality. Objects contain code that you can use in your scripts. However, the manner in which you access the functionality contained in an object is called black-box reuse. When you use the functionality provided by an object, you never need to see the code that it contains.

Compiled Objects

The most common types of objects that you will use in your Microsoft® Visual Basic® Scripting Edition (VBScrpt) files are compiled objects. With these types of objects, you will never need to see the code that they contain. The code that provides the functionality is compiled into a binary file, which is usually a dynamic link library (DLL) or a Microsoft ActiveX® Control file (with the file extension .ocx). All that you need to do is create script in VBScript that communicates with the object to reuse the prepackaged functionality that it provides.

In addition to containing code that provides reusable functionality, objects also contain data. You can manipulate this data in a manner similar to reusing the packaged functionality. You do not need to know how the object implements its data. You only need to know how to communicate with the object to manipulate the data values. Again, this is all part of the black-box reuse concept.

You will communicate with the functionality provided by an object by using its methods. You will manipulate the data that an object contains by working with its properties. Methods and properties are described in the following section.

Note   Each object that you work with has a well-defined list of methods and properties associated with it. For example, one object might contain a **Color** property and a **Paint** method, while another object might contain a **Name** property and a **Play** method. The methods and properties that each individual object contains are designed by the developer of that object.

Methods and Properties

- ■ **Methods**
  - ● Invoking a method
  - ● Using parentheses
- ■ **Properties**

To manipulate objects, you work with their methods and properties.

Methods

Objects expose their functionality as methods. To use the functionality provided by a particular method, you need to know how to call it. You do not need to know how the method works internally. The term invoke is often used to describe the process of calling a method.

When you invoke a method in your script, the compiled method code runs in its entirety at the point in your code where you call it. It is important to understand the benefits that this affords you as a script developer. The method might contain thousands of lines of code hidden from you by the object. You can simply access this code by calling the method. You can achieve this by using a single line of script. The term used to describe the approach of hiding complex code is encapsulation.

Invoking a method

There are three different ways to invoke a method. Which approach you use in your script depends upon how the method is exposed. The three approaches are described below.

Syntax

Object.Method

In this approach, the method is invoked with a simple call. The call uses the dot notation to specify the name of the object and the name of the method that you want to invoke. In this simple call, the method does not need any inputs from your script, nor does it return data to your script.

Syntax

`Object.Method Param1 [, Param2, … ,Paramn]`

In this approach, the method is invoked with a call similar to the previous call. Again, the call uses the dot notation to specify the name of the object and then the name of the method that you want to invoke. However, this approach passes data into the method from your script by using one or more parameters. The method accepts the data and works with it internally, encapsulated from your script.

The parameters are provided as a comma-separated list.

Syntax

`MyVariable = Object.Method([Param1, Param2, … ,Paramn])`

In this approach, a Visual Basic Scripting Edition variable is used to hold the return value of the method call. Again, the dot notation is used, but this time the value of the variable is set to the result of the method call.

Note   For more information about variables, see Using Objects later in this module and in Module 3, "Script Logic," in Course 2433A, *Microsoft Visual Basic Scripting Edition and Microsoft Windows Script Host Essentials*.

Using Parentheses

An important addition to this syntax is the inclusion of the parentheses that follow the method call. The parentheses indicate that your script must evaluate the method call. In this case, it holds the evaluated data in the variable.

Methods that return data to the calling script might require parameters. If this is the case, then those parameters must be supplied as a comma-separated list inside the parentheses, as shown in the previous syntax. However, some methods might return data and not require parameters. If this is the case, then you still must use the parentheses, although the code does not contain any parameters, as the following syntax illustrates:

Syntax

`MyVariable = Object.Method()`

Properties

Objects expose their data to your script in their properties. To manipulate this data, all you must know is how to retrieve and set the property value. You do not need to know how the object actually stores or handles the data. Again, this reinforces the black-box reuse concept.

The following syntax illustrates some standard approaches to setting and retrieving the values of an object's properties:

Syntax   *Object.Property = Value*

In this syntax, using the dot notation sets the property's value. The value might take one of a number of forms, but you must be able to evaluate it as a discrete value. Some of forms that the value takes are described as follows:

- A literal value

  You can set the property of an object to a literal value, such as the number 10 or the string "Cat."

- A simple expression that can be evaluated as a discrete value

  You can set the property of an object to the result of an expression that your script can evaluate as it runs, such as the result of 18 + 9 or the result "London" concatenated with " United Kingdom."

- A property of another object

  You can set the property of one object to the property of another object. You can achieve this in the following single line of code:

Syntax   *Object1.Property1 = Object2.Property2*

- The return value of an object's method call

  You can set the property of one object to the return value of another object's method. You can achieve this in the following single line of code:

Syntax   *Object1.Property1 = Object2.Method([Param1])*

If you want to retrieve the property value and store it in one of your variables, use the following code. The syntax is very similar to that used to retrieve the return value of a method. However, in this case, you do not use parentheses.

Syntax   MyVariable = Object.Property

Understanding Instantiation Terminology

- **Classes**
  - Blueprints for your objects
- **An Analogy–Architect Drawings and Buildings**
- **Type Libraries**
  - A collection of classes
- **Instantiation**
  - Multiple instances

To use objects and their corresponding methods and properties, you must write code that creates the object. Object creation involves referring to the object's type library and class. These terms are explained below.

Classes

A class is the blueprint for an object. The developers who allow you to reuse their code as objects do not write the code in the object itself. They actually write code in a class. When you want to reuse code, your script creates an object based on a class. The object code is written in the class in such a way that it provides you with the methods and properties for your object.

An Analogy–Architect Drawings and Buildings

One way to think about the purpose of a class is to consider a real-world analogy. Imagine the process involved in planning and constructing a building: The architect has a vision of what she wants the building to look like and how she wants the building to be structured. To convey her ideas to the builders, she creates an architect drawing, or blueprint, in which she specifies the materials to be used and the dimensions of the building.

At this point, her job is done. She can now hand the blueprint to the builders, who construct the building according to the plans. In fact, the builders can construct many similar buildings, all based on the same drawing. They can reuse the blueprint many times. After the building has been constructed, the owner can decide to paint the building with a color of his choice. He might also decide to install alarms, add furniture, and so on.

In this analogy, the architect's blueprint is analogous to a class. Objects are analogous to the buildings that are created from the blueprint.

The blueprint makes allowances that alarms can be installed and furniture can be added. These actions are analogous to methods. The object is manipulated after it has been created by performing these actions.

Furthermore, the blueprint of the building does not specify a fixed color for the paint used to decorate it. The blueprint allows this color to be chosen after the building has been constructed. The paint color is analogous to a property.

Type Libraries

A type library is a collection of classes that can be redistributed to allow you to build objects based on those classes. Type libraries are compiled files that expose their classes to your script. They are usually compiled into dynamic link libraries (DLL) or ActiveX Controls files.

A Collection of Classes

Using the earlier analogy of a blueprint, the architect might produce many blueprints for different building types. She might develop one blueprint for a house, one for an apartment building, and one for a skyscraper office complex. She might then store all of these blueprints in a folder that is named Buildings.

When she completes these blueprints, she can give the whole folder to the builder. When the builders want to build a house, they can get the house blueprint from the folder. They could also access the skyscraper or apartment blueprints to construct those types of buildings, as well.

In this analogy, the folder is the type library. It contains the blueprints for many different types of buildings. Each building type has its own set of distinct features and attributes. In object terminology, the methods and properties are these distinct features and attributes.

You must know the name of any type library that you use in your scripts.

Note   For examples of the names of type libraries, see Working with Objects later in this module.

Instantiation

The process of creating an object from its class is termed instantiation. When an object is instantiated, it inherits the properties and methods that the class defines. This functionality is held in memory by your computer. As a result, it is efficient for you to manipulate the object.

After the object is instantiated, it no longer needs to refer back to its class, nor is it desirable that it should do so. The premise behind this fact is that after the object is created, you can manipulate it without affecting the class upon which the object was based.

Using the architect drawing analogy, imagine that the builders have constructed a house and that the decorator paints it yellow. It is sensible that this action should affect only that house and should not affect the blueprint. If it does affect the blueprint, then all of the new houses would now be yellow, which is obviously not desirable.

Multiple Instances

You will often use multiple instances of the same class in your script. If you create multiple instances of the same class, then you can manipulate each instance, or object, independently of the others.

Using the above analogy, the builders might construct a whole street of houses from the same blueprint. The decorator might then paint house Number 1 yellow. This will not affect the other houses, even though they are based on the same blueprint. The decorator might paint house Number 2 green, and so on.

Note   Objects are usually instantiated with a single line of code written in Visual Basic Scripting Edition. For more information about how to write this instantiation code, see Creating and Using Objects later in this module.

◆ Creating and Using Objects

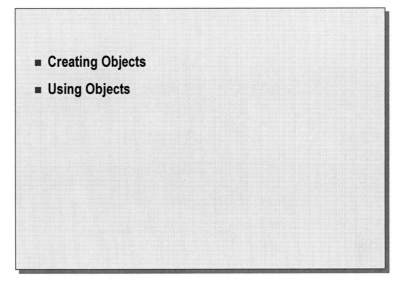

- **Creating Objects**
- **Using Objects**

Once you understand the programming terms that relate to objects, you can use objects in your scripts.

This section explains how to create and use objects in your scripts.

Creating Objects

- **Libraries**
  - Example-Wshom.ocx
- **Classes**
  - Example-WScript.Network
- **Object Usage Example**

```
Dim oNetwork
Set oNetwork = CreateObject("WScript.Network")
oNetwork.MapNetworkDrive "z:", \\London\Lab2Share
```

A type library commonly used by administrative scripts is the Microsoft Windows Script Host (WSH) library.

Libraries

The WSH library is distributed in the Wshom.ocx file, and is installed by default on all Microsoft Windows 2000 computers.

This type library is accessed in a script that uses the following name:

Example

```
WScript
```

Classes

The WScript type library contains multiple classes that you use in your scripts. An example is the **Network** object. This allows a script to perform simple network tasks. The object is instantiated using the following syntax:

Syntax

```
Set <Object Variable> = CreateObject("<Library>.<Class>")
```

An example of how to create the **Network** object is as follows:

Example

```
Set oNetwork = CreateObject("WScript.Network")
```

The above syntax uses the **CreateObject()** function that is part of the Visual Basic Scripting Edition language. It accepts a string parameter that specifies the type library and the class to be used to create the object. An object variable is set to the result of this function so that you can then use the variable to refer to the newly created object in subsequent lines of script.

Note For more about object variables, see Using Objects later in this module.

After this object has been instantiated, you can use the object to perform network tasks, such as mapping a network drive or printer. This is achieved by using methods, such as **MapNetworkDrive** and **AddPrinterConnection**. The **oNetwork** object variable also exposes properties such as **ComputerName** and **UserName**, which you can use in the script to identify the user running the script and the computer that it is running on. The following example illustrates how you can use these methods and properties:

Example

```
Set oNetwork = CreateObject("WScript.Network")
oNetwork.MapNetworkDrive "Z:", "\\MyServer\MyShare"
Wscript.Echo oNetwork.ComputerName
```

The first line of code instantiates the new object and sets the **oNetwork** object variable to it.

The next line of code uses the **MapNetworkDrive** method to create a new drive mapping. The parameters supplied indicate that the Z drive is to be mapped to the shared folder called MyShare on the server called MyServer.

The third line of script retrieves the value of the **ComputerName** property from the **oNetwork** object variable. In the same line of code, the result of this operation is displayed to the user with the **Echo** method of the built-in **WScript** object.

Note   Although WScript is the name of a type library, there is also an object called **WScript** that exposes useful methods like **Echo**. Since this object is related to the host itself, there is no need to instantiate it (as you must do with most objects). It is automatically instantiated by the host that your scripts run in and can therefore be used directly.

Using Objects

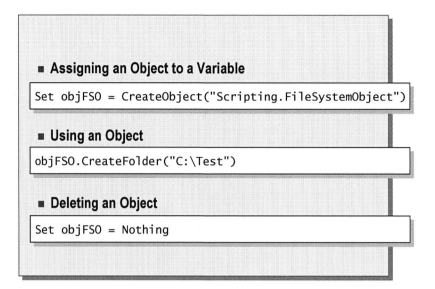

To use the properties and methods of an object, you must be able to refer consistently to your instance of it. To do this, you use a named pointer to your instance of the object. The named pointer is known as an object variable, and it points to the object code and data in memory.

Assigning an Object to a Variable

You will use the **set** keyword to assign an object to a variable in your code. The **set** keyword informs the script that the variable points to an in-memory object structure.

The following example instantiates a **FileSystemObject** object and points the objFSO variable to it, so that it can be manipulated in subsequent lines of code:

Example

```
Set objFSO = CreateObject ("Scripting.FileSystemObject")
```

Using an Object

After the object has been created in the memory space of the running script, it is possible to access the methods and properties that it exposes by using the object variable that points to it.

The following example uses the **CreateFolder** method to create a new folder called Test in the root of the C drive:

Example

```
objFSO.CreateFolder ("C:\Test")
```

Deleting an Object

Objects consume memory on the computer that they are running on. Therefore, it is good practice to delete them when you are done using them.

To delete an object, you set its object variable to the keyword **Nothing**, as shown in the following:

Example

```
Set objFSO = Nothing
```

Note Objects that are not explicitly set to **Nothing** are deleted automatically by WSH when the script terminates. However, it is considered best practice to delete objects explicitly when the script no longer requires them, because this frees up the disk space that is used by the object. Complex objects can use a substantial amount of disk space, so you should delete complex objects as soon as possible.

◆ Understanding Object Models

- ■ **Defining Object Models**
- ■ **COM Objects**
- ■ **COM Objects in Practice**
- ■ **Using an Object Browser**
- ■ **Demonstration: Using an Object Browser**
- ■ **The Scripting Object Model**
- ■ **The WSH Object Model**

An object model describes a collection of objects that are designed to perform a related set of tasks. This section examines how these models function and how you can use them when you are writing scripts.

This section also provides an introduction to the Component Object Model (COM).

In addition, you will learn more about the Microsoft Scripting runtime object model and the WSH object model. An understanding of these object models increases the range of administrative tasks that you will be able to perform with scripts.

Defining Object Models

- **Describing Object Models**
- **Examples of Object Models**
  - WSH
  - ADSI
  - ADO

Many of the objects that you will use in your scripts are presented to you in an object model.

Describing Object Models

An object model is a collection of objects that are designed to perform a related set of tasks, such as managing the file system or reading information from a database. The object classes, methods, and properties are grouped together by the developer and presented as an object model.

In many cases, the objects in the object model are organized into a hierarchy. The higher level, or root, objects provide access to the objects further down. For example, the **FileSystemObject** object provides access to the drive object. It is not possible to call the drive object without using the **FileSystemObject** object.

While many existing object models implement hierarchies that require you to access one object through another object, a more modern approach is to access all objects directly. For example, all of the objects in the ActiveX Data Objects (ADO) model can be accessed directly. They are not organized into a hierarchy.

Examples of Object Models

Some of the most commonly used object models in administrative scripts are described below:

- Windows Script Host (WSH)

  This object model provides you with functionality that you can use to perform basic administrative tasks, such as creating folders and mapping network drives.

- Active Directory™ Service Interface (ADSI)

  This object model provides you with functionality that you can use to access and configure the Active Directory service features, such as users and groups.

- ActiveX Data Objects (ADO)

  This object model provides you with functionality that you can use to access data sources, such as Microsoft SQL Server™.

COM Objects

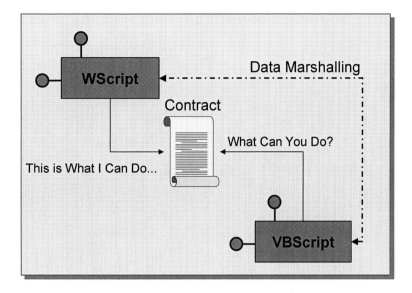

The Component Object Model (COM) provides a specification and set of rules that define how software systems can be constructed from reusable components. The COM specification also describes the precise way in which clients, such as WSH scripts, can communicate with objects that are located inside components.

Contracts

A contract consists of a definition of the methods and properties supported by objects. COM allows a contract to be defined and specifies the services that the component provides to its clients. The rules of COM mandate that the contract, after it is published or made generally available to client software, cannot change. This alleviates many of the versioning issues prevalent in most software systems, particularly those developed prior to the component era.

COM also governs how data is transferred between the client and object. The process of passing data into and out of an object is called marshalling.

DCOM and Component Services

Distributed COM (DCOM) extends marshalling support of COM so that objects can be accessed over a network.

Windows 2000 integrates Component Services to provide additional functionality to component developers and support for distributed transactions, resource management, security, and so on.

COM Objects in Practice

- **Object Identification**
  - ProgID
- **Automation**
  - Required for script
- **Type Libraries**
  - Defines component's metadata

Classes are identified by using a label called a Programmatic Identifier, or ProgID.

Object Identification

The ProgID is stored in the **HKEY_CLASSES_ROOT** section of the registry. It tells the system which .dll, .exe, or .ocx file contains the associated class definition that is used to construct the object. A ProgID consists of a type library and a class name that are separated by a dot, as in the following example:

Syntax

```
Library.Class
```

The following example uses the **Scripting.FileSystemObject** ProgID to create an instance of the object. The registry contains information about the compiled file that defines this type of object:

Example

```
Set MyObject = CreateObject("Scripting.FileSystemObject")
```

Automation

Scripting environments, such as WSH, impose certain restrictions on COM objects. One of the key restrictions is the range of data types that can be passed to and from the object. This, and other restrictions, means that script code cannot communicate with all COM objects. Those COM objects complying with the requirements of script are called automation objects.

Automation defines a restricted set of data types and imposes one or two other requirements on the developer of COM objects. From the administrator's perspective, this is not a significant issue, since nearly all of the object models that an administrator might want to use from a WSH script are automation-compliant.

For example, all of the applications in Microsoft Office, such as Microsoft Word and Microsoft PowerPoint®, support automation. As a result, Visual Basic Scripting Edition can be used to control their functionality. The following script takes the first slide from an active PowerPoint presentation, copies it, and pastes it into a Word document called Demo.doc that is located in the C:\My Documents\ folder:

Example

```
Set oPres = CreateObject ("PowerPoint.Application")
oPres.Visible=True
oPres.ActivePresentation.Slides(1).Copy
Set oWord = CreateObject ("Word.Application")
oWord.Visible=True
oWord.Documents.Open "c:\My Documents\Demo.doc"
oWord.Selection.Range.Paste
```

Type Libraries

As mentioned previously, you can use type libraries to define the set of classes, methods, and properties that a component supports. This type of information is the component's metadata, the data that describes data.

Although it is typically saved as part of the component's .dll or .ocx file, it can reside in a stand-alone type library file, usually with a .tlb file extension. By examining the metadata inside a type library, it is possible to discover the objects, methods, and properties that you can use in a script. Object browsers can use this type information to depict a graphical view of an object model.

Using an Object Browser

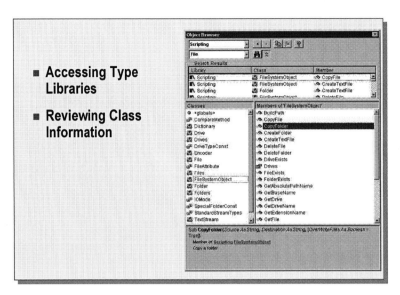

- **Accessing Type Libraries**
- **Reviewing Class Information**

It is helpful to view what objects are available in a type library when you write script. Many tools can give you this functionality.

The Microsoft Object Browser is a tool that you can use to look inside a type library. It displays the information in a readable, graphical form. The object browser ships with Microsoft Visual Basic for Applications in Microsoft Office.

Note Another browser tool called the object linking and embedding (OLE)/COM Object Viewer ships with Microsoft Visual Studio® development system. It is a developer-oriented tool and will not be used in this course.

You can download it as a stand-alone application from the Microsoft Web site at www.microsoft.com.

Demonstration: Using an Object Browser

In this demonstration, you will see how to use an object browser.

▶ **To use an object browser to view an object model**

1. Click **Start**, point to **Programs**, and then click **Microsoft Word**.

2. In the Microsoft Word window, on the **Tools** menu, point to **Macro**, and then click **Visual Basic Editor**.

3. In the Microsoft Visual Basic window, on the **View** menu, click **Object Browser**.

4. Click the **<All Libraries>** list.

   The libraries available to Microsoft Word are the following:

   • Normal

   • Office

   • stdole

   • VBA

   • Word

▶ **To add the Scripting library**

1. In the Microsoft Visual Basic window, on the **Tools** menu, click **References**.

2. In the **References–Project** dialog box, select the **Microsoft Scripting Runtime** check box, and then click **OK**.

3. Click the **<All Libraries>** list.

   Note that **Scripting** library has been added to the list.

4. Click **Scripting**.

5. In the empty list, type **FileSystemObject** and then press ENTER.

6. In the Members of 'FileSystemObject' pane, click **CreateFolder**.

   Notice the data in the Search Results pane as you click the item.

7. Close the Microsoft Visual Basic window.

8. Close the Microsoft Word window.

The Scripting Object Model

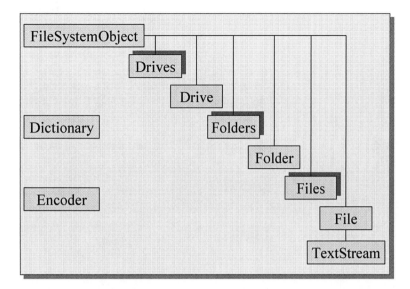

The type information describing the scripting object model, or the Microsoft Scripting Runtime object model, is defined in Scrrun.dll. The primary object that this object model provides is the **FileSystemObject** object. You will sometimes use the **Dictionary** object and the **Encoder** object from this object model.

FileSystemObject

You can use the **FileSystemObject** object to manage files and folders on the local computer. In addition to manipulating existing folders and files, the **FileSystemObject** object enables you to create new folders and text files.

You can only create text files by using the **FileSystemObject** object. If you want to create a new Word document, you must use the Word object model.

The **FileSystemObject** object also does not provide support for managing NTFS file systems permissions. If you need to change the security permissions on the file, you must use an extra utility.

Dictionary

The **Dictionary** object is a container object that you can use to store arbitrary items of data. You associate each item with a name or unique key value. You can use the key to retrieve the stored data.

For example, you can use the **Dictionary** object to store the details about all of the administrators in an enterprise. Details might include a name, phone number, and e-mail address. You can associate each dictionary entry with the unique site the administrator is responsible for.

The site in the following example acts as the key with which the data item can be retrieved. It uses the **Dictionary** object. The example creates an instance of the **Dictionary** object and then stores the details of three administrators, Alan, Kathie, and Don, in it.

Example

```
Set AdminsList = Wscript.CreateObject("Scripting.Dictionary")
AdminsList.Add "UK", "Alan : +44 (0)117 555-0100"
AdminsList.Add "Europe", "Kathie : +33 (0)122 555-0105"
AdminsList.Add "US", "Don : +1 (0)25 555-0115"
```

To display, for example, the details about the administrator who is responsible for the UK, use the following line of code. This line of script uses the associative feature of the **Dictionary** object to retrieve the detail about the UK administrator. The retrieved data is then concatenated with a string literal and displayed by using the **WScript.Echo** method.

Example

```
WScript.Echo "The UK administrator is: " & AdminsList("UK")
```

Encoder

Scripts that have been encoded use the **Encoder** object. The encoding process is done with the Windows Encoder utility. This enables script writers to encode their script so that the script cannot be viewed, copied, or modified but can still be executed.

The WSH Object Model

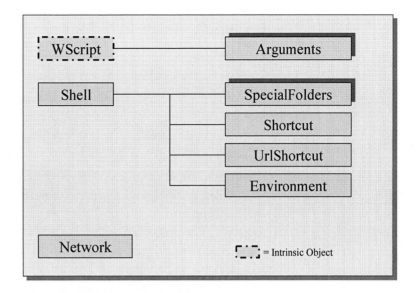

The type library Wshom.ocx provides the object model for WSH. This object model provides some of the objects, methods, and properties that are most often used in scripting.

WScript

The **WScript** object is an intrinsic object, which means that it is automatically created when a script is executed and requires no explicit instantiation. The **WScript** object supports the following methods:

- **CreateObject.** This enables the creation of an object for use in the script.

Note   The **WScript CreateObject** method is accessed by using the following ProgID: WScript.CreateObject(""). If the "Wscript" is left out, the Visual Basic Scripting Edition **CreateObject** method is used. For most standard actions, both methods are interchangeable.

- **ConnectObject.** This connects WSH to an existing object.
- **DisconnectObject.** This disconnects WSH from an existing object connected by **ConnectObject**.
- **GetObject.** This enables the retrieval of an existing object from a file, for example the opening of an existing Word document.
- **Echo.** This is used to display a message on the screen, either by a command line if the host is CScript or by a message box if the host is WScript.
- **Quit.** This terminates the execution of the script.
- **Sleep.** This causes the script execution to pause for the stated number of milliseconds. This can very useful when sending keystrokes to an external program from a script.

Shell

This object is instantiated with the following statement:

Example

```
Set objShell = WScript.CreateObject("WScript.Shell")
```

You can use this object to start a new process, create shortcuts, and provide the environment collection to handle access to useful environmental variables, such as WINDIR, COMPUTERNAME, and USERNAME. This is done by using the following objects:

- **SpecialFolders**. Returns the paths for Windows shell folders such as the Desktop folder, Start menu folder, and personal My Documents folder.

- **Shortcut**. Creates an object reference to a shortcut.

- **UrlShortcut**. Creates an object reference to a Uniform Resource Locator (URL) shortcut.

- **Environment**. Retrieves environment variables from the operating system.

Network

This object is instantiated with the following statement:

Example

```
Set objNetwork = WScript.CreateObject( "WScript.Network" )
```

The **Network** object exposes the Microsoft Windows network functionality to your scripts, which provides methods that you can use to:

- List all mapped drives.

- Connect and disconnect remote drives.

- List all mapped printers.

- Connect and disconnect remote printers.

- Set the default printer.

◆ Common Object Models

- Collaboration Data Objects
- ActiveX Data Objects
- Active Directory Service Interfaces
- Windows Management Instrumentation
- Internet Explorer and Internet Information Server
- Other Applications

The object models discussed so far provide the basic functionality that you can use to write useful administrative scripts.

In this section, you will be introduced to some of the other automation object models that you can use for specific tasks, such as sending e-mail messages and accessing databases.

Collaboration Data Objects

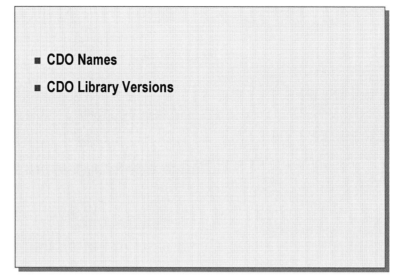

- CDO Names
- CDO Library Versions

Collaboration Data Objects (CDO) are designed to simplify the creation of applications or scripts with e-mail messaging functionality. The CDO libraries expose messaging objects, such as folders, messages, recipient addresses, and attachments.

CDO Names

CDO has gone through the following name changes in its lifetime:

- Previous versions of CDO were called OLE Messaging. OLE Messaging was first available in Exchange version 4.0.

- CDO version 1.1 was named Active Messaging. Active Messaging was installed with Exchange version 5.0. There were a few feature enhancements in Active Messaging, but the core functionality of the library remained unaltered.

- The current version 1.2 has the name Collaboration Data Objects (CDO). CDO 1.2 is installed with Exchange version 5.5. This version has added functionality over CDO 1.1, including support for scheduling meetings and appointments.

Note   To download CDO version 1.21, go to http://www.microsoft.com/exchange/55/downloads/cdo.htm

CDO Library Versions

The following four versions of the CDO library are available:

- CDO version 1.2.1 (Cdo.dll).

  This version is installed with Microsoft Outlook® 98, Outlook 2000, and Exchange 5.5 Server. It can be used on all Windows platforms, and it uses Messaging Application Programming Interface (MAPI) to perform its tasks.

- CDONTS (Cdonts.dll).

  CDO for NT Server is installed with Internet Information Services (IIS), Microsoft Commercial Internet Server (MCIS) and Exchange 5.5 Server. It uses Simple Mail Transfer Protocol (SMTP) and is designed for use by IIS applications. It does not support user interfaces, such as profile dialogs. Also, it does not use MAPI and therefore has no concept of Address Books, Authenticated Users or other MAPI features.

- CDO For Windows 2000 (Cdosys.dll).

  CDO 2.0 ships with Windows 2000 platforms. It supports SMTP and Network News Transfer Protocol (NNTP) but does not support MAPI. It is designed for administrators, because it enables you to do the following:

  - Append disclaimers or other notices to e-mail messages sent through a server.

  - Create Active Server Pages (ASP) applications with messaging capabilities.

  - Detect and discard unsolicited bulk mailings.

  - Detect and discard inappropriate newsgroup postings.

  - Check incoming messages for viruses.

  - Forward and filter messages automatically.

- CDO for Exchange 2000 (Cdoex.dll).

  The latest version is CDO version 3.0 for Exchange 2000. This is installed with Exchange 2000 Server. CDOEX upgrades the features of CDO for Windows 2000 to include features such as calendar objects and contact management and support for the new Exchange 2000 Web Storage System.

ActiveX Data Objects

- ■ **Data Sources**
- ■ **Examples of Data Providers:**
  - ● ODBC
  - ● Index Server
  - ● SQL Server
  - ● Active Directory directory service
  - ● Exchange 2000

ActiveX Data Objects (ADO) enables the fast and efficient access to and manipulation of data in a data source.

Data Sources

Data sources are often relational databases, such as SQL Server 2000. However, ADO enables you to access a variety of other nonrelational data sources, such as Active Directory. You can use ADO to search Active Directory for objects and properties, such as users and phone numbers. Because it enables you to search Active Directory, ADO is of interest to administrators who write scripts.

Note   The current ADO provider for ADSI only provides read-only access to objects in Active Directory.

Examples of Database Providers

To access data that is stored in different formats, ADO requires an OLE database (DB) provider for each type of data source. The current ADO OLE DB providers include:

- ■ Open Database Connectivity (ODBC), for databases without a specific OLE DB provider
- ■ Microsoft Index Server
- ■ SQL Server
- ■ Active Directory directory service
- ■ Exchange 2000

The ADO model consists of the following objects:

- **Connection**. Represents a connection to an OLE DB data source such as ADSI.

- **Command**. Defines a specific command to execute against the data source.

- **Error**. Contains details about data access errors and is refreshed each time that an error occurs in a single operation.

- **RecordSet**. Represents the results of a command object execution and consists of a sequence of records.

- **Fields**. Represents the collection of fields or columns within a record set.

- **Parameters**. Represents a collection of parameters, which can be supplied to the command object to modify its execution.

- **Properties**. Represents values supplied by the provider for a data source.

Note   For more information about how to use ADO to search for information in Active Directory, see Module 5, "Understanding ADSI," in Course 2433A, *Microsoft Visual Basic Scripting Edition and Microsoft Windows Script Host Essentials*.

Active Directory Service Interfaces

> - **Active Directory Service Interface**
> - **Gives Access to Multiple Directory Service Providers Through an Open Set of Interfaces**
> - **ADSI Providers Include:**
>   - LDAP
>   - Windows NT
>   - NDS
>   - NetWare 3 bindery

Active Directory Service Interface (ADSI), previously called OLE Directory Services, gives developers and administrators access to the information stored within multiple directory service providers through an open set of interfaces. Applications or scripts, written by using ADSI, work with any directory service that has an ADSI provider.

For example, with ADSI, scripts can access Lightweight Directory Access Protocol (LDAP), Novell Directory Services (NDS), Active Directory, and Microsoft Windows NT® version 4.0–based directories with a single interface. The only prerequisite for accessing these types of directory structures is that there is an appropriate ADSI provider available. Examples of available ADSI providers include:

- LDAP

  The LDAP provider works with any LDAP version 2 or version 3 directory, such as Exchange 5.0 and 5.5. This provider is also used to provide the access to Active Directory.

- Windows NT (WinNT)

  The WinNT provider supports the Windows NT 4.0 directory and server-based objects such as the Lanman Server.

- NDS

  This provider gives you access to the Novell Directory Service.

- NetWare 3 bindery (NWCOMPAT)

  This provider gives access to Novell's legacy bindery (3.x) servers.

ADSI compatible products include Active Directory, Exchange 5.5, IIS, and Site Server.

Note You will learn more about ADSI in Module 5, "Understanding ADSI".

Windows Management Instrumentation

- **Web-Based Enterprise Management**
  - Standard management API

- **Windows Management Instrumentation**
  - Can monitor and configure the Windows operating system, system devices, Active Directory, the registry, performance counters, and so on
  - Execute methods on managed objects
  - Receive event notification

Windows Management Instrumentation (WMI) is a single, consistent application programming interface (API) that is designed to make the Windows 2000 server family the most manageable Microsoft operating system to date.

Web-Based Enterprise Management (WBEM)

WBEM is an industry initiative to develop a standard technology for accessing management information in an enterprise. The aim is to lower the total cost of ownership (TCO) of computers in an enterprise. Many companies are participating in the WBEM initiative.

Windows Management Instrumentation (WMI)

WMI is the Microsoft implementation of WBEM. WMI can be used to write management scripts by using a single, object-oriented, remote-enabled, and scriptable interface that provides the following functionalities:

- Monitor, configure, and control management information about:

  - The Windows operating system.

  - System devices.

  - Active Directory.

  - The registry.

  - Performance counters.

- Execute methods on managed objects to perform complex operations; for example, to compress a file or reboot a remote system.

- Receive and act on events based on changes in any management data visible through WMI and events from Simple Network Management Protocol (SNMP) devices and the Windows Event Viewer service.

Note   This level of functionality makes WMI complex to script. WMI scripting is a major topic on its own and falls outside the scope of this course. For more information about WMI scripting, see Module 8, "Beyond the Basics" in Course 2433A, *Microsoft Visual Basic Scripting Edition and Microsoft Windows Script Host Essentials*.

For more information about WMI in general, go to the following Web site and download the WMI software development kit (SDK): http://msdn.microsoft.com/downloads/c-frame.htm?007#/downloads/sdks.

Internet Explorer and Internet Information Server

- **Internet Explorer**
  - Script host
  - No access to WSH
- **Internet Information Server (IIS)**
  - Active Server Pages

Prior to WSH, the primary application for Visual Basic Scripting Edition and Microsoft JScript® was for Web scripting.

Internet Explorer

Since Microsoft Internet Explorer version 3.0, Internet Explorer has had a scripting host embedded in it. Due to this historical link with the Web browser, a great deal of VBScript documentation still assumes that you are using script only in the context of a Web browser.

This may be misleading for systems administrators, because the functionality provided by WSH could be very different to that provided by Internet Explorer. For example, the functionality of the Internet Explorer host has been limited for security reasons, because it is not desirable if a remote Web script can access the **FileSystemObject** object and delete files or folders.

IIS

IIS has the ability to run VBScript if this script is embedded in an Active Server Page (ASP). Unlike Internet Explorer, the ASP page has full access to WSH, because the script is being run only on the server. As a result, ASP pages can be used very successfully to provide a central management Web site that administrators can use to manage an enterprise.

Note For more information about the administrative use of ASP pages, see Module 8, "Beyond the Basics," in Course 2433A, *Microsoft Visual Basic Scripting Edition and Microsoft Windows Script Host Essentials*.

Other Applications

Many applications and utilities expose a COM automation interface. This makes scripted control of the application possible.

Microsoft Office

It is possible to control Microsoft Word, Microsoft Excel, Microsoft PowerPoint®, Microsoft Access, Microsoft Outlook, and Microsoft FrontPage® with script. A comprehensive help file is included with Microsoft Office to help you understand the many possibilities involved in scripting these applications.

The help file is aimed at Visual Basic and Web developers, so some experimentation with different versions of the examples might be needed to make them work with WSH.

Note For examples of scripting with Microsoft Office, see Module 8, "Beyond the Basics," in Course 2433A, *Microsoft Visual Basic Scripting Edition and Microsoft Windows Script Host Essentials*.

Utilities

Many utilities also expose a COM interface, which makes scripting possible. The Microsoft Windows Media™ Player is an example of such a utility. To find the possibilities for scripting these utilities, use the Object Browser and examine the object model for the program that you want to script. This shows you the object, methods, and properties that you can use in your scripts.

Lab 2: Working with Objects

Objectives

After completing this lab, you will be able to:

- Manipulate the scripting object model by using Visual Basic Scripting Edition.

- Manipulate the WSH object model by using VBScript.

- Automate Microsoft Office applications by using VBScript.

Scenario

In this lab, you will use VBScript to manipulate various object models. Specifically, you will instantiate objects from the scripting object model, the WSH object model, and the Microsoft Word object model. You will then manipulate the methods and properties of these objects to perform administrative tasks.

Estimated time to complete this lab: 45 minutes

Exercise 1
Manipulating the Scripting Object Model

In this exercise, you will write code in Visual Basic Scripting Edition that manipulates the scripting object model. You will instantiate a **FileSystemObject** object and a **Folder** object and manipulate them by using their methods and properties.

▶ **To open a partially completed script file**

1. Click **Start**, point to **Programs**, point to **SAPIEN Technologies, Inc.**, and then click **PrimalSCRIPT 2.0**.

   PrimalSCRIPT appears.

2. In the **PrimalSCRIPT 2.0** dialog box, click **OK**.

3. On the **File** menu, click **Open**.

4. In the **Open** dialog box, browse to the *install_folder*\Labs\Lab02\Starter folder (*install_folder* is C:\ Program Files\MSDNTrain\2433A by default).

5. Click **ScrOM.vbs**, and then click **Open**.

▶ **To instantiate scripting objects**

1. Locate the comment **TODO Instantiate a FileSystemObject**.

2. On the line immediately below this comment, type the following:

   ```
   Set oFSO = CreateObject("Scripting.FileSystemObject")
   ```

3. Locate the comment **TODO Instantiate a Folder Object**.

4. On the line immediately below this comment, type the following:

   ```
   Set oFolder = oFSO.GetFolder("C:\WINNT")
   ```

▶ **To retrieve scripting object properties**

1. Locate the comment **TODO Retrieve the Drive property of the Folder object**.

2. Add the following code to the end of the line immediately below this comment:

   ```
   & oFolder.Drive
   ```

   You have now concatenated the drive property of the **Folder** object to a string literal. The script written in VBScript joins them together and then uses them as a parameter for the **WScript.Echo** method. The whole line of code should read:

   ```
   WScript.Echo "The Folder's Drive is: " & oFolder.Drive
   ```

3. Locate the comment **TODO Retrieve the Path property of the Folder object**.

4. Add the following code to the end of the line immediately below this comment:

```
& oFolder.Path
```

You have concatenated the path property of the **Folder** object to a string literal. The script written in VBScript joins them together and then uses them as a parameter for the **WScript.Echo** method. The whole line of code should read:

```
WScript.Echo "The Folder's Path is: " & oFolder.Path
```

5. Locate the comment **TODO Retrieve the Count property of the Folder object's Subfolders collection**.

6. Add the following code to the end of the line immediately below this comment:

```
& oFolder.SubFolders.count & " subfolders"
```

You have concatenated the **Count** property of the **Folder** object's **SubFolders** collection to two string literals. The script written in VBScript joins them together and then uses them as a parameter for the **WScript.Echo** method. The whole line of code should read:

```
Wscript.Echo "The Folder has " & oFolder.SubFolders.Count &
↪" subfolders"
```

Tip   The line continuation character (↪) indicates that the text following it should be written on the same line as the code that precedes it.

---

7. On the **File** menu, click **Save**.

8. On the **Script** menu, click **Run Script**.

9. Review the message boxes as your script runs.

You have now successfully manipulated the scripting object model.

Exercise 2
Manipulating the WSH Object Model

In this exercise, you will write code in Visual Basic Scripting Edition that manipulates the WSH object model. You will instantiate a **Shell** object and a **Network** object and manipulate them by using their methods and properties.

▶ **To open a partially completed script file**

1. On the **File** menu, click **Open**.

2. In the **Open** dialog box, browse to the *install_folder*\Labs\Lab02\Starter folder.

3. Click **WSHOM.vbs**, and then click **Open**.

▶ **To instantiate and manipulate the Shell object**

1. Locate the comment **TODO Instantiate a Shell object**.

2. Type the following code on the line immediately below this comment:

   ```
   Set oShell=WScript.CreateObject("Wscript.Shell")
   ```

3. Locate the comment **TODO Use the Shell's RegRead method to read values from the Registry**.

4. Type the following lines of code immediately below this comment:

   ```
   sOS = oShell.RegRead("HKLM\Software\Microsoft\
   ↪Windows NT\CurrentVersion\ProductName")

   nBuildNo = oShell.RegRead("HKLM\Software\Microsoft\
   ↪Windows NT\CurrentVersion\CurrentBuildNumber")

   sOrg = oShell.RegRead("HKLM\Software\Microsoft\
   ↪Windows NT\CurrentVersion\RegisteredOrganization")
   ```

   These three lines of code retrieve data from the registry and store them in VBScript variables.

   Note   There are only three lines of code for you to type. The continuation arrows indicate that the subsequent code should be typed on the same line as the preceding code.

   For more information about variables, see Module 3, "Script Logic," in Course 2433A, *Microsoft Visual Basic Scripting Edition and Microsoft Windows Script Host Essentials*.

▶ **To instantiate and manipulate the Network object**

1. Locate the comment **TODO Instantiate a Network object**.

2. Type the following code on the line immediately below this comment:

```
Set oNetwork = CreateObject("WScript.Network")
```

3. Locate the comment **TODO Map z: to the LabShare folder on the instructor machine (London)**.

4. Type the following code on the line immediately below this comment:

```
oNetwork.MapNetworkDrive "z:", "\\London\LabShare"
```

5. On the **File** menu, click **Save**.

6. On the **Script** menu, click **Run Script**.

7. Review the message boxes as your script runs.

8. Using Windows Explorer, verify that your Z drive has been successfully mapped to the LabShare folder on the Instructor computer.

   You have now successfully manipulated the WSH object model.

Exercise 3
Automating Microsoft Word

In this exercise, you will write code in Visual Basic Scripting Edition that manipulates the Microsoft Word object model. You will instantiate an **Application** object. You will create and modify a **Document** object. You will then save the **Document** object and review its contents.

▶ **To create a new script file**

1. Switch to PrimalSCRIPT.

2. On the **File** menu, click **New**.

3. In the New dialog box, click **VBScript**, and then click **OK**.

   Note that PrimalSCRIPT enters some comments into the file for you.

4. On the **Edit** menu, click **Select all**, and then press DELETE.

▶ **To automate Microsoft Word**

1. Type the following lines of code:

```
Dim wApp, wDoc, wRange, sName, sDate, sTime

Set wApp = CreateObject("Word.Application")
Set wDoc = wApp.Documents.Add
Set wRange = wDoc.Range

sName = "VBScript Student"
sDate = Date()
sTime = Time()
sContent = "Document created by " & sName & " at " & sTime
↪& " on " & sDate & "!"

wRange.Style = -3
wRange.Font.Color = 255
wRange.Text = sContent
wDoc.SaveAs "C:\Automating Word.doc"
wApp.Quit

Set sRange = Nothing
Set wDoc = Nothing
Set wApp = Nothing

WScript.Echo "Your Document has been saved as C:\Automating
↪Word.doc"
```

> **Tip**   This code uses the following three objects from the Microsoft Word object model:
>
> - An **Application** object, which is Microsoft Word itself
> - A **Document** object that is saved to the hard disk
> - A **Range** object that allows the text of a document to be manipulated
>
> Note that the value -3 indicates a Microsoft Word style of Heading 2 for the **Range** object. Also note that the value 255 indicates that the text is red. All of this information can be obtained by using the Object Browser.

2. On the **File** menu, click **Save As**.
3. Go to the *install_folder*\Labs\Lab02\Starter folder.
4. In the **File name** box, type **WordOM.vbs** and then click **Save**.
5. On the **Script** menu, click **Run Script**.
6. You are notified that your document has been saved. Click **OK**.

► **To review the results of your script**

1. Using Windows Explorer, go to the root of your C drive.
2. Click **Automating Word.doc**, and then press ENTER.
3. Review the contents of the document, and then close Microsoft Word.

   You have now successfully manipulated the Microsoft Word Object Model.

Review

■ Object Terminology

■ Creating and Using Objects

■ Understanding Object Models

■ Common Object Models

1. What is missing from this line of script?

   ```
   MyFSO = CreateObject("Scripting.FileSystemObject")
   ```

2. What ADSI provider is used to access the Active Directory?

3. What protocols does the Cdosys.dll allow scriptable access to?

4. What object model provides access to the Windows **Shell** and **Network** objects?

msdn® training

Module 3: Script Logic

Contents

Overview

- **Fundamental VBScript Rules**
- **Variables, Constants, and Data Types**
- **Operators**
- **Conditions and Loops**
- **Procedures**
- **Script Layout**

Microsoft® Visual Basic® Scripting Edition (VBScript) is a powerful scripting language. It provides an effective, efficient, and powerful framework that you can use to write administrative scripts.

After completing this module, you will be able to:

- Describe the rules of the VBScript language.
- Declare and use variables, constants, and data types in your scripts.
- Use VBScript language operators.
- Construct conditional code structures.
- Construct looping structures.
- Declare and use **Sub** and **Function** procedures.
- Determine an effective script layout.

Fundamental VBScript Rules

> ■ **The Basic Rules**
>
> - VBScript is not case sensitive
>
> - VBScript ignores extra white space
>
> - VBScript does not impose a maximum line length
>
> - VBScript allows you to split long lines
>
> - A name written in VBScript cannot exceed 255 characters

Before looking at the mechanics of Visual Basic Scripting Edition, it is important to understand the basic rules that should be obeyed.

■ VBScript is not case sensitive.

The following commands are equivalent:

Example

```
WSCRIPT.ECHO
WScript.echo
wscript.echo
```

Although VBScript is not case sensitive, it is considered bad practice to use all uppercase or all lowercase characters, because this makes the script difficult to read.

■ VBScript ignores extra white space.

The script engine ignores extra white space in any lines of script when it is parsed.

For example:

Example

```
WScript.    Echo            "Hello"
```

is the same as:

Example

```
WScript.Echo "Hello"
```

This gives the scriptwriter flexibility when laying out the script in a manner that is easy to read.

■ VBScript does not impose a maximum line length.

Unlike other languages, such as Microsoft Visual Basic, VBScript does not impose a maximum number of characters per line. In addition, you can write what are effectively separate lines of code on a single line by using the colon as a divider. The following combines two logical lines by using the colon divider:

Example

```
WScript.Echo "Test One" : WScript.Echo "Test Two"
```

■ VBScript enables you to type a line of code over several lines in the script.

Long statements can be broken into multiple lines by using the line-continuation character (a space followed by an underscore). Using this character can make the script easier to read. The following example shows a long line of code split into four lines by line-continuation characters:

Example

```
WScript.Echo "Message to " _
& vUserName & _
" Please lock your workstation"
```

If you split a long string across multiple lines, you must manage the string data on each line as a separate string. You can achieve this by ending each string with double quotes, and then concatenating the subsequent string to the previous line by using the string-concatenation character (&). The following example illustrates how to split a string across multiple lines:

Example

```
WScript.Echo "Message to" _
& vUserName _
& " Please make sure that you remember" _
& " to logoff or lock your workstation" _
& " if you leave it unattended, Thanks"
```

■ VBScript imposes a limit on the length of names.

VBScript imposes a limitation of 255 characters on any names used to identify items, such as variables, constants, and procedures.

◆ Variables, Constants, and Data Types

- **Variables**
- **Constants**
- **Data Types**
- **Naming Conventions**
- **Arrays**
- **Dynamic Arrays**

Before you can successfully write powerful administrative scripts by using Visual Basic Scripting Edition, you must be able to use variables, constants, and data types.

In addition, you must understand what an array is and how to work with both single-dimension and multi-dimensional arrays.

In this section you will learn about variables, constants, data types, and arrays. In addition, you will learn about naming conventions.

Variables

> ■ **Containers for Values That May Change**
>   ● Value is accessible by the variable name
> ■ **String Data**
>   ● strServer = "MyServer"
> ■ **Dates and Times**
>   ● dDOB = #05-06-1966#
> ■ **Naming Restrictions**
> ■ **Declaring Variables**
>   ● Implicit or explicit?
>   ● Option Explicit

Variables are names that you define, which point to memory locations that your script can access. Visual Basic Scripting Edition shields the actual memory locations from you. You can define variables in your script to hold data in memory in a convenient and easy to use manner. After data is held in variables, you can manipulate any data needed by your script.

Container for Values That May Change

Variables are used to store data items. As the term variable implies, the values stored may change during the lifetime of the script. The value of the data is accessed by using the variable name. For example:

Example

```
nMyAge = nMyAge + 10
WScript.Echo nMyAge
```

In this example, you manipulate the variable nMyAge by retrieving its current value and adding 10 to it. The new value is then echoed to the screen. The scriptwriter does not need to know the value of nMyAge in advance. In fact, a user could provide it to the script at run time through a pop-up box. Variables that contain a single value, such as nMyAge, are described as scalar variables.

String Data

A string is a data type that indicates that the variable contains characters, rather than numeric values. To store string data in a variable, you must enclose the data in double quotes as shown in the following example:

```
strServer = "MyServer"
```

Example

Dates and Times

When assigning dates or times to variables, they should be enclosed by the # character, as shown in the following example:

Example

```
dToday = #05-06-2000#
```

This indicates that the script written in VBScript interprets the value as a date or time, rather than as a string or a calculation, such as 5–6–2000.

Naming Restrictions

When naming variables in Visual Basic Scripting Edition, the following rules apply. A variable name:

- Must begin with an alphabetic character.
- Cannot contain an embedded period.
- Must not exceed 255 characters.
- Must be unique within the current scope.

You will learn more about scope later in the module.

Note A variable cannot be assigned the name of a VBScript keyword. For a list of VBScript keywords, see the VBScript documentation.

Declaring Variables

By default, script written in Visual Basic Scripting Edition implicitly creates a variable the first time that it reads a name that is not a reserved word or procedure name. This sort of behavior can easily result in script errors due to mistyped variable names.

In the following example, the scriptwriter has mistakenly typed **nMiAge** instead of **nMyAge** on the second line. The result of this typographical error is that instead of echoing a value of 45, as expected, a value of 10 is returned. This is because the script written in VBScript implicitly created a new variable called nMiAge. It is initialized with a value of zero.

Example

```
nMyAge = 35
nMyAge = nMiAge + 10
WScript.Echo nMyAge
```

This type of error can be very difficult to trace, so it is considered good practice to force the script written in VBScript to require explicit variable declarations by using the following line at the top of the script:

Example

```
Option Explicit
```

After the **Option Explicit** command has been added to the script, any undeclared variables will cause the script to generate an error rather than implicitly create a variable.

After **Option Explicit** has been added, you must explicitly declare all new variable names before they can be used. You can declare variables by using any of the following statements:

- Dim
- Private
- Public
- Static

You will see the difference between these statements later in this module. You can use all of the statements to declare the name of the variable and reserve some memory to hold the value of the variable; for example:

Example

```
Dim nMyAge
```

You can include multiple variables in a single declaration statement by using the comma as a separator between each name. The following illustrates how you can achieve this:

Example

```
Dim nMyAge, nMyName, nMyAddress
```

Constants

> - **Constants Do Not Change During Script Execution**
>   - Makes scripts easier to read and debug
>   - Assigned at the start of the script
> - **The CONST Statement**
>   Const COMP_NAME = "Microsoft"
> - **Type Library Constants**
> - **Intrinsic Constants**
>   Examples: vbCrLf , vbRed

Along with declaring and using variables in your scripts, you can declare and use constants.

Values Do Not Change During Script Execution

A constant is a name that you assign to a memory location in a manner similar to variables. Like variables, constants hold your data. However, the value assigned to a constant cannot change during the execution of a script.

Using constants helps make your scripts manageable. If a constant value, such as a tax rate, is used in several places in a script and the value must be modified in the future, the scriptwriter must only change the value at the location where the constant is defined. All of the other instances of the constant will contain the new value.

Constants can also make script easier to read, and therefore easier to debug, as long as you have used meaningful constant names.

The CONST Statement

A constant can represent a string, a number, or a combination that includes most arithmetic, comparison, and logical operators.

The following is an example of the syntax used for setting constants:

Example
```
Const COMP_NAME = "Microsoft"
```

If you attempt to change a constant's value in the script, the script written in Visual Basic Scripting Edition generates the following compilation error:

Example
```
Microsoft VBScript compilation error: Name redefined
```

Type Library Constants

Many type libraries describing object models expose constant values that can be legitimately passed as method parameters.

For example, in the Active Directory™ Service Interface (ADSI) object model, many of these constants are exposed to help with the creation of new objects, such as users and groups in Active Directory. When a new group is created, ADSI determines the type of group (Domain Local, Global, or Universal) by using a creation flag. If the flag has the value 2, ADSI knows to create a new Global Group. Other constant values correspond to the other group types. To help with readability, the ADSI type library exposes these constant values by using meaningful names; for example:

Example

ADS_GROUP_TYPE_GLOBAL_GROUP

The type library itself declares the above constant and assigns it a value of 2.

Visual Basic and Microsoft Visual C++® provide support for directly referencing the type library. This enables developers to use the predefined constants in their code.

Visual Basic Scripting Edition is unable to read information directly from a type library.

Note   Microsoft Windows® Script Host (WSH) version 2.0 provides Extensible Markup Language (XML) support in .wsf files. This enables you to reference type library constants.

For further details, see Module 8, "Beyond the Basics", in Course 2433A, *Microsoft Visual Basic Scripting Edition and Microsoft Windows Script Host Essentials.*

If a standard script written in VBScript is being used, the values of these constants must be discovered and explicitly defined as equivalent constants at the top of the script file as shown in the following example:

Example

CONST ADS_GROUP_TYPE_GLOBAL_GROUP = &H2

This line declares the following constant and assigns it the value of 2:

ADS_GROUP_TYPE_GLOBAL_GROUP

The &H tells the script that this is a hexadecimal value so that it is stored correctly. In this instance, &H2 is the same as a decimal value of 2. If the value is &H32, the decimal value stored by the script is 50. After this definition is in place, you can use the more meaningful constant name.

Note These constant values are published in the Microsoft Windows 2000 Platform software development kit (SDK). A quick way to find the value is to search for the constant name or search for ENUM for a list containing all the enumerations available.

Alternatively, if you know the type library that exposes the constants, you can use the Object Browser to discover the values directly. For example, the ADSI constants are stored in activeds.tlb, which has a Programmatic Identifier (ProgID) of ActiveDs.

For more information about ADSI constants, see Module 5, "Understanding ADSI," in Course 2433A, *Microsoft Visual Basic Scripting Edition and Microsoft Windows Script Host Essentials*.

Intrinsic Constants

Along with the constants that are defined by the scriptwriter, there are a number of useful constants built into Visual Basic Scripting Edition. These constants, referred to as intrinsic constants, provide a convenient way to use specific values without having to remember the value itself. Because these constants are already defined in VBScript, there is no need to explicitly declare them in the script. You can simply use them in place of the values that they represent.

Note Because it is not possible to disable intrinsic constants, the names of the constants are treated as reserved words.

For a full list of these intrinsic constants, refer to the VBScript documentation. The following table illustrates the various categories of constants and a brief description of each.

Constant grouping	Definition
Color Constants	Defines eight basic colors that can be used in scripting. For example, vbRed represents the number 255, which is interpreted as red.
Date and Time Constants	Defines date and time constants that are used by various date and time functions. For example, vbMonday represents the value 2, vbSunday equals 1, and vbTuesday equals 3.
Date Format Constants	Defines constants used to format dates and times.
Miscellaneous Constants	Defines constants that do not conveniently fit into any other category.
MsgBox Constants	Defines constants used in the **MsgBox** function to describe button visibility, labeling, behavior, and return values.
String Constants	Defines a variety of nonprintable characters that are used in string manipulation.
Tristate Constants	Defines constants that are used with functions that format numbers.
VarType Constants	Defines the various **Variant** subtypes.

One useful example of a VBScript constant is:

Example

```
vbCrLf
```

This constant represents the value of Chr(13) and Chr(10), which are the ASCII characters for the carriage return and line-feed characters. This is useful when formatting the text that is displayed in a message box as follows:

Example

```
sMessage = "Welcome to the world of VBScript" & vbcrlf & _
   "and all the useful commands that it provides" & _
   vbcrlf & "Please press the OK button to continue"
MsgBox sMessage
```

The first line assigns the message string to a variable called sMessage. Then, the **MsgBox** function displays the string as three lines of text rather than one long line.

Data Types

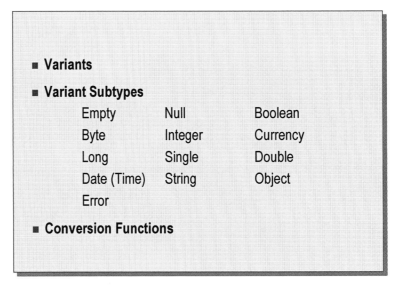

- **Variants**
- **Variant Subtypes**

  Empty   Null   Boolean

  Byte   Integer   Currency

  Long   Single   Double

  Date (Time) String   Object

  Error

- **Conversion Functions**

Unlike most modern compiled languages, such as Visual Basic and Visual C++, Visual Basic Scripting Edition uses one data type for all data. This type is called the **Variant** data type.

Variants

A **Variant** can contain numeric data, dates and times, objects, Boolean variables, or strings. In most cases, VBScript will automatically detect the type of data stored and will deal with it accordingly.

In the following example, vAnswer contains the string "MyServer," because vDemoA and vDemoB contain string values declared in quotes. The addition operator in this example performs a string concatenation.

Example

```
vDemoA = "My"
vDemoB = "Server"
vAnswer = vDemoA + vDemoB
WScript.Echo vAnswer
```

The next example looks very similar, but the vDemoA and vDemoB variables contain numeric data. This time, the result of the addition operation generates another number. As a result, vAnswer holds data that is numeric.

Example

```
VDemoA = 5
vDemoB = 10
vAnswer = vDemoA + vDemoB
WScript.Echo vAnswer
```

Variant Subtypes

It is possible to divide the **Variant** data type into subtypes. These subtypes allow a finer level of control on how data is manipulated by your script.

For example, you can have numeric data that represents currency, a date, or a time. The **Variant** interprets the data accordingly.

A **Variant** contains many subtypes, as illustrated in the following table.

Subtype	Description
Empty	Variant is uninitialized.
Null	Variant contains no valid data.
Boolean	Contains either **True** (-1) or **False** (0).
Byte	Contains an integer between the range of 0 and 255.
Integer	Contains an integer between the range of 32,768 and 32,767.
Long	Contains an integer between the range of –2,147,483,648 and 2,147,483,647.
Currency	Contains a fixed decimal number between the range of –922,337,203,685,477.5808 and 922,337,203,685,477.5807.
Single	Contains a single-precision, floating-point number between the range of –3.402823E38 and –1.401298E-45 for negative values and 1.401298E-45 and 3.402823E38 for positive values.
Double	Contains a double-precision, floating-point number between the range of –1.79769313486232E308 and –4.94065645841247E-324 for negative values and 4.94065645841247E-324 and 1.79769313486232E308 for positive values.
Date (Time)	Contains a number that represents a date or time between the range of January 1, 100 and December 31, 9999.
String	Contains a variable-length string that can be up to approximately two billion characters in length.
Object	Points to an object.
Error	Contains an error number.

Conversion Functions

Sometimes, a strict level of control over the exact data type is required. In these situations, you can use conversion functions to convert data from one subtype to another.

A typical example of when this might be required is when you extract a particular set of digits from a number. This is much easier to achieve by using string handling functions such as **Left**, **Right**, and **Len**. To use these functions, the numeric value must first be converted to a string by using the **CStr** function. After the digits have been extracted, you can then convert them back into an integer by using the **CInt** function.

The following table lists the functions that can convert data into a **Variant** of a specific subtype.

Function name	Conversion
CInt	Returns a **Variant** of subtype **Integer**
CBool	Returns a **Variant** of subtype **Boolean**
CByte	Returns a **Variant** of subtype **Byte**
CCur	Returns a **Variant** of subtype **Currency**
CDate	Returns a **Variant** of subtype **Date**
CDbl	Returns a **Variant** of subtype **Double**
CLng	Returns a **Variant** of subtype **Long**
CSng	Returns a **Variant** of subtype **Single**
CStr	Returns a **Variant** of subtype **String**

Note For more information about conversion functions, see the VBScript documentation.

Naming Conventions

- **Not Required, but Good Practice**
- **Hungarian Naming Convention**
  - Prefix names with a type identifier
  - Example: Wscript.Echo objMyServer.Name
  - Constants must be capitalized
- **Be Consistent**

Another method that you can use to help improve the readability of script is to employ a naming standard for your variables and constants.

Not Required, but Good Practice

A naming convention is not required by Visual Basic Scripting Edition. However, it is generally accepted that implementing some sort of naming convention is good practice.

Hungarian Naming Convention

Some of the rules laid of this standard are:

- Variable names should begin with one or more lowercase letters. These letters are used to indicate the type of data stored in the variable, as shown in the following table.

Prefix	Data Type
str	**String**
Fn	**Function**
c (or capitalize each letter in the constant name)	**Constant**
b	**Boolean** (**True** or **False**)
d	**Date**
obj	An object reference
n	A numeric value

- Function, method names, and each word in a multiword name should begin with a capital letter, as the following examples show:

Example

```
WScript.Echo objMyServer.Name
```

Example

```
Sub CheckDateSub()
```

- Early versions of VBScript had no specific **Const** command, so constants were simply defined as variables that were named in uppercase, and underscores were used to separate words; for example:

Example

```
COMPANY_NAME
DEFAULT_PATH
```

VBScript now has a **Const** command but this format has become the preferred naming standard for constants.

Note   There is a great deal more to this naming convention, most of which is not relevant to scripting due to the limited data types available to script. For more information about this subject, go to:

http://msdn.microsoft.com/library/partbook/win98dh/
variablenameshungariannotation.htm

Be Consistent

You do not have to use the Hungarian naming convention. You can easily develop your own naming convention. For example, you can use dtm as the prefix for dates and times. However, whatever naming standard you use, it is important that you apply it consistently in all scripts. This will aid in the reading and debugging of the scripts in the future.

Arrays

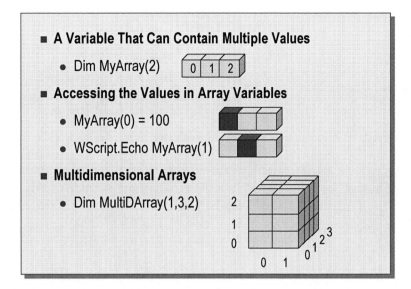

- ■ **A Variable That Can Contain Multiple Values**
  - ● Dim MyArray(2)
- ■ **Accessing the Values in Array Variables**
  - ● MyArray(0) = 100
  - ● WScript.Echo MyArray(1)
- ■ **Multidimensional Arrays**
  - ● Dim MultiDArray(1,3,2)

You may want to store multiple values in memory. In some cases, the values will be related. Rather than declaring and using multiple, separate variables to achieve your aims, you can instead make use of arrays.

A Variable That Can Contain Multiple Values

Arrays are a type of variable that can contain multiple values. You can specify the number of discrete values that an array can store when you declare it. You do this by specifying a number in brackets after the variable name. The number you supply is one less than the number of values that you want to store. For example, the following syntax specifies that the array can handle three discrete values:

Example

```
Dim MyArray(2)
```

The number is known as the upper bound of the array. The array can store discrete values by using any number between zero and the upper bound, including zero and the upper bound itself. Therefore, it can store a number of values that is one greater than the upper bound.

Accessing the Values in Array Variables

The values in an array are accessed by using a notation that uniquely identifies each value inside the array. You use a number between zero and the upper bound of the array to access a discrete value that it contains. The following example sets the first element (element number zero) to a value of 100:

Example

```
MyArray(0) = 100
```

The next example retrieves the value in the second element (element number one) and uses it as a parameter to the **Echo** method of the **WScript** object:

Example

```
WScript.Echo MyArray(1)
```

Multidimensional Arrays

It is possible to have multidimensional arrays. You declare a multidimensional array by providing a comma-separated list of upper bounds, as the following example shows:

Example

```
Dim MyTable(4, 9)
```

This example shows two numbers being used as the upper bounds, which indicates that this is a two-dimensional array. You can visualize a two-dimensional array as a table. The following table is a representation of how you can visualize the two-dimensional array.

	0	1	2	3	4	5	6	7	8	9	10
0											
1											
2											
3											
4											
5											

You can use up to 60 dimensions for an array in Visual Basic Scripting Edition. An array with three dimensions can be visualized as a cube. It becomes harder to visualize an array with four or more dimensions. However, most arrays you will use in VBScript will have no more than four or five dimensions and will often contain only one or two.

Note Arrays can contain variables of different data types. This is useful if you are storing values related to the same object. For example, the first value can be a person's name, and the rest of the row can be the values relating to that person, such as a telephone number. The next row can be the next person.

Dynamic Arrays

- **Creating Dynamic Arrays**
  - Dim MyArray()
- **Resizing an Array**
  - ReDim MyArray(6)
  - ReDim Preserve MyArray(6)
- **Array Statement**
  - Dim MyArray
  - MyArray = Array (Value1, Value2, Value3)
- **Emptying an Array**
- **The UBound Function**

The previous section, Arrays, described how to declare array variables by providing upper bound arguments in the declaration statement. However, providing the upper bound in this manner results in a fixed-size array. After the array has been declared, you can no longer change the number of elements that it contains or the number of dimensions that define the array's dimensionality. This approach is ideal if you know the number of dimensions and elements for your array in advance.

Creating Dynamic Arrays

You may want to use arrays in your scripts but may not know the upper bound or the dimensions of the array when you are writing the code. For these situations, you can use a dynamic array.

There are three basic steps to using a dynamic array in Visual Basic Scripting Edition.

1. Declare the array, but omit the upper bound argument.

Example

```
Dim MyArray()
```

2. Initialize the array to the required size by using the **ReDim** statement.

Example

```
ReDim MyArray(4)
```

You can use **ReDim** on its own to create and initialize an array in one step.

3. Use the array as in the previous section, Arrays.

Resizing an Array

The ReDim statement can also be used to resize the array if required. For example, you may start with an array that has five elements, but at some point, it may need to be resized to hold eight values. You can reissue the **ReDim** statement, as the following example shows:

Example

```
Dim MyArray()
RedDim MyArray(4)
MyArray(0)=100
MyArray(1)=200
MyArray(2)=300
MyArray(3)=400
MyArray(4)=500
...
...
ReDim MyArray(7)
...
...
```

It is extremely important to understand that using the **ReDim** statement removes the existing values in the array. In the previous example, the five-element array was populated with the data as shown, but then this data was lost when the array was resized.

The **Preserve** keyword can be used in conjunction with the **ReDim** statement to alter this behavior. As the name of the keyword implies, it preserves the contents of the array, if possible, when the resizing takes place.

In the following example, **ReDim** sets the initial number elements in the dynamic array to 5. A subsequent **ReDim** statement resizes the array but makes use of the **Preserve** keyword to protect the data already in the array.

Example

```
Dim MyArray()
RedDim MyArray(4)
MyArray(0)=100
MyArray(1)=200
MyArray(2)=300
MyArray(3)=400
MyArray(4)=500
...
...
ReDim Preserve MyArray(7)
...
...
```

Caution   If you resize a fully populated array so that it contains fewer elements than before, then you will inevitably remove some data, even if you use the **Preserve** keyword.

The Array Statement

Dynamic arrays can also be achieved by using the **Array** statement. This has the advantage that it can initialize and populate an array at the same time; for example:

Example

```
Dim MyArray
MyArray = Array(100, 200, 300, 400, 500)
```

The **Dim** statement declares the variable name. The variable is then converted into an array, initialized to contain five elements, and populated with the values shown in the parentheses, all in one line. Note that the statement does not require an upper bound to be explicitly declared. The upper bound of the array will be created to fit the number of elements in the parentheses.

Emptying an Array

The **Erase** statement is used to delete the contents of an array.

Example

```
Erase MyArray
```

This clears the contents of a fixed-size array. The array itself still exists. However, if using the Erase statement empties a dynamic array, the data is removed and the array is uninitialized. The array must be redimensioned with the **ReDim** statement before it can be used again.

The UBound Function

With dynamic arrays, you often do not know how many elements they contain when you write your scripts. However, you often must work this out in code. For example, you must know the upper bound when using a loop to iterate through all of the elements in the array. The **UBound** function can be used in these situations. This function returns the number of the highest element in the array, as the following syntax shows:

Syntax

UBound(_arrayname_[, _dimension_]**)**

In this syntax, _arrayname_ is the name of the array, and _dimension_ is the required dimension that you want to check. If only one dimension exists, _dimension_ is optional.

◆ Operators

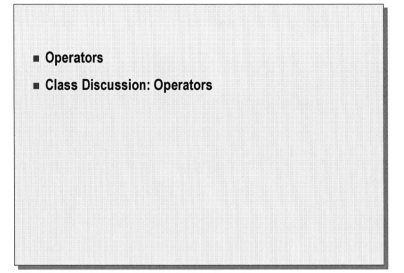

- **Operators**
- **Class Discussion: Operators**

If you want to successfully manipulate your data, you must understand the use of variables, arrays of variables, and constants, as well as the operators that Visual Basic Scripting Edition provides.

In this section, you will learn about the operators that VBScript provides.

Operators

> ■ **Main Operator Types:**
>
> - Arithmetic: ^ - * / \ Mod + -
> - Concatenation: &
> - Comparison: = <> < > <= >= IS
> - Logical: Not And Or XOr Eqv Imp
>
> ■ **Operator Precedence**
>
> - Parentheses

Operators are the reserved characters that you use along with variables and other data in your scripts. The operators provided by Visual Basic Scripting Edition can be categorized into four types: arithmetic, concatenation, comparison, and logical.

Arithmetic Operators

Arithmetic operators perform basic arithmetic functions such as addition, subtraction, or multiplication. The following table describes the arithmetic operators.

Operators	Description	Symbol
Exponentiation	Raises a number to the power of an exponent	^
Unary negation	Indicates the negative value of a numeric expression.	-
Multiplication	Multiplies two numbers.	*
Division	Divides two numbers and returns a floating-point result.	/
Integer division	Divides two numbers and returns an integer result.	\
Modulus arithmetic	Divides two numbers and returns only the remainder.	Mod
Addition	Sums two numbers.	+
Subtraction	Finds the difference between two numbers.	-

Concatenation Operator

You often must create a string by concatenating or joining together two or more other strings. The string concatenation operator is the ampersand (&). A space must follow the ampersand for the concatenation to work correctly. For example, the following script sample concatenates two string literals and a string variable into a single string that is then echoed to the screen:

Example

```
WScript.Echo "The path is, " & strPath & " on Server B"
```

Numeric variables can also be concatenated with string values.

Example

```
nAge = InputBox("Please enter your Age.")
nTogo = 65 - nAge
MsgBox "You have " & nTogo & " years until you retire!"
```

In this example, the variable nAge is assigned the value entered into the input box. A simple calculation is then done to calculate the years left until the age of 65. The result is stored in the variable nTogo. This number is then concatenated with two string literals, and the resulting string is displayed in a message box.

Warning   It is possible to use the plus sign (+) to provide concatenate strings. However, this is not recommended because it will generate errors when mixing string and numeric values.

Comparison Operators

Comparison operators are used to compare values. By using these operators, an expression can be built that will test for a condition and return either **True** or **False**. The following table describes the available operators.

Description	Symbol
Equality	=
Inequality	<>
Less than	<
Greater than	>
Less than or equal to	<=
Greater than or equal to	>=
Object equivalence	IS

The syntax for these operators is the following:

Syntax

```
result = value1 operator value2
```

Logical Operators

Logical operators are used in a similar way to comparison operators. For example, the **Not** operator performs logical negation on an expression as follows:

Example

```
bNegResult = Not bResult
```

If the value of **bResult** is **True**, the value of **bNegResult** is set to **False**.

The following table describes the logical operators supported by Visual Basic Scripting Edition.

Operators	Description	Symbol
Negation	Performs logical negation on an expression	Not
Conjunction	Performs a logical conjunction on two expressions	And
Disjunction	Performs a logical disjunction on two expressions	Or
Exclusion	Performs a logical exclusion on two expressions	XOr
Equivalence	Performs a logical equivalence on two expressions	Eqv
Implication	Performs a logical implication on two expressions	Imp

Operator Precedence

You will often build complex tests by using a mixture of operators. It is important to understand how the various operators are resolved and the order in which each part of the expression is evaluated. This is determined by the order of operator precedence that VBScript defines.

The following list presents the operators in the order of precedence that is defined by VBScript:

- ^

- −

- *, /, and \

- MOD

- +, -

- &

- =, <>, < >, <=, >=, and IS

- NOT

- AND

- OR

- XOR

- EQV

- IMP

By using parentheses, you can control the order of precedence. Expressions in parentheses are evaluated before expressions that are not in parentheses.

Class Discussion: Operators

A. **1+4+10*6-4/2**

B. **(1+4+10)*6-(4/2)**

C. **1+4+10*(6-4)/2**

D. **(1+4+10) & (6-4)/2**

E. **1+4+10 & (6-4)/2**

In this discussion, you will review five calculations with the rest of the class. Each calculation looks similar, but by using the various rules of precedence, different results are achieved. Record the value of each expression in the space below it.

1+4+10*6-4/2

_____

(1+4+10)*6-(4/2)

_____

1+4+10*(6-4)/2

_____

(1+4+10) & (6-4)/2

_____

1+4+10 & 6-4/2

_____

◆ Conditions and Loops

- ■ **Conditional Statements: If...Then**
- ■ **Conditional Statements: Select Case...End Select**
- ■ **Looping: For...Next**
- ■ **Looping: Do...Loop / While...Wend**
- ■ **Built-in Functions**

It is essential that you can apply standard programming techniques, such as decision-making and looping, to your administrative scripts.

In this section, you will learn how to write conditional code by using two standard programmatic approaches. You will then learn how to construct effective looping structures by applying a variety of techniques. In addition, you will learn about some of the built-in functions that Visual Basic Scripting Edition provides to enable you to write manageable and effective code.

Conditional Statements: If...Then

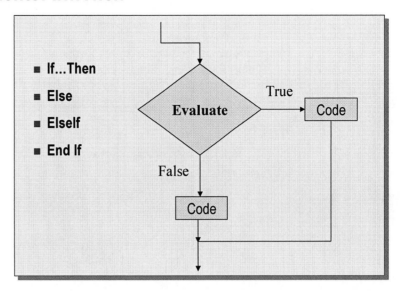

- If...Then
- Else
- ElseIf
- End If

Conditional structures are used to control the flow of the code in your scripts. You often must write code that can only be run in certain circumstances. You can achieve this with conditional structures.

If...Then

You will often use the **If...Then** statement in Visual Basic Scripting Edition, because it provides a simple test to evaluate if a condition is **True** or **False**. The basic syntax for the **If...Then** structure is:

Syntax

```
If <condition> Then <action>
```

For example:

Example

```
If MyVar = 5 Then WScript.Echo "MyVar = 5"
```

In this example, the message **MyVar = 5** is echoed to the screen only if the MyVar variable contains the value 5. If the variable has any other value, the message will not be displayed.

Else

The **Else** statement can be added to the **If...Then** statement. This enables statements to be executed if the condition within the **If** statement is not met; for example:

Example

```
If MyVar = 5 Then
  WScript.Echo "MyVar = 5"
Else
  WScript.Echo "MyVar does not equal 5"
End If
```

In this script, the message **MyVar does not equal 5** is displayed unless the MyVar variable contains the value 5.

Note   The expansion of the structure from the single-line syntax, shown previously, to the multiple-line format, as shown in this example, is known as a **Block If** structure. When you develop **Block If** structures, you must always remember to include the keyword **End If** at the end of the structure.

ElseIf

The **ElseIf** construct extends the functionality of the **If** statement by allowing the condition to have more than two different results; for example:

Example

```
If MyVar = 0 Then
    WScript.Echo "MyVar = 0"
ElseIf MyVar = 1 Then
    WScript.Echo "MyVar = 1"
ElseIf MyVar = 2 then
    WScript.Echo "MyVar = 2"
Else
    WScript.Echo "Sorry value is out of range"
End If
```

End If

The **End If** statement can be added if you want to combine multiple steps in a single test. For example:

Example

```
If MyVar = 5 Then
  WScript.Echo "MyVar = 5"
  WScript.Echo "Reseting MyVar"
  MyVar =  0
End If
```

In this example, three lines of script are executed if the condition evaluates to **True**. These lines are indented for clarity. Indentation is particularly beneficial when several conditional statements are nested, as shown in the following example:

Example

```
If MyVar = 5 Then
  WScript.Echo "MyVar = 5"
  If MyVar2 = 10 Then
      WScript.Echo "MyVar2 = 10"
  End If
End If
```

If MyVar contains the value 5, the first message is echoed to the screen. Then, a second test is performed on a second variable. If that also returns **True**, a second message is displayed. An **End If** statement is required for each **If** statement.

Conditional Statements: Select Case...End Select

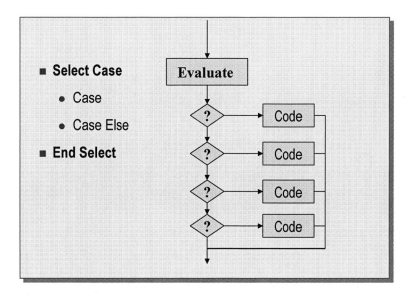

- **Select Case**
  - Case
  - Case Else
- **End Select**

Although you can rely exclusively on the **If** statements described in the previous section for conditional coding, there is an alternative. You can use the **Select Case** structure. Although it is true that any **Select Case** structure can be rewritten by using **If** statements, and vice versa, there are times when one structure is more appropriate than the other, because one or the other is easier to code, read, or debug.

The **Select Case** statement works with a single condition that is evaluated once in the first line of the statement. The result of the expression is then compared with the values for each **Case** statement listed below the original **Select Case** statement. If there is a match, the block of statements associated with that **Case** statement is executed; for example:

Example

```
Select Case MyVar
    Case "0"
        WScript.Echo "MyVar = 0"
    Case "1"
        WScript.Echo "MyVar = 1"
    Case "2"
        WScript.Echo "MyVar = 2"
    Case Else
        WScript.Echo "Sorry value is out of range"
End Select
```

This script is clearer than the previous example that uses the **If...Then...ElseIf** structure. Notice that substituting an **If...Then...ElseIf** structure with a **Select Case** structure only works in this example, because the same condition is being tested all the way down the **ElseIf** tree. If more than one condition is being tested, the **If...Then** structure is more appropriate.

Select Case statements can be nested. Like the **If** statement, each nested **Select Case** statement must have a matching **End Select** statement.

Looping: For...Next

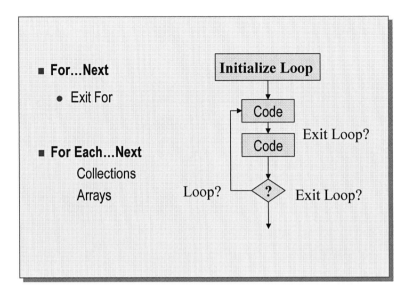

Along with writing decision-making code, you often must write code that runs multiple times in each execution of your script.

For...Next

The **For...Next** loop is used to execute one or more statements a specific number of times. The number of times that the statements are executed is determined by the counter variable of the **For...Next** loop, which is set up when the loop is initialized. This counter is then increased or decreased with each repetition of the loop.

The syntax of the **For...Next** construct is:

Syntax

```
For counter = start to finish [Step n]
  action(s)
Next counter
```

For example, the following code illustrates a loop that runs ten times:

Example

```
For iCounter = 1 To 10
  WScript.Echo "This is loop number " & iCounter
Next
```

The variable iCounter is set to 1 when the loop is initialized. The **WScript.Echo** statement is then executed. When the **Next** statement is reached, the variable automatically increases by 1 and the loop is executed again. This continues until the value of counter is greater than 10. Then, the loop is exited, and execution continues at the line after the **Next** statement. By default, iCounter will increment by one each time around the loop. This default behavior can be modified by using the **Step** statement as follows:

Example

```
For iCounter = 1 to 10 Step 2
  WScript.Echo "Odd number " & iCounter
Next
```

This **Step** statement results in only five iterations of the loop. As the loop runs, iCounter has the value of 1, 3, 5, 7, and 9.

The **Step** statement can also be used to decrement a counter simply by the addition of a minus sign (-).

Example

```
For iCounter = 10 to 2 Step -2
  action(s)
Next
```

In this example, the loop is iterated five times, starting at the value of 10 and finishing with the value of 2.

Exit For

You can optionally exit a loop at any time before it is finished by using the **Exit For** statement; for example:

Example

```
vInput = InputBox ("Enter the Value to stop the loop at")
iStop = CInt(vInput)
For iCounter = 1 to 10
  WScript.Echo "Current iCounter Value = " & iCounter
  If iStop = iCounter Then Exit For
  WScript.Echo "Around we go again"
Next
WScript.Echo "Loop exited at value of " & iCounter
```

This script uses a variable called vInput that takes a value from the user of the script. This value is then converted into an integer and stored in the iStop variable. A **For...Next** loop is then set up and the current value of the counter variable iCounter is echoed to the screen. A test is then done to see if iCounter equals iStop. If it is equal, the loop is exited. Otherwise, a message is echoed, and the loop continues. After the loop is exited, a message is echoed that displays the value of iCounter.

For Each...Next

The **For Each...Next** structure is used to iterate through the items in a collection of objects or for each element of an array. This is very useful when you do not know how many elements there will be in the collection prior to running the script; for example:

Example

```
For Each File in objFiles
   WScript.echo File.Name
Next
```

The above example shows a snippet of a script that has a collection object called **objFiles**. Collection objects usually contain multiple items, so the **For Each...Next** structure is used to loop through each item in the collection. In this example, a collection of files is looped through, and the name of each file is displayed. Once all of the items in the collection have been displayed, the loop is exited.

Looping: Do...Loop / While...Wend

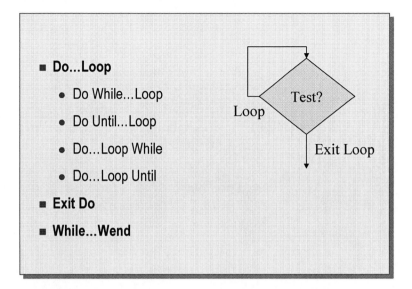

- **Do...Loop**
  - Do While...Loop
  - Do Until...Loop
  - Do...Loop While
  - Do...Loop Until
- **Exit Do**
- **While...Wend**

As described in the previous section, Looping: For...Next, you often write code that executes a given number of times. You have seen how to use the **For...Next** loop to run code a specific number of times. However, that type of loop is only useful when you know how many times a loop must be executed or when you know that you can work out the number of times a loop must be executed as part of your code.

Often, you must execute code in a loop, but you do not know how many times the loop must be run when you are actually writing the code. Additional looping structures are available to you when you encounter this situation.

Do...Loop

The **Do...Loop** structure iterates a number of script statements in a similar fashion to the **For...Next** structure. The main difference between the **Do...Loop** structure and the **For...Next** structure is that the **Do...Loop** structure does not require you to know the number of times the loop must be run when you write the code. There are two basic forms of this structure: **Do While...Loop** and the **Do Until...Loop**.

Do While...Loop

This loop repeatedly executes a statement while a condition is true. The condition is evaluated each time that the loop begins.

Example

```
Do While vMyVar < 100
  vMyVar = vMyVar + 1
  WScript.Echo "vMyVar = " & vMyVar
Loop
```

Do Until...Loop

This statement repeats the script in the loop until a condition becomes true. The previous examples can be converted into the **Do Until...Loop** structure by making the following changes to the script test conditions:

Example

```
Do Until vMyVar >= 100
  vMyVar = vMyVar + 1
  WScript.Echo "vMyVar = " & vMyVar
Loop
```

Note It is possible to rewrite a **Do While** structure as a **Do Until** structure by negating the condition, as shown above.

Do...Loop While

You can check the expression that represents the exit condition at the end of the **Do While** loop, rather than at the beginning; for example:

Example

```
Do
  vMyVar = vMyVar + 1
  WScript.Echo "vMyVar = " & vMyVar
Loop While vMyVar < 100
```

Checking the condition at the end of the loop, rather than at the beginning, forces the loop to be executed at least once. Imagine that the condition is already satisfied when the loop begins. If you check for the condition at the beginning of the loop, the code inside the loop is not executed at all.

However, if you check the condition at the end of the loop, even if the condition is already met, the code inside the loop runs once. If, by the end of the loop, the condition is still satisfied, the loop is finished. However, note that the code inside the loop may alter the state of the condition. The loop continues until the condition is satisfied once more.

Do...Loop Until

As with the **Do While** loop, you can check the expression that represents the exit condition at the end of the **Do Until** loop, rather that at the beginning; for example:

Example

Example

```
Do
  vMyVar = vMyVar + 1
  WScript.Echo "vMyVar = " & vMyVar
Loop Until vMyVar >= 100
```

Exit Do

Just as there is an **Exit For** statement, there is an **Exit Do** statement that is useful for exiting a loop if another condition is met while the loop is executed. For example:

Example

```
vInput = InputBox ("Enter the Value to stop the loop at")
iStop = CInt(vInput)
Do While iCounter < 10
 iCounter = iCounter + 1
  WScript.Echo "Current iCounter Value = " & iCounter
  If iStop = iCounter Then Exit Do
  WScript.Echo "Around we go again"
Loop
WScript.Echo "Loop exited at value of " & iCounter
```

While...Wend

The **While...Wend** structure was introduced in the early days of Visual Basic and has since been superseded by the **Do** loops and the **For** loops. It is available for backwards compatibility.

It works in the following way:

- If the test condition is true, all of the statements in the loop are executed until *t*he **Wend** statement is encountered.

- The script then returns to the **While** statement and the test condition is checked again.

- If the condition is still true, the process is repeated.

- If it is not true, the loop is exited, and the execution of the script that follows the **Wend** statement runs.

For example:

Example

```
While vMyVar < 100
  vMyVar = vMyVar + 1
  WScript.Echo "vMyVar = " & vMyVar
Wend
```

Generally, **Do...Loop** is considered to be better than **While...Wend**, because it is more structured and flexible.

Built-in Functions

- ■ **Date and Time Functions**
  - Now, Time, Date, DateDiff
- ■ **String Manipulation Functions**
  - LCase, UCase
- ■ **Mathematical Functions**
  - Rnd, Round

Visual Basic Scripting Edition contains various special functions that can be used in script to provide certain features that are either difficult to write yourself or required by many scripts. These special functions are known as built-in functions. They can be used in expressions with variables and other values to calculate and return values.

Date and Time Functions

There are functions that make handling dates and times in your script easy.

Now

The **Now** function returns the current date and time on the computer system clock, as the following example shows:

Example

```
WScript.Echo Now
```

This function returns a value like 26/06/2000 15:23:41

The format of the return value depends on your regional settings.

Time

The **Time** function returns a **Variant** of subtype **Date** that indicates the current time on the computer system clock, as the following example shows:

Example

```
WScript.echo Time
```

This function returns a value such as 15:24:27

Date

The **Date** function returns the current date on the computer system clock; for example:

Example

```
WScript.Echo "Today's Date is : " & Date
```

This function returns a value such as 26/06/2000

DateDiff

The **DateDiff** function returns the number of intervals between two dates.

Example

```
vDate = DateDiff("d", Date, "01/01/3000")
WScript.Echo "Days until the next Millennium: " & vDate
```

The "d" argument indicates that the function must return a number that represents the number of days between the two dates. Other valid argument values include:

- "yyyy" for the number of years between the two dates.
- "m" for the number of months between the two dates.
- "h" for the number of hours between the two dates.

String Manipulation Functions

Because you often must manipulate and compare strings with Visual Basic Scripting Edition, several string manipulation functions are provided.

These functions return a string value that has been converted to lowercase (**LCase**) or uppercase (**UCase**). This is useful when you compare one string to another string and the scriptwriter does not know what case will be used.

A user that typed one of the strings may have mixed the case of his or her input. This can cause any test to fail, because a string comparison of a lower and an upper case letter always returns **False**. By using the **LCase** or **UCase** functions, the scriptwriter is assured that the comparison is performed by using lower or upper case only.

Example

```
vName = InputBox("Please enter your home country?")
   vName = LCase(vName)
Select Case vName
    Case "uk"
        WScript.Echo "Welcome to the UK!"
    Case "usa"
        WScript.Echo "Welcome to the States!"
    Case "germany"
        WScript.Echo "Welcome to Germany!"
    Case "france"
        WScript.Echo "Welcome to France!"
    Case Else
        WScript.Echo "Sorry, try again! "
End Select
```

Mathematical Functions

Because you often must perform mathematical manipulations with Visual Basic Scripting Edition, several mathematical functions are provided.

Rnd

The **Rnd** function returns a random number between 0 and 1 to seven decimal places. This function only works correctly if the random number generator has been initialized before the **Rnd** function is called. To initialize the random number generator, use the **Randomize** statement as shown in the following example:

Example

```
Randomize
WScript.Echo Rnd
```

By multiplying the value that the **Rnd** function returns, you can generate random numbers within a given range. For example:

Example

```
Randomize
WScript.Echo Rnd * 100
```

This generates a random number between 0 and 100, including fractions of a number.

Round

If a script requires you to use whole numbers, you can use the **Round** function to convert a number to the nearest integer.

Example

```
Randomize
vRnd = Rnd * 100
WScript.Echo Round(vRnd)
```

Note   There are many more functions available in VBScript. For the complete list of functions, see the VBScript documentation.

◆ Procedures

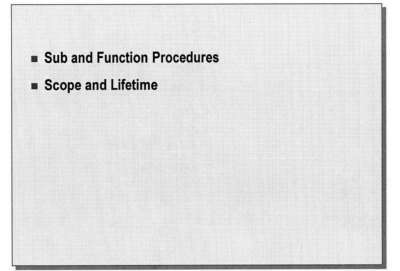

- Sub and Function Procedures
- Scope and Lifetime

You have learned how to write scripts by using the Visual Basic Script Edition language. When you write your code, you often encounter a situation where you must run similar blocks of code multiple times. When this is the case, you can encapsulate this code into reusable blocks, called procedures.

In this section, you will learn about **Sub** and **Function** procedures. You will also learn how procedures and variables interact to create the concepts of scope and lifetime.

Sub and Function Procedures

- **Sub Procedures**
- **Function Procedures**
  - Returns a result
- **Exiting a Procedure**
- **Passing Parameters**
  - ByRef
  - ByVal

In Visual Basic Scripting Edition, there are two kinds of procedures: **Sub** procedures, sometimes called subroutines, and **Function** procedures.

Procedures are used to encapsulate code block that you need often.

Sub Procedures

Sub procedures contain code that you can reuse in your scripts many times without having to rewrite the code every time that it is needed. Instead, you write the code once inside the procedure, and then call the procedure from other places in your code to indicate that the contents of the procedure should be run at that point.

The following example shows how **Sub** procedures can be used in your scripts. Note that the **Sub** procedure named Status is called twice. The Call statement is optional.

Example

```
Dim sStausMessage
Call Welcome
sStausMessage = "Starting..."
Call Status
sStausMessage = "Ending..."
Call Status
Call Farewell
Sub Welcome()
  WScript.Echo "Hello"
End Sub
Sub Status()
  WScript.Echo sStausMessage
End Sub
Sub Farewell()
  WScript.Echo "Goodbye"
End Sub
```

Note The **Call** statement is optional.

Function Procedures

Function procedures are very similar to **Sub** procedures. You write the code once inside the procedure, and then simply call the procedure from other places in your code. The only important difference between a **Sub** and a **Function** procedure is that the latter returns a result to the script that called it, while the former does not.

Consequently, you use the **Function** procedure most often as part of a larger expression, because the call to it results in a value being returned in place of the **Function** name. The following example illustrate how the function call returns a value that can be used in any expression:

Example

```
Dim dDate
dDate=Tomorrow
WScript.Echo dDate
Function Tomorrow()
  Tomorrow= DateAdd("d",1,Date())
End Function
```

Exiting a Procedure

If a test, such as an **If...Then** structure, determines that the procedure must be exited, the procedure is exited by using the exit statement. When you reach the end of the procedure, the **End Sub** statement returns the execution of the script back to the point in the script immediately after the procedure was called.

Passing Parameters

The code examples shown so far do not enable you to pass any additional data into the procedures when they are called. However, passing additional data that the procedure works with is a very useful and common practice.

To pass parameters to your procedures, you must define the parameters that the procedure will receive when you write the procedure. You do this by providing a comma-separated list of parameter names inside the parentheses for the procedure, as the following example shows:

Example

```
Function GrossValue(NetValue, TaxRate)
  GrossValue=NetValue + (NetValue * TaxRate)
End Function
```

You must pass the values of the parameters to the procedure when you call the procedure. The following example calls the **GrossValue** function and passes a value of 100 for the *NetValue* parameter and 0.175 for the *TaxRate* parameter:

Example

```
WScript.Echo "Gross Value is: " & GrossValue(100,0.175)
```

ByRef and ByVal

You pass data into procedures by using variable names that contain the relevant data rather than the literal values themselves. By default, variables are passed to procedures by reference. As a result, if you make any changes to the parameters in the **Sub** procedure or **Function** procedure, the original variable in the calling code is altered, as well.

Although this is the default behavior in VBScript, you can explicitly qualify each argument by using the **ByRef** keyword, as shown in the following example:

Example

```
Function GrossValue(ByRef NetValue, ByRef TaxRate)
  GrossValue=NetValue + (NetValue * TaxRate)
End Function
```

The second method for parsing an argument is by value. With this approach, any argument passed to the **Sub** procedure or **Function** procedure is a copy of the original variable. If you make any changes to the parameters in the procedure, the variable in the calling code is not changed.

To specify this option, you use the **ByVal** keyword in front of each argument, as shown in the following example:

Example

```
Function GrossValue(ByVal NetValue, ByVal TaxRate)
  GrossValue=NetValue + (NetValue * TaxRate)
End Function
```

You will note that in the examples used so far, both **ByRef** and **ByVal** result in identical script behavior. This is because the procedures themselves do not internally modify the values of the parameters that have been passed to them. However, this is not always the case. For example, the following code, which uses **ByRef**, results in a message of "Two times 60 is 60," which is obviously not intended:

Example

```
Dim iNumber, iResult
iNumber=30
iResult = Doubler(iNumber)
WScript.Echo "Two times " & iNumber & " is " & iResult
Function Doubler(ByRef InputNum)
  InputNum = 2 * InputNum
  Doubler = InputNum
End Function
```

The *InputNum* parameter points to the same memory location as the iNumber variable, because *InputNum* was passed by using **ByRef**. Therefore, any changes made to the *InputNum* parameter also results in those changes being applied to the iNumber variable.

The following example is almost identical. However, the parameter is passed by using **ByVal**. This results in a message of "Two times 30 is 60," which is intended.

Example

```
Dim iNumber, iResult
iNumber=30
iResult = Doubler(iNumber)
WScript.Echo "Two times " & iNumber & " is " & iResult
Function Doubler(ByVal InputNum)
  InputNum = 2 * InputNum
  Doubler = InputNum
End Function
```

Scope and Lifetime

- **Script-Level Variables**
  - Dim
  - Private
  - Public
- **Procedure-Level Variables**
  - Dim

The scope of a variable defines where it can be used in your script. The lifetime of a variable determines the time period that the variable exists in memory and the time period it is available to your script.

The scope and lifetime of a variable are determined by where in the script the variable is declared and the keyword used to declare the variable.

Script-Level Variables

When declaring a variable in the main body of the script, it can be referenced from anywhere else in the script. Variables can be used by other statements in the main body and also in any procedures that are called. These variables are known as script-level variables that have script-level scope.

You can declare script-level variables with either the **Dim** keyword or the **Private** keyword. These keywords are synonymous when used to declare script-level variables.

There is also a **Public** keyword that can be used to define variables that are available outside the scope of the script itself. However, you can only do this if the script is going to be used with other scripts that can reference these variables, such as .wsf files. If this is not the case, then script-level variables that are declared with the **Public** keyword behave identically to variables that are declared with the **Private** and **Dim** keywords.

The names of script-level variables must be unique throughout the script. The lifetime of a script-level variable is from the time the variable is declared to the time when the script terminates.

Procedure-Level Variables

When a variable is declared in a procedure, only script within that procedure can access or change the value of the variable. It has local scope and is called a procedure-level variable. A procedure-level variable exists only when the procedure is running. When the procedure is finished, the variable is destroyed. The variable has procedure-level lifetime.

You can have local variables of the same name in several different procedures, because each variable is recognized only by the procedure in which it is declared. Declaration of procedure-level variables is usually undertaken at the very start of the procedure itself. This is a good practice, because it makes tracking the variables easier.

It is also a good practice to declare variables with the smallest scope possible. This prevents you from having to make a long list of variable names that is visible to the whole script and helps to minimize the memory that variable names consume.

Procedure-level variables cannot be declared with the **Public** or **Private** keywords. You must use the **Dim** keyword to declare procedure-level variables.

◆ Script Layout

- **Script Sections**
- **Using a Template**
- **Best Practices for VBScript**

You can organize your scripts in a manner that makes them easy to deal with and easy to read and debug.

In this section, you will learn about organizing the code in your scripts. You will also learn about some good practices for coding.

Script Sections

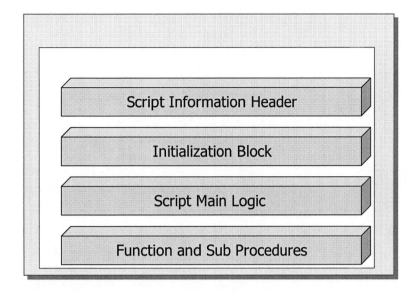

As your scripts get larger and more complex, it becomes increasingly important to have a standard and logical layout for your scripts. There are several recommended standards, but you are free to decide whether you want to use them or not. However, remember that ultimately these standards are there to make working with script easier.

One simple recommended standard is to organize the script into four main blocks:

- Script information header
- Initialization block
- Main logic
- **Function** and **Sub** procedures

Script Information Header

This script information header contains information about the script itself. It is not required for the execution of the script as it is commented out. The information in the script information header is there to help whoever is reading the script identify what the script is, who wrote it, and what it should do. An example of a script header is shown below:

Example

```
'============================================================
'
' LANG        : VBScript
' NAME        : MyScript.wsf
' AUTHOR      : My Name
' DATE        : 21/06/2000
' Description : Demonstration Script Header
' COMMENT     : Add comments here
'
' KEYWORDS    : Indexing Keywords here
'============================================================
```

The use of the KEYWORDS field is to enable an indexing engine to search and retrieve all related scripts.

Initialization block

The next block of the script is the initialization block. In this section, script-level variables, constants, and object names are declared. This provides a single reference area where all variable names can be looked up when working on the script. For example:

Example

```
'============================================================
'Variable Declarations

Dim nNetValue
'Used to store the net value of a product

Dim nGrossValue
'Used to store the gross value of a product

Dim nTaxRate
'Used to store the tax rate that must be applied to net value


'============================================================
```

Script Main Logic

The script main logic section is where you type the main body of the script. Note that this section is not always the biggest part of the script. If the script uses a lot of procedures to complete its task, this section might be no more than a list of procedure calls and a **WScript.Quit** statement. The following is an example of the main body of a script:

Example

```
'==========================================================
' Main Body

' Set the net value
nNetValue = 100

' Set the tax rate
nTaxRate = 0.175

' Call the GrossValue function
nGrossValue = GrossValue(nNetValue, nTaxRate)

' Display the result to the user
WScript.Echo "The Gross Value is: " & nGrossValue


'==========================================================
```

Function and Sub Routines

This section is made up of all of the procedures that are called from within the main script logic. They are not executed in a top-down manner, but are executed when called. You can also store procedures that are not currently used in the script, but can be used at some point in the future. If the main script logic does not call the procedure, it will be ignored.

The following example shows the final script, complete with all of the sections:

Example

```
'===============================================================
'
' LANG          : VBScript
' NAME          : MyScript.wsf
' AUTHOR        : My Name
' DATE          : 21/06/2000
' Description   : Demonstration Script Header
' COMMENT       : Add comments here
'
' KEYWORDS      : Indexing Keywords here
'===============================================================
'===============================================================
'Variable Declarations

Dim nNetValue
'Used to store the net value of a product

Dim nGrossValue
'Used to store the gross value of a product

Dim nTaxRate
'Used to store the tax rate that must be applied to net value


  '===========================================================
  '===========================================================
' Main Body

' Set the net value
nNetValue = 100

' Set the tax rate
nTaxRate = 0.175

' Call the GrossValue function
nGrossValue = GrossValue(nNetValue, nTaxRate)

' Display the result to the user
WScript.Echo "The Gross Value is: " & nGrossValue


  '===========================================================
  '===========================================================
' Procedures

' Returns a gross value based on a net value and a tax rate
Function GrossValue(nNet, nRate)
  GrossValue=nNet + (nNet * nRate)
End Function


  '===========================================================
```

Note   You can also use another type of layout, which defines the procedures directly after the initialization of the variables, with the main script logic at the end of the script. It makes little difference to the execution of the script which layout you use. Ultimately, it is a matter of personal preference.

Using a Template

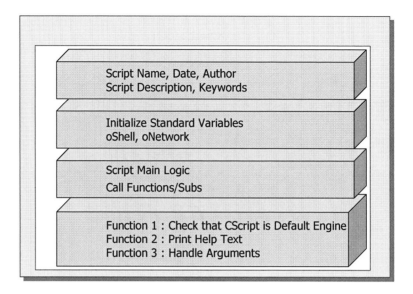

After you have defined the basic script layout, you can create a template that can be reused as the basis for future scripts. This template can be as simple or as complex as required. Fundamentally, it should help you create scripts in a standard way.

The template is not restricted to the script outline. If there are script segments or procedures that are regularly used, such as common variable definitions or usage display procedures, these could also be included as part of the template.

A typical template might have separate sections for:

- Script name, description, date, author, and keywords.
- Script level variable and constant declarations.
- The main script body.
- Procedures.

Some Integrated Development Environment (IDE) tools, such as Primal Script, allow for the definition of a template as part of creating a new script file. If you are using one of these tools, it is worth spending a few minutes setting up this feature, because ultimately this feature can save you a great deal of typing.

Note Lab 3, "Working with VBScript," uses an example script template that you can customize to meet your needs.

Best Practices for VBScript

- **Using Option Explicit**
- **Giving Variables Meaningful Names**
- **Commenting Your Scripts**
- **Using a Consistent Naming Standard**
- **Creating a Useful Script Store**

Coding by using Visual Basic Scripting Edition is flexible. You can achieve the same results in many different ways. However, there are some best practices that you should adhere to.

Using Option Explicit

Always set **Option Explicit** in your script, because you are required to declare all of your variable names. This greatly reduces bugs caused by mistyped variable names.

Giving Variables Meaningful Names

When possible, give the variables and objects in your script meaningful and user-friendly names. This will make it easier to understand what a script is trying to do.

Commenting Your Script

Commenting your script not only makes it easier for other people to understand what a script is trying to achieve, but it will also help you if you must reuse a script after many months.

Using a Consistent Naming Standard

Whether or not you choose to use the Hungarian naming standard, adopt a consistent standard. This makes your scripts easy to understand over time.

Creating a Useful Script Store

As you learn script, you will come across many examples of script that solve a specific problem. When you come across these examples, cut and paste them into a script template and store them in a folder that you can then index. By doing this, you can build up a store of examples that you can quickly copy into your script when required.

Lab 3: Working with VBScript

Objectives

In this lab, you will create a script template file and use it to create a script that tests a user's name against a known list.

You will use the following concepts and features of Visual Basic Scripting Edition to achieve this:

- Script templates
- Constants
- Variables
- Decision-making structures
- Looping structures
- Intrinsic VBScript constants
- Procedures

Estimated time to complete this lab: 30 minutes

Exercise 1
Creating Script Templates

In this exercise, you will use PrimalSCRIPT to create an administrative script template.

▶ **To create a PrimalSCRIPT template**

1. On the **Start** menu, point to **Programs**, point to **SAPIEN Technologies, Inc**, and then click **PrimalSCRIPT 2.0**.

   PrimalSCRIPT appears.

2. On the **File** menu, click **New**.

3. In the **New** dialog box, click **Text**, and then click **OK**.

   A new text document is created.

4. Type the following code in the new document:

```
'=============================================================
' LANG          : VBScript
' NAME          :
' AUTHOR        : NWind Traders Administrator
' DATE          :
' Description      :
' COMMENT       :
' KEYWORDS      :
'=============================================================
'=============================================================
'Variable Declarations


'=============================================================
'=============================================================
' Main Body


'=============================================================
'=============================================================
' Procedures

' Function Template
Function FName(arg1, arg2)

End Function

' Sub Template
Sub SName(arg1, arg2)

End Sub

'=============================================================
```

▶ **To save the script template**

1. On the **File** menu, click **Save As**.

2. In the **Save As** dialog box, browse to the
   C:\Program Files\SAPIEN\PrimalSCRIPT\Templates folder.

3. In the **File name** box, type **NWind Script.vbs**

4. In the **Save as type** box, click **VBScript files (*.vb, *.vbs)**, and then click
   Save.

5. On the **File** menu, click **Close**.

▶ **To create a new script based on your template**

1. On the **File** menu, click **New**.

   Note that your template, NWind Script, is now available as a template for
   new script documents.

2. In the **New** dialog box, click **NWind Script**, and then click **OK**.

   A new document is created, based on your template. Note that the text is
   color-coded and formatted as VBScript. Changes you make to this new
   document will not affect the NWind Script template.

3. Leave the script open, because you will use it in the next exercise.

You have now created a template and have seen how to create a new script that
is based upon it.

Exercise 2
Using Constants, Variables, Loops, and Conditional Structures

In this exercise, you will use the new file that was written in Visual Basic Scripting Edition and that was created from the template in exercise 1. You will then use variables and constants to manipulate data that is entered by the script user.

In addition, you will create decision-making and looping structures that will compare the user's name with a list of pre-approved administrators. You will enable the user to enter his or her name up to three times. If the user enters an administrator's name, the script continues to run. If the user fails to enter a valid name three times in a row, the user is notified that he or she has not been validated.

▶ **To complete the script description section**

1. Modify the script description section so that it reads as follows:

```
'===========================================================
'
' LANG         : VBScript
' NAME         : Validate.vbs
' AUTHOR       : NWind Traders Administrator
' DATE         :
' Description  : Validates administrative users
' COMMENT      : Lab 03
'
' KEYWORDS     : Loops, variables, constants
'===========================================================
```

2. Type today's date in the DATE field.

▶ **To declare constants and variables**

1. Under **Variable Declarations**, declare the following variables:

   - iLoopCount

   - sUserName

   - iAnswer

2. In the same section, declare a constant named **ADMIN_1**, with a value of **FRANK LEE**

3. Declare another constant named **ADMIN_2**, with a value of **STEPHANIE HOOPER**

   The complete section should resemble the following code:

```
Dim iLoopCount, sUserName, iAnswer
Const ADMIN_1 = "FRANK LEE"
Const ADMIN_2 = "STEPHANIE HOOPER"
```

▶ **To use a decision-making structure**

1. Under **Main Body**, construct nested **If** statements by typing the following:

```
iLoopCount = iLoopCount + 1
If iLoopCount > 3 then
    WScript.Echo "Maximum attempts exceeded!" & vbCrLf
↳& "This script will now end..."
    WScript.Quit
ElseIf iLoopCount > 1 then
    iAnswer = MsgBox("You must be an Administrator to run
↳this script." _
    & vbCrLf & "Do you want to try again?", vbYesNo)
    If iAnswer = vbNo then
        WScript.Quit
    End If
End If
```

Tip In the text above, the line-continuation characters (↳) are used to denote that you should type the subsequent code on the same line as the preceding code. The text has simply wrapped around in the printed document

---

2. Immediately below the final **End If** statement, add the following line to gather user input and assign it to the variable sUserName:

```
sUserName = InputBox (
↳"Please enter your name (firstname lastname)")
```

3. On the **File** menu, click **Save As**.

4. Navigate to the *install_folder*\Labs\Lab03\Starter folder (*install_folder* is C:\ Program Files\MSDNTrain\2433A by default).

5. In the **File name** box, type **Validate.vbs** and then click **Save**.

▶ **To use a Do...Loop**

1. Locate the comment **Main Body**, and on the line immediately below, add a **Do** statement as follows:

```
Do
```

2. Immediately below the **InputBox** statement, type the following line of code, which controls the termination of the loop:

```
Loop While UCase(sUserName) <> ADMIN_1 _
    And UCase(sUserName) <> ADMIN_2
```

3. Immediately below the **Loop** statement, type the following:

```
WScript.Echo "You have been validated!" & vbCrLf _
    & "The script will now continue..."
```

4. On the **File** menu, click **Save**.

▶ **To test the script**

1. On the **Script** menu, click **Run Script**.

2. In the input box, type **Don Funk**

   Don Funk is not one of the administrators. You will be notified of this with a message box.

3. In the message box, click **No**.

   The script ends.

4. Repeat steps 1 and 2

5. Click **Yes** to try again.

6. In the input box, type **Don Funk** again.

7. Click **Yes** to try again.

8. In the input box, type **Don Funk** one more time.

9. On the **Script** menu, click **Run Script**.

10. In the input box, type **Stephanie Hooper**.

You have now created and tested a script that validates users.

Exercise 3
Using Procedures

In this exercise, you will create a reusable function that carries out the process of validating a user against a known list of administrators. The function will return either **True** or **False**, thereby making it easy to use in the calling code.

▶ **To create a validate function**

1. In the script, under **Procedures**, modify the template of the function so that it reads:

```
Function Validate(sUser)
If UCase(sUser) = ADMIN_1 Or UCase(sUser) = ADMIN_2 then
        Validate = True
    Else
        Validate = False
    End if
End Function
```

2. Under **Main**, modify the **Loop** statement so that it uses the function, as follows:

```
Loop While Not Validate(sUsername)
```

3. On the **File** menu, click **Save**.

4. On the **Script** menu, click **Run Script**.

5. In the input box, type **Don Funk**

   Don Funk is not one of the administrators. You will be notified accordingly in a message box.

6. In the message box, click **Yes**.

7. In the input box, type **Frank Lee**

   You are successfully validated.

You have now successfully used constants, variables, loops, procedures, and decision-making code by using Visual Basic Scripting Edition.

Review

- **Fundamental VBScript Rules**
- **Variables, Constants, and Data Types**
- **Operators**
- **Conditions and Loops**
- **Procedures**
- **Script Layout**

1. Where is VBScript case-sensitive.

2. What is the primary data type used in VBScript?

3. What would be the result of the following:

   (10-5+10)*2-(4*5/2)

4. The following script causes a compilation error. What is the problem?

```
If MyVar = 5 Then
        WScript.Echo "MyVar = 5"
If MyVar = 7 Then
        WScript.Echo "MyVar = 7"
End If
```

msdn® training

Module 4: Error Handling and Debugging

Contents

Microsoft®

Overview

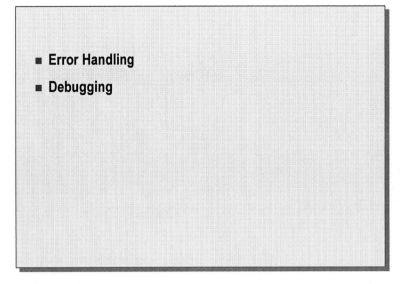

- **Error Handling**
- **Debugging**

It is inevitable that you will sometimes encounter errors in your scripts. When errors occur, you must know how to deal with them.

This module deals with error handling. It also deals with some approaches to debugging, including the use of a debugger application.

After completing this module, you will be able to:

- Describe the types of errors that may be present in code written in Microsoft® Visual Basic® Scripting Edition (VBScript).

- Write code that handles run-time errors.

- Use the Microsoft Script Debugger to locate and fix logic errors.

◆ Error Handling

- ■ Type of Errors
- ■ Handling Run-Time Errors
- ■ The Err Object
- ■ Setting an Error Trap

Errors that prevent your code from performing as intended will be present in some of the code that you develop. Even professional programmers sometimes encounter errors.

This section describes the different types of errors that can occur in VBScript. It also describes some approaches for dealing with run-time errors.

Types of Errors

- **Syntax Errors**
- **Run-Time Errors**
- **Logic Errors**

Programming errors fall into three categories: syntax, run-time, and logic errors.

Syntax Errors

Syntax errors result from code that is written incorrectly, such as a mistyped keyword, the omission of required punctuation, or an incorrect construct, such as a **Next** statement without a corresponding **For** statement.

VBScript detects these errors when your script is compiled. If syntax errors are found, the script cannot start. Instead you will be notified that a compilation error has occurred. VBScript reports detailed information about the syntax error, such as its location in your script and a description of the type of error.

Run-Time Errors

Run-time errors occur when your code is syntactically correct, but a statement attempts an operation that is impossible to execute. For example, attempting a calculation that includes a division by zero, or attempting to save a file to the floppy disk drive when no disk is present, results in a run-time error. For these types of errors, you must create an error trap. You will learn how to create an error trap in Setting an Error Trap later in this module.

Logic Errors

Logic errors occur when code does not perform the way that you intended. Your code may be syntactically correct, and no run-time errors may be encountered, but it does not produce the results that you anticipated. You must test and debug your code to determine why the results are different than those that you intended. You will learn how to debug scripts in the Debugging later in this module.

Handling Run-Time Errors

- Creating Robust Scripts
- Enabling Graceful Exits
- Implementing Error Handling

By detecting run-time errors, you can make your script responsive to common run-time errors.

Creating Robust Scripts

Scripts that trap run-time errors can handle common user errors without stopping program execution. Anticipating common errors, such as trying to open a nonexistent file, and protecting the code against these errors, makes the program less likely to stop running.

Enabling Graceful Exits

Sometimes the error-handling code in your script cannot resolve a run-time error. When this happens, your code can still perform other actions, such as closing any open data files and saving data that would be lost otherwise. In addition, you can inform the user that an error has occurred and give the user more descriptive messages than they may otherwise receive.

Implementing Error Handling

To implement error handling, you must anticipate what lines of code run-time errors may occur in. In addition, you must anticipate the type of error that may occur. The basic process for implementing error handling is to:

- Set an error trap.
- Determine which error has occurred.
- Take some remedial action or exit the script gracefully.

The Err Object

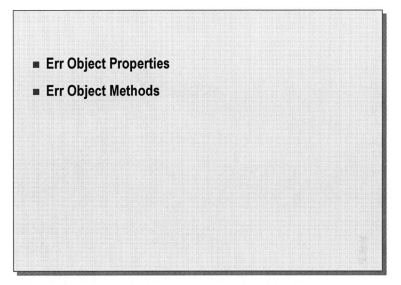

- **Err Object Properties**
- **Err Object Methods**

Run-time errors can originate from the code that you write in Visual Basic Scripting Edition. When a run-time error occurs, you can check the properties of the **Err** object to see what error has occurred.

Err Object Properties

The following table lists the most commonly used properties of the **Err** object.

Property	Description
Number	Returns a valid error number. **Number** is the default property of the **Err** object.
Description	The error message that corresponds to the **Number** property.

Err Object Methods

In addition to using the properties of the **Err** object, you can use its methods to control errors.

The following table lists the most commonly used methods of the **Err** object.

Method	Description
Clear	Clears all of the property settings of the **Err** object. **Clear** is equivalent to Err = 0.
Raise	Generates a run-time error. You can use this method when you test your error-handling code.

Setting an Error Trap

- **On Error Resume Next**
- **Fixing the Error**

The default behavior of Visual Basic Scripting Edition, when it encounters a run-time error, is to halt its execution and display a message to the user of the script. The message is often regarded by the user as being cryptic, especially if the user has no VBScript or programming experience. In addition, the user cannot choose to recover from the error.

On Error Resume Next

To modify the default way in which VBScript handles run-time errors, you can set a trap. Once the trap is set, the default behavior of VBScript run-time error handling is overridden. This enables your error-handling code to control the sequence of actions that is taken to either fix the error or to provide a safer, more graceful, and more meaningful exit for the user.

You set the error trap with the **On Error Resume Next** statement. This enables your code to continue running.

If you use the **On Error Resume Next** statement, you should trap potential errors after each line of code that you anticipate may cause possible errors. The following example shows the approach to handling errors in this manner:

Example

```
On Error Resume Next
Dim intNumberOfTests, intTotalPoints, nAverage
' collect test information
intTotalPoints = InputBox("Enter the Total points scored.")
intNumberOfTests = InputBox("Enter the number of exams.")
' calculate average
nAverage = intTotalPoints / intNumberOfTests
' check for runtime errors by zero
Select Case Err.Number
Case 0 'No error occurred
  WScript.Echo "Average score = " & Str(lngAverage)
Case 11 'Division by zero
  WScript.Echo "Cannot divide by zero."
Case 13 ' Type mis-match
  WScript.Echo "Only numeric data is allowed."
Case Else
  WScript.Echo "Unexpected error."
  WScript.Quit
End Select
```

Fixing the Error

The example shown above successfully traps the error. However, it does not make any attempt to fix the error. It merely enables a graceful exit. The example on the following page illustrates an approach to fixing run-time errors, namely by allowing the user to try again. It uses several advanced approaches:

- The script starts by making a call to the procedure named **MainProc**.

- **MainProc** then makes a call to the function named **CalcAvg**, and stores the result of this function in the iResult variable.

- The **CalcAvg** function performs the main task of the script. It prompts the user for two numbers and then attempts to divide one number by the other number. The line that attempts the division is where common run-time errors occur, such as division by zero and type mismatches.

- The **CalcAvg** function is protected by the **On Error Resume Next** error trap.

- After the line that performs the division is executed, the script queries the value of the **Err** object's **Number** property. If it is 0, then no error has occurred. If it is 11, then you know that a division by zero has been attempted. A value of 13 indicated that a type mismatch occurred, such as dividing a number by a string.

  The function returns a number to the calling Sub procedure, depending on the value of the **Err** object's **Number** property. The codes 0, 1, 2, and 3 have been arbitrarily chosen for this script. You can choose to return whatever data you want to.

- Based on the value returned from the function, the **MainProc** procedure takes some action. If the value is 1, 2, or 3, an error occurred in the function. In these cases a suitable message is displayed to the user. The user is then prompted as to whether he or she wants to try again. If the user answers **No**, the script ends.

  However, if the user answers **Yes**, the **MainProc** procedure calls itself. This is an advanced technique, known as iterative programming. When you use iterative programming techniques such as this, you must ensure that the code does not enter an endless loop.

Example

```
Call MainProc
Sub MainProc()
Dim iResult, iAnswer
iResult = CalcAvg()
Select Case iResult
Case 1
  WScript.Echo "Cannot divide by zero"
  iAnswer = Msgbox("Do you want to try again?",vbYesNo)
  If iAnswer = vbYes then
      Call MainProc
  Else
      WScript.Quit
  End IF
Case 2
  WScript.Echo "Only numeric data is allowed"
  iAnswer = Msgbox("Do you want to try again?",vbYesNo)
  If iAnswer = vbYes then
      Call MainProc
  Else
      WScript.Quit
  End IF
Case 3
  WScript.Echo "An unexpected error occurred"
  iAnswer = Msgbox("Do you want to try again?",vbYesNo)
  If iAnswer = vbYes then
      Call MainProc
  Else
      WScript.Quit
  End IF
End Select
End Sub

' code continued on next page
```

```
' code continued from previous page

Function CalcAvg()
On Error Resume Next
Dim intNumberOfTests, intTotalPoints, nAverage
' collect test information
intTotalPoints = InputBox("Enter the Total points scored.")
intNumberOfTests = InputBox("Enter the number of exams.")
' calculate average
nAverage = CInt(intTotalPoints)/CInt(intNumberOfTests)
' check for runtime errors by zero
Select Case Err.Number
Case 0 'No error occurred
  WScript.Echo "Average score = " & nAverage
  CalcAverage = 0
Case 11 'Division by zero
  CalcAvg = 1
Case 13 ' Type mis-match
  CalcAvg = 2
Case Else
  CalcAvg = 3
End Select
End Function
```

◆ Debugging

- **The Microsoft Script Debugger**
- **Debugging Techniques**

Usually the most difficult errors to find and fix are logic errors. However, it is inevitable that logic errors, sometimes referred to as bugs or glitches, will be introduced into your code, especially as your code becomes more complex.

The Microsoft Script Debugger is an invaluable tool that helps you to debug your scripts.

In this section, you will learn how to use the Microsoft Script Debugger.

The Microsoft Script Debugger

- **Processing Errors in WSH Scripts**
- **Using the Microsoft Script Debugger**

The Microsoft Script Debugger is installed as part of the Microsoft Windows® 2000 setup process. It enables you to find logic errors in your code. You can use the debugger to:

- View the source code of the script that you are debugging.
- View and control script flow.
- View and change variable and property values.
- View the order of execution of procedures in a script.

Processing Errors in WSH Scripts

The following describes the events that occur when a Windows Script Host (WSH) script is processed:

- The script is loaded into WSH and parsed.

  Parsing involves reading code segments, analyzing them, and compiling them into an executable binary format.

- The browser reports any syntax errors that it finds during the parsing stage.

- After successfully parsing a section of script, WSH executes it.

  Global or inline scripts that are not part of an event-handling **Sub** procedure or function are executed immediately.

  Event-handling **Sub** procedures or functions and procedures that are called by other procedures are parsed immediately, but they are not executed until they are triggered by an event or called by another procedure.

- If a run-time error occurs when a client script runs, an error message is displayed and the script containing the error stops.

Using the Microsoft Script Debugger

If an error occurs in a script, WSH displays an error message indicating the error and the number of the line on which it is found. If you have the debugger installed on your computer, you will be prompted about whether you want to debug the script. If you choose to debug the script, WSH starts the debugger and displays the current script in a read-only window.

Once the script is loaded into the debugger, you can move through the document, set breakpoints, return to the document to run scripts, and step through the script. By doing this, you can locate run-time and logic errors.

Note   You cannot edit the source code directly in the debugger. You must edit the original .vbs file and then rerun it.

Debugging Techniques

- ■ **Setting Breakpoints and Stepping Through Code**
- ■ **Using the Command Window**
- ■ **Viewing the Call Stack**

The Microsoft Script Debugger provides the following features that you can use to debug your scripts to find logic errors:

- ■ Breakpoints
- ■ Line-stepping functions
- ■ The Command window
- ■ The Call Stack window

Setting Breakpoints and Stepping Through Code

You can specify breakpoints in your script. A breakpoint is a point at which you want your script to temporarily stop running. You can then use stepping options to execute your code on a line-by-line basis. By doing so, you can examine the effects of each line of code and locate and resolve logic errors. You can set breakpoints on specific lines to pinpoint problems in your scripts.

To set a breakpoint on a specific line, take the following actions:

- ■ In the Microsoft Script Debugger, place the insertion point in the line where you want the breakpoint.
- ■ On the **Debug** menu, click **Toggle Breakpoint**.

  The line where you set the breakpoint is displayed in red to indicate that it is a breakpoint.

You can then repeat the procedure for each breakpoint that you want to set in the document. After you set your breakpoints, you can continue running the script.

The debugger stops at the first breakpoint that it encounters. You can then use the stepping options to execute the lines according to your requirements.

The script debugger toolbar has the following line-stepping options:

- **Step Into**

  This option enables you to step through your code one line at a time. When a call to a **Sub** or **Function** procedure is encountered, this option indicates that you want to step through that procedure line-by-line.

  This is useful if you have not already debugged the procedure.

- **Step Over**

  This option also enables you to step through your code one line at a time. However, when a call to a **Sub** or **Function** procedure is encountered, this option indicates that you do not want to step through that procedure line-by-line. Instead, that procedure is run at full speed, and you can continue to step through subsequent lines of code that follow the procedure call.

  This is useful if you have already debugged the procedure.

- **Step Out**

  If you have stepped into a lengthy procedure, but at some point you want to run the rest of the procedure at full speed, you can use this option. You can continue to step through subsequent lines of code that follow the procedure call.

  This is useful if you have found the error in the procedure, or if you stepped into the procedure when you wanted to step over it instead.

Using the Command Window

Another valuable debugging technique is viewing and changing the values of variables or properties as you step through your code. Viewing the values stored in variables or properties can help you determine if the script is running properly.

You can affect the way the script runs by making changes directly to values in the variables contained in a running script. After changing these values, you can continue running the script and see the effects of your changes.

To view and change values, you use the Command window. You can evaluate any expression in the window, enter script commands, and see their effects. Because the Command window is active, changes you make in the window directly affect the script that is currently running.

You can use the Command window to run script commands any time that you are at a breakpoint or have stepped from a breakpoint to other statements.

Viewing the Call Stack

There are advantages in creating reusable procedures in your script code. However, breaking up scripts into procedures can complicate debugging. When you use the debugger to step through your script, you may encounter code whose execution threads from procedure to procedure. The call stack enables you to track the order of procedures calls.

The Microsoft Script Debugger has a special window for viewing the call stack. You can open the Call Stack window from the **View** menu. You can then use the list of procedure calls to trace the execution of the program and locate any procedures that cause errors.

Lab 4: Debugging and Error Handling

Objectives

After completing this lab, you will be able to:

- Write run-time error-handling code.
- Use the Microsoft Script Debugger.
- Find and fix logic errors.

Scenario

In this lab, you will write error-handling code that traps common run-time errors, such as divisions by zero and type mismatches. These types of errors are typically caused by invalid user input, so the approach used in the lab is useful whenever you write code that interacts with users.

You will also use the Microsoft Script Debugger application to find logic errors and bugs in code written in VBScript. You will see how to fix these errors.

Estimated time to complete this lab: 30 minutes

Exercise 1
Trapping Run-Time Errors

In this exercise, you will create and implement a run-time error trap.

▶ **To change the default script host**

1. On the **Start** menu, click **Run**.

2. In the **Open** box, type **cmd** and then click **OK**.

3. Enter the following command to change the default host to WScript:

   CScript //H:WScript

4. Close the command window.

▶ **To execute a script that can cause run-time errors**

1. Using Windows Explorer, go to the
   install_folder\Labs\Lab04\Starter folder (*install_folder* is C:\ Program
   Files\MSDNTrain\2433A by default).

2. Double-click **ExamMarker.vbs**.

3. In the **Enter the Total points scored** box, type **1284** and then click **OK**.

4. In the **Enter the number of exams** input box, type **0** and then click **OK**.

   A Division by Zero run-time error occurs.

5. Click **OK**.

6. Repeat steps 2 and 3.

7. In the **Enter the number of exams** box, type **banana** and then click **OK**.

8. Click **OK**.

▶ **To open the script**

1. On the **Start** menu, point to **Programs**, point to **SAPIEN Technologies,
   Inc**, and then click **PrimalSCRIPT 2.0**.

2. On the **File** menu, click **Open**.

3. Navigate to the *install_folder*\Labs\Lab04\Starter folder (*install_folder* is
   C:\ Program Files\MSDNTrain\2433A by default).

4. Click **ExamMarker.vbs**, and then click **Open**.

▶ **To write error-handling code**

1. Locate the **CalcAvg** function.

2. On the line immediately below the function name, type the following code:

   ```
   On Error Resume Next
   ```

3. Locate the following line of code in the function:

   ```
   nAverage = CInt(intTotalPoints)/CInt(intNumberOfTests)
   ```

4. On the line immediately below this calculation, type the following code:

```
Select Case Err.Number
Case 0 'No error occurred
   Msgbox "Average score = " & nAverage
   CalcAvg = 0
Case 11 'Division by zero
   CalcAvg = 1
Case 13 ' Type mis-match
   CalcAvg = 2
Case Else
   CalcAvg = 3
End Select
```

5. On the **File** menu, click **Save**.

▶ **To test your division by zero error-handling code**

1. On the **Script** menu, click **Run Script**.

2. In the **Enter the Total points scored** box, type **1284** and then click **OK**.

3. In the **Enter the number of exams** box, type **0** and then click **OK**.

4. Click **OK**.

   You are prompted as to whether or not you want to try again.

5. Click **Yes**.

▶ **To test your type-mismatch error-handling code**

1. In the **Enter the Total points scored** box, type **1284** and then click **OK**.

2. In the **Enter the number of exams** input box, type **banana** and then click **OK**.

3. Click **OK**.

   You are prompted as to whether or not you want to try again.

4. Click **Yes**.

▶ **To test the recoverability of your code**

1. In the **Enter the Total points scored** box, type **1284** and then click **OK**.

2. In the **Enter the number of exams** input box, type **20** and then click **OK**.

3. Click **OK**.

▶ **To change the default script host**

1. On the **Start** menu, click **Run**.

2. In the **Open** box, type **cmd** and then click **OK**.

3. Run the following command to change the default host to WScript:

   CScript //H:WScript

4. Close the command window.

   You have now successfully handled run-time errors for this script.

Exercise 2
Debugging VBScript

In this exercise, you will use the Microsoft Script Debugger to find and fix logic errors.

▶ **To create a script that contains logic errors**

1. Switch to PrimalSCRIPT.

2. On the **File** menu, click **New**.

3. Click **VBScript**, and then click **OK**.

4. On the **Edit** menu, click **Select all**.

5. Press DELETE.

6. Type the following code:

```
Dim iDays, iHours(), iTotal, iAverage, iLoop
Do
    iDays = InputBox("How many days did you work last
↪week?")
Loop While Not IsNumeric(iDays)
ReDim iHours(iDays)
For iLoop = 0 to iDays
    iHours(iLoop) = CSng(InputBox("Enter hours for day " &
iLoop))
    iTotal = iTotal + iHours(iLoop)
Next
iAverage = iTotal/iDays
WScript.Echo "Total hours worked: " & iTotal
WScript.Echo "Average daily shift: " & iAverage
```

7. On the **File** menu, click **Save As**.

8. In the **Save** dialog, go to the *install_folder*\Labs\Lab04\Starter folder (*install_folder* is C:\ Program Files\MSDNTrain\2433A by default).

9. In the **File name** box, type **TimeSheet.vbs** and then click **Save**.

▶ **To test your code for run-time errors**

1. On the **Script** menu, click **Run Script**.

2. Type **5** as the number of days worked last week, and then click **OK**.

3. Type **7.5** as the number of hours worked, and then click **OK**.

4. Repeat step 3 for each input box.

5. Click **OK** in the message box that informs you how many hours were worked in total.

6. Click **OK** in the message box that informs you what the average daily shift was.

The script does not have any run-time errors. However, it prompts you for details about the hours worked for more than five days, which can be considered a logic error.

▶ **To debug the script**

1. On the **Script** menu, click **Debug Script**.

   The Microsoft Script Debugger appears. Execution is halted on the first executable line of code.

2. On the **View** menu, click **Command Window**.

   The Command window appears.

3. On the **Debug** menu, click **Step Into**.

   The VBScript input box appears. Note that it may be hidden behind the debugger window, so switch to the input box if necessary by using the Windows taskbar.

4. Enter **5** as the number of days worked last week, and then click **OK**.

5. In the Command window, type **?iDays** and then press ENTER.

   The Command Window displays the current value of the iDays variable. Note that the iDays variable is correctly set to five at this point in the code

6. From the **Debug** menu, click **Step Into**.

   Note that the highlighted code is about to redimension the **iHours()** array. If this line of code executes, the array contains six elements.

   You have found the first logic error. The array should contain five elements rather than six. It should contain one element for each day of the week that was worked. Remember that arrays are zero-based in VBScript.

▶ **To fix the logic error in your code**

1. On the **Debug** menu, click **Stop Debugging**.

2. Close the Microsoft Script Debugger.

3. Using Primal Script, switch back to the VBScript window and modify the line of code that redimensions the **iHours()** array so that it reads as follows:

   ```
   ReDim iHours(iDays-1)
   ```

4. Modify the subsequent line so that it reads:

   ```
   For iLoop = 0 to iDays - 1
   ```

5. Modify the next line so that it reads:

   ```
   iHours(iLoop) = CSng(InputBox("Enter hours for day " &
   ↪iLoop + 1))
   ```

6. On the **File** menu, click **Save**.

▶ **To test your fixed code**

1. On the **Script** menu, click **Run Script**.

2. Enter **5** as the number of days worked last week, and then click **OK**.

3. Enter **7.5** as the number of hours worked, and then click **OK**.

4. Enter the following data for the other input boxes:
   - Day 2: **8**
   - Day 3: **8**
   - Day 4: **7**
   - Day 5: **7**

5. Verify that you are now only prompted for hours worked on 5 days.

6. Close PrimalSCRIPT.

You have now successfully debugged a script written in VBScript with the script debugger.

Review

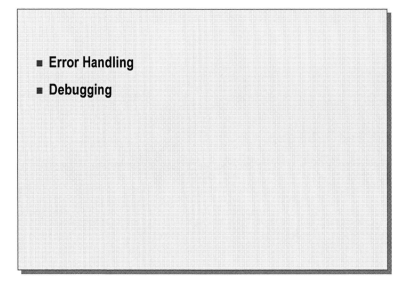

- **Error Handling**
- **Debugging**

1. What is the name of the object that holds the details about run-time errors?

2. Name two commonly used properties of the **Err** object?

3. What are the three stepping options that are supported by the Microsoft Script Debugger?

msdn®training

Module 5:
Understanding ADSI

Contents

Microsoft®

Overview

- **ADSI Overview**
- **Binding with ADSI**
- **ADSI Objects**
- **Searching Active Directory**
- **Creating New ADSI Objects**
- **Setting Security in Active Directory**
- **Managing Shares Using ADSI**
- **Controlling Services Using ADSI**
- **ADSI Resources**

You can access the functionality of Microsoft® Active Directory™ by using the Active Directory Services Interface (ADSI) in your administrative scripts. ADSI enables you to achieve many administrative tasks for which you will want to write scripts.

This module provides you with the knowledge necessary to:

- Describe how ADSI works.
- Bind to ADSI objects.
- Search Active Directory.

Create and modify objects in Active Directory.Manage shares with ADSI.Control services with ADSI.

◆ ADSI Overview

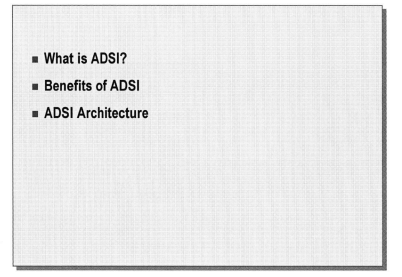

- **What is ADSI?**
- **Benefits of ADSI**
- **ADSI Architecture**

Before you write code that interacts with ADSI, you must understand how ADSI works and how it can help you to create administrative scripts.

In this section, you will learn about the uses of ADSI. You will also learn about the benefits of using ADSI in your administrative scripts. In addition, you will learn about the ADSI architecture.

What Is ADSI?

- **ADSI**
  - The primary interface to Active Directory
  - Version 2.5 released with Windows 2000
  - Available for Win9x and Windows NT 4.0
- **Provides Access to Directory Service Objects**
- **Support For Multiple Directory Service Providers**
  - **LDAP**
  - **Windows NT**
  - **NDS**
  - **Bindery**

ADSI (previously called OLE Directory Services) is an abstraction layer that exposes the objects of different directory services through a single set of Application Programming Interfaces (API).

ADSI

Microsoft Windows® 2000 ships with ADSI version 2.5, which is also available as a download for Microsoft Windows NT® 4.0, Microsoft Windows 95, and Microsoft Windows 98 at the following Web site:

- http://www.microsoft.com/ntserver/nts/downloads/other/ADSI25/

Provides Access to Directory Service Objects

You can use ADSI to manage the resources in a directory service, regardless of which network environment contains the objects. By using ADSI and scripting, administrators can automate common directory service setup and administrative tasks.

Support for Multiple Directory Service Providers

Scripts written to ADSI will work with any directory service that offers an ADSI provider.

ADSI can provide access to any Lightweight Directory Access Protocol (LDAP) service, such as Windows NT 4.0 and the NetWare Directory Services (NDS) and NetWare 3 Bindery-based servers from Novell. These providers enable communication between the directory service and client as follows:

- Lightweight Directory Access Protocol

  The LDAP provider works with any LDAP version 2 or version 3 directory, such as Microsoft Exchange versions 5.0 and 5.5. This provider also works for the Windows 2000 Active Directory. The LDAP provider dynamic-link libraries (DLL) are adsldp.dll and wldap32.dll.

An LDAP address can be divided into three basic components:

- The first component is the *Common Name* (CN). This represents the leaf object, which is an object that contains no other objects. Examples of CNs are users or printers.

- The second component is the *Organization Unit* (OU). This is the container object in the directory.

- The final component is the *Domain Component* or (DC).

  The following is an example of an LDAP address:

  ```
  LDAP://CN=Alan,OU=Test,DC=Microsoft,DC=COM
  ```

  This LDAP address refers to the object called **Alan** in the Organizational Unit called "Test" in the domain named microsoft.com.

- Windows NT (WinNT)

  This is the easiest provider to use because of its simple address format. It provides access to both Windows NT 4.0 and Windows 2000 computers and domains. The local provider DLL for Windows NT is ADSNT.DLL.

- Novell NetWare Directory Services (NDS)

  The NDS provider works with Novell Netware version 4.x or greater to give access to objects in the Novell Directory Service (NDS). The provider DLL is ADSNDS.DLL.

- NetWare 3 Bindery (NWCOMPAT)

  Access to the Novell legacy network operating system is achieved through use of the NWCOMPAT provider. This provider allows ADSI to access objects stored in Bindery-based servers such as Netware versions 3.11 and 3.12. The provider DLL is ADSNW.DLL.

Benefits of ADSI

- ■ **Ease of Use**

- ■ **Namespace Portability**

- ■ **Powerful Functionality**

    - ● Can script common admin and end-user tasks:
        - • List all objects in a directory
        - • Add new objects to a directory
        - • Manage security on objects in a directory
        - • Create a network share
        - • Control machine services remotely

ADSI provides several major advantages to scriptwriters.

Ease of Use

ADSI exports a comprehensive but straightforward set of interfaces that you can use to easily access objects within a directory service.

Namespace Portability

ADSI abstracts the complexity of the directory service interfaces, allowing you to use the same set of methods to access multiple directories. This greatly simplifies script writing because the basic methods can be reused with different directory objects in different namespaces.

Powerful Functionality

ADSI provides a set of powerful features that enable you to develop sophisticated script solutions. These solutions may include simple tasks such as finding objects in an OU through complex scripts that create entire enterprise directory services and populate them with many objects.

Note Microsoft used ADSI scripting when testing the scalability of Active Directory to help create the massive directory structures required.

The following are examples of ADSI tasks:

- ■ Read/write properties (attributes) to and from a directory service object:

    - • Change the department name for all users in an OU.

    - • Update a group's membership.

    - • Create new user accounts.

- Manage the schema:
  - Create a report that generates a complete schema list.
  - Add objects to the schema.
- Manage security on directory service objects:
  - Set permissions for all user objects in a domain.
  - Change the permissions on a printer object in an OU.
  - Assign new permissions to a group in a domain.

ADSI Architecture

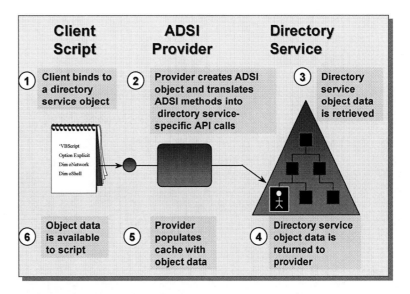

Before examining how to script ADSI, it is important to understand how the ADSI architecture works.

Binding

The ADSI client must first find and connect (bind) to an object. The client can be an application, such as a script, a custom application, or one of the support tools supplied on the Windows 2000 CD-ROM.

The Provider

After the client has bound to an object, the ADSI provider DLL on the local computer processes the bind request from the client and translates it into the directory-specific API call to retrieve the required object. The client script or application can then use the methods and properties of the object.

The following steps are involved in this process:

1. The client script or application makes a request to bind to an object in a directory service.

2. The ADSI provider on the client computer receives the request and creates an ADSI object in the client's address space. The provider then makes a connection to the required directory service by using the API calls of that particular directory service.

3. The directory service object information, such as the object methods and properties, are retrieved from the directory.

4. The directory service object information is returned to the ADSI provider.

5. The ADSI provider creates an instance of the ADSI object in the memory space of the client application.

6. The object methods are now available for the client script to use.

◆ Binding with ADSI

■ Binding

■ Server-Less Binding

■ Binding with Alternative Credentials

A process called *binding* must take place before you can use ADSI methods and properties.

In this section, you will learn how to bind to directory service objects. You will also learn about server-less binding, and how to pass security credentials to ADSI as you bind to ADSI objects.

Binding

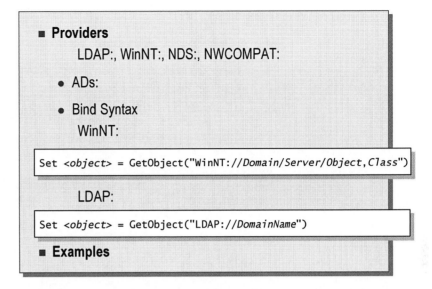

The binding process creates an object in the client's memory address space. After your script has bound to an object, it can invoke any method relevant to that particular type of object and can read or modify its properties.

Providers

An important part of the binding request from your script is to specify the provider that should be used to bind to the object. As discussed earlier, ADSI includes four different providers:

- WinNT:
- LDAP:
- NDS:
- NWCOMPAT:

Important   These names are all case-sensitive.

Ads:

There is also an **Ads:** name that can be used to resolve all of the available providers on the local computer. For example, if an enterprise uses a new provider called NewProv, the following code could be inserted into any scripts that require this non-standard provider:

Example

```
Set objProviders = GetObject("ADs:")
For Each provider In objProviders
    If provider.name = "NewProv:" Then
        WScript.Echo "The required provider is installed"
        WScript.Quit
    End If
Next
WScript.Echo "The required provider is missing"
WScript.Quit
```

Binding Syntax

The ADSI binding syntax for the WinNT provider is as follows:

Example

```
Set <Object> = _
  GetObject ("WinNT://Domain/Server/Object,Class")
```

where:

- <Object> is the object variable that will contain the reference to the retrieved Active Directory object.

- **GetObject** is the method used to bind to the ADSI namespace and create the local copy of the object that will be used in the script.

- "WinNT" is the ProgID for the required ADSI provider. This name is sometimes referred to as the *Moniker*. (Moniker is a Component Object Model (COM) term that describes the mechanism that is used to bind to COM objects, in this case the ADSI providers.)

- "Domain" is the domain name.

- "Server" is the computer name.

- **Object** is the object name.

- **Class** is the class specification. This is optional, but it is useful for preventing ambiguity where different objects have the same names. Using this class specification can also speed up the binding process.

Together, the provider name and path are referred to as the *ADSPath* or *bind string*.

WinNT and LDAP Binding examples:

The following examples show a number of ways that you can bind to WinNT and LDAP objects:

- To bind to the root of the WinNT namespace:

Example
```
Set oMyObj = GetObject("WinNT:")
```

- To bind to the root of the LDAP namespace:

Example
```
Set oMyObj = GetObject("LDAP:")
```

- To bind to the root of a specific Windows NT domain:

Example
```
Set oMyObj = GetObject("WinNT://MyDomain")
```

- To bind to the root of a specific Windows 2000 domain:

Example
```
Set oMyObj = GetObject("LDAP://MyDomain.com")
```

- To bind to the root of a specific Windows 2000 domain, by providing the *class* parameter:

Example
```
Set oMyObj = GetObject("LDAP://DC=MyDomain, DC=com")
```

- To bind to the root of a specific Windows 2000 domain, by providing a computer name instead of the domain name:

Example
```
Set oMyObj = GetObject("LDAP://MyServer")
```

Note The preceding example binds to the domain that includes the server. This differs from the WinNT provider, which binds to the computer object if a computer name is used.

- To bind directly to a specific computer with WinNT:

Example
```
Set oMyObj = GetObject("WinNT://MyServer,computer")
```

- To bind directly to a specific computer with LDAP:

Example
```
Set oMyObj = GetObject("LDAP://CN=MyServer,OU=Domain
↪Controllers,DC=MyDomain,DC=com")
```

Note If the computer to which you bind is not a domain controller, the provider binds to the Security Accounts Manager (SAM) of the local computer.

- Binding to a user object on a server with WinNT:

Example
```
Set oMyObj = GetObject("WinNT://MyDom/MyServer/Alan,user")
```

- Binding to a user object on a server with LDAP:

Example
```
Set oMyObj = GetObject
↪("LDAP://MyServer.MyDom.com/CN=Alan,OU=CM,DC=MyDom,DC=com")
```

Server-Less Binding

- **Preferred Binding Method**
  - No hard-coded server name
- **RootDSE Binding**
  - No hard-coded domain name

    Portable, site-aware, fault-tolerant
  - Directory Service client required for non-Windows 2000 clients
- **Global Catalog Server Binding**
  - GC://

In the topic "Binding" you learned how to bind to specific computers. This may not always be possible or desirable for the reasons described in this section.

Preferred Binding Method

The preferred method of binding is called *server-less binding*. With this approach, no server name is specified or hard-coded in the script. The following shows an example of a server-less binding with a specified domain name, but no server name. This method relies on the Windows 2000 location server that uses the Domain Name Service (DNS) to bind to the best server for the requested domain.

Example

```
Set oMyObj = GetObject("LDAP://DC=MyDomain, DC=com")
```

Server-less binding is a very useful mechanism to include in your scripts, because it provides the following benefits:

- Site awareness

  DNS uses Windows 2000 site information to determine if a domain controller exists in the same physical site as the client that runs the script. If no domain controller exists in the site, DNS finds any available domain controller for the script to use, and returns that domain controller for binding to the provider.

- Fault tolerance

  Because server-less binding binds to a namespace rather than a specific domain controller, if any domain controller is temporarily unavailable, the locator service attempts to find another one in the same domain.

RootDSE Binding

The server-less binding approach works well in a single domain environment. However, if your script is to be run from multiple domains, you must use an object called **RootDSE** that eliminates the need for a hard-coded reference to the domain, as well as the server. You can use the **RootDSE** object to resolve the current domain name before binding to it. Each Windows 2000 domain controller has a unique **RootDSE** object that you can use to provide information about the various namespace objects in the domain, which can then be used in scripts.

Note   DSE stands for "DSA-Specific Entry," where DSA is an X.500 term for the directory server.

Retrieving the **DefaultNamingContext** property from the **RootDSE** object enables you to bind to the current domain. The following is an example of server-less binding, using the **RootDSE** object:

Example

```
Set oRootDSE = GetObject("LDAP://RootDSE")
Set oMyDomain = GetObject( "LDAP://" & _
oRootDSE.Get("defaultNamingContext"))
WScript.echo oMyDomain.name
```

This example displays the name of the domain in which the script is running. First, the script binds to the **RootDSE** object. Then, it creates a new object called **oMyDomain** that binds to the current domain by using the **DefaultNamingContext** property of the **RootDSE** object. Finally, WScript.echo displays the domain name.

The **RootDSE** object enables the script to be run from any domain and to successfully receive a binding for the script to use. The following is a list of some of the most commonly used properties of the **RootDSE** object on a Windows 2000 domain controller.

Property	Description
namingContexts	Multi-valued. Distinguished names for all naming contexts stored on this directory server. By default, a Windows 2000 domain controller contains at least three namespaces: Schema, Configuration, and one for the domain that includes the server.
defaultNamingContext	The distinguished name for the domain that includes this directory server.
schemaNamingContext	The distinguished name for the schema container.
configurationNamingContext	The distinguished name for the configuration container.
RootDomainNamingContext	The distinguished name for the first domain in the forest that contains the domain that includes this directory server.
SupportedLDAPVersion	Multi-valued. LDAP versions (specified by major version number) supported by this directory server.
HighestCommittedUSN	The highest USN used on this directory server. Used by directory replication.
DnsHostName	The DNS address for this directory server
ServerName	The distinguished name for the server object for this directory server in the configuration container.
currentTime	The current time set on this directory server.
dsServiceName	The distinguished name of the **NTDS settings** object for this directory server.

Note   Clients of Windows 95, Windows 98, and Windows NT cannot use server-less binding unless they have the Directory Service client installed in addition to the ADSI Services download.

Global Catalog Server Binding

If your scripts need to search for objects in multiple domains in a forest, you can bind to a Global Catalog (GC) server in the domain in which the script is running. Global Catalog servers contain a list of all objects in a domain. Each object in a GC includes a complete subset of attributes. Storing the required attribute in this subset makes querying the local GC considerably faster than relying on a complete cross-domain search.

To bind to a GC server, use its name as shown in the following example:

Example

```
Set oGC = GetObject("GC://DC=MyDomain, DC=com")
```

Any searches performed against this GC server will return all objects in the forest that match the criteria, including objects from the client's local domain.

Binding with Alternative Credentials

- **Binding as a Different User**
  - Use **OpenDSObject** method

```
Set oMyDS = GetObject("LDAP:")
Set oMyObj = oMyDS.OpenDSObject _
(AdsPath,UserName,Password,ADS_SECURE_AUTHENTICATION)
```

- **Using ADSI Constants**

In all of the examples shown so far, ADSI binds to the directory by using the logon credentials of the user who is running the script. However, there are situations where your scripts must bind to a particular directory service by using different security credentials from those of the logged-on user.

Binding as a Different User

ADSI provides an **OpenDSObject** method that allows binding to take place with different security credentials than those of the user who is running the script.

OpenDSObject takes as arguments the **ADSpath** of the object or subtree to be binded, the username, the password, and the authentication method. To use this method, you must bind directly to "LDAP:" as shown in the following example:

Example

Set oMyDS = Getobject("LDAP:")
Set oMyObj = oMyDS.OpenDSObject(AdsPath, UserName, Password,
↪ADS_SECURE_AUTHENTICATION)

Note This method requires that the user's name and password be entered as clear text into the script. This presents a security issue that you should consider when planning.

Using ADSI Constants

The last argument in the preceding example specifies the authentication flags to govern how the authentication takes place for the **OpenDSObject** method. You achieve this by using constants that are not intrinsically available to Microsoft Visual Basic® Script (VBScript). These constants should be defined at the top of the script. Possible values for the authentication parameter are listed in the following table.

Constant	Description	Value
ADS_SECURE_ AUTHENTICATION	Requests secure authentication. When set, the WinNT provider uses NT LanManager (NTLM) to authenticate the client. Active Directory will use Kerberos, and possibly NTLM.	1
ADS_USE_ENCRYPTION	Forces ADSI to use encryption for data exchange over the network.	2
ADS_USE_SSL	Encrypts the channel with Secure Sockets Layer (SSL) technology. Certificate Server must be installed to support SSL encryption.	2
ADS_READONLY_ SERVER	For a WinNT provider, ADSI tries to connect to a Primary Domain Controller or Backup Domain Controller. For Active Directory, this flag indicates that a server is not required for a server-less binding.	4
ADS_NO_ AUTHENTICATION	Requests no authentication. Setting this flag is the same as requesting an anonymous binding. The WinNT provider does not support this flag.	16
ADS_FAST_BIND	When this flag is set, ADSI will not attempt to query the **ObjectClass** property. Therefore, only the common properties and methods supported by all ADSI objects are available, not the object-specific properties. This improves the performance of the binding process if this information is all that is required by the script.	32
ADS_USE_SIGNING	Verifies data integrity to ensure that the data received is the same as the data sent. The ADS_SECURE_AUTHENTICATION flag also must be set to use the signing.	64
ADS_USE_SEALING	Encrypts data by using Kerberos. The ADS_SECURE_AUTHENTICATION flag also must be set in order to use the sealing.	128

◆ ADSI Objects

- ■ **Object Methods**
- ■ **Object Properties**
- ■ **Demonstration: Using ADSVW.EXE**

As you have seen in the section, "Binding with ADSI," you can manipulate various directory services by binding to a directory and then manipulating the objects contained in the directory.

In this section, you will learn more about the objects available to your scripts as you write code that interacts with ADSI. You will see how to invoke object methods and how to set and retrieve the values of object properties.

Object Methods

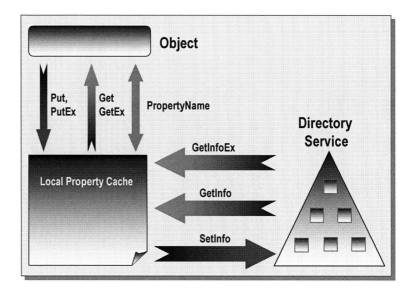

After your script has completed the binding process (as described in the section, "Binding with ADSI"), the instance of the object becomes available for the script to use. The methods that the script can use provide access to both the instance of the object in memory and the object in the directory by means of a local property cache that is used to store the values being worked with. Understanding the relationship between these three components is essential to understanding how to develop ADSI scripts.

Working with the Local Property Cache

To avoid making a call to a domain controller every time information about an object is read or modified, ADSI caches object properties locally on the client. When you first bind to an object with **GetObject**, the properties of that object are empty into the local cache. When you explicitly instruct ADSI to populate the cache, or when you first try to retrieve an absent property value, ADSI automatically retrieves all property values that have been set for that object, and places them in the cache.

Further handling of the object properties will retrieve the values from the local cache, thus requiring no additional calls across the network to the domain controller.

The following table lists the seven ADSI object methods that are used to work with ADSI objects and the local property cache.

Method	Description
Get	Retrieves the value of a property.
	variable = oMyObj.Get("*PropName*")
GetEx	Retrieves the values of a multivalue property.
	Array() = oMyObj.GetEx("*PropName*")
Put	Sets the value of a property.
	oMyObj.Put "*PropName*", "*Value*"
PutEx	Sets the values of a multivalue property.
	oMyObj.PutEx ADSProp,"*PropName*",Array("Value1","Value2")
GetInfo	Retrieves the values of all of the object's properties from the directory service and puts them in the local property cache.
	oMyObj.GetInfo
GetInfoEx	Retrieves the values of the specified object's properties from the directory service and puts them in the local property cache.
	oMyObj.GetInfoEx Array("*PropName*"), 0
SetInfo	Saves changes to an object's properties back to the directory service.
	oMyObj.SetInfo

The following ADSI script example demonstrates the methods that can be used to read the values of properties that belong to an object in Active Directory.

Example

```
'Create an instance of an OU object from existing AD OU
Set oOU = GetObject _
  ("LDAP://cn=Admin10,OU=WST,DC=Microsoft,DC=local")
'Get a value from AD into the Local Property cache (LPC)
WScript.Echo oOU.PropertyCount ' 0 Properties cached
oOU.GetInfoEx Array("memberOf"), 0
WScript.Echo oOU.PropertyCount ' 1 Property cached
'Fill the Local Property Cache
oOU.GetInfo
WScript.Echo oOU.PropertyCount ' all Properties cached
'Get a value from the LCP
WScript.Echo oOU.Get("cn")
'Same as above using different method
WScript.Echo oOU.cn
'Get & echo a multivalued property from Local Property Cache
aMemberOf = oOU.GetEx("memberOf")
For Each grp In aMemberOf
  WScript.Echo grp
Next
```

This script starts by creating an instance of an existing user object from an LDAP directory service. The property count of the object's local property cache is then echoed to the screen. At this stage, it will be zero, because no request to populate the local property cache has been made.

Next, the **GetInfoEX** method is used to populate the local property cache with a single property, **memberOf**. This is checked by echoing out the property count once again. The **GetInfo** method is then used to pull from the directory all properties that contain a set value. The property count shows the number of these values now in the local property cache. The next two lines echo the value of the **CN** property stored by using two different techniques, the **Get** method and the **.PropertyName** property.

The last method that is demonstrated is **GetEx**, which is used to access the values of multivalue properties. This method returns the values of a property as an array that can then be stepped through in any number of ways. The script demonstrates the use of a **For...Each** loop.

Writing Information into the Directory

The following script demonstrates the methods that you can use to create, update, or append property values for objects in the local property cache. The script then updates the properties back to the directory.

Example

```
'Setup ADSI Constant
Const ADS_PROPERTY_APPEND = 3
'Create an instance of an OU object from AD
Set oOU = GetObject _
  ("LDAP://cn=Admin10,OU=WST,DC=Microsoft,DC=local")
'Update the local property cache value
oOU.Put"Description", "Cache Demo OU"
'Same as above using different method
oOU.Description, "Cache Demo OU again"
'Update LPC with a multivalue property
oOU.PutEx ADS_PROPERTY_APPEND, "otherTelephone", _
  Array("(0)1234 5678900", "(0)0098 7654321")
'Write the local property cache back to AD
oOU.SetInfo
```

The first task of this script is to define the ADSI constants that will be used in the script. These constants will be used by the **PutEx** command, which will be discussed later.

After the instance of the Admin10 user has been created, the script writes a new value for the **Description** property, by using the **Put** method and then the .PropertyName syntax. Notice that you can use the .PropertyName technique to both read and write values in ADSI scripting. The **PutEx** method is then used to append an extra value into an existing multivalue property. The syntax for this method is shown in the following example:

Syntax

```
oOU.PutEx ADSProp, "property", Array("Val1", "Val2")
```

In this example, "ADSProp" is a constant value that is used to indicate how the value should be updated. It can consist of any of the values in the following table.

Constant name	Value
ADS_PROPERTY_CLEAR	1
ADS_PROPERTY_UPDATE	2
ADS_PROPERTY_APPEND	3
ADS_PROPERTY_DELETE	4

In the preceding example, "property" is the schema name of the property to be set. "Val1" and "Val2" are the values that will be used to modify the property. These values are passed to the method as elements of an array.

The last line of the preceding example uses the **SetInfo** method to write the updated local property cache back to the directory service.

Note Failing to call **SetInfo** is a common mistake in ADSI scripting that results in all updates to the cached object being discarded. Also note that if a call is made to **GetInfo** (either explicitly or implicitly through a **Get** method) before **SetInfo** has updated the directory service object, all property values in the local cache will be overwritten by the fresh call to the directory service object.

Object Properties

- **Six Standard Properties**
  - Name
  - Class
  - Guid
  - ADsPath
  - Parent
  - Schema
- **Additional Properties Are Specific to the Class Type**
- **Reading Multiple Properties**
- **Script Uses Schema Names, Not Display Names**

The next major step in using ADSI is to directly access the values stored in the properties for the directory objects. To do this, you must first know the names of the properties to use.

Six Standard Properties

Most ADSI objects expose six standard properties, as described in the following table.

Property	Description
Name	The name of the object.
Class	The schema class name of the object.
GUID	A globally unique identifier structure that uniquely identifies the object.
AdsPath	The string form of the object's path in the directory service. This path uniquely identifies the object.
Parent	The ADsPath name of the object's parent container.
Schema	The ADsPath of this object's schema class object.

The following example displays these standard properties for an OU:

Example

```
Set oMyObj = GetObject("LDAP://ou=WST,dc=contentm,dc=com")
WScript.Echo "Name is    " & oMyObj.Get "Name"
WScript.Echo "Class is   " & oMyObj.Get "Class"
WScript.Echo "GUID is    " & oMyObj.Get "GUID"
WScript.Echo "ADsPath is " & oMyObj.Get "ADsPath"
WScript.Echo "Parent is  " & oMyObj.Get "Parent"
WScript.Echo "Schema is  " & oMyObj.Get "Schema"
```

Additional Properties Are Specific to the Class Type

The standard ADSI properties are useful for identifying an object and its location in the directory hierarchy. However, most of the useful information about an object is stored in other properties that are specific to the class of that object.

For example, user objects support a **FullName** property that can be used as follows:

Example

```
Set oMyUser = _
  GetObject("LDAP://cn=UserName,ou=WST,dc=contentm,dc=com")
WScript.Echo "The full name is = " & oMyUser.Get("FullName")
```

Reading Multiple Properties

Sometimes you might require a list of all properties that have had their values set for a specific object. To achieve this, you can write code that counts all of the properties in the local cache by using the **PropertyCount** and **Item** methods as shown in the following example:

Example

```
Option Explicit
Dim objGroup, i, sPropList, count
On Error Resume Next
Set objGroup = _
  GetObject("LDAP://cn=Admin10,ou=WST,dc=NWTraders,dc=msft")
objGroup.GetInfo
i = objGroup.PropertyCount
sPropList = "There are " & i _
  & " values in the local property cache:" & vbCrLf & vbCrLf
For count = 0 To (i-1)
  sPropList = sPropList & objGroup.Item(CInt(count)).Name _
  & vbCRLF
Next
WScript.Echo sPropList
```

Script Uses Schema Names, Not Display NamesIf you run the preceding example code, you will find that the property names returned are not the same as those shown through the Microsoft Management Console (MMC) snap-in Active Directory Users and Computers. The property names used in the script example are the schema names, not the display names. Because the Windows 2000 user interface tools use the display names, it can be useful to be able to browse an object in Active Directory and display the schema names that will be used in the script. The demonstration at the end of this section uses a tool (Adsvw.exe) that displays schema names.

Demonstration: Using ADSVW.EXE

Using ADSVW.EXE to Examine Active Directory Objects

You can use a number of tools to browse object details in Active Directory. These include ADSI Edit from the Windows 2000 support tools provided on the Windows 2000 CD-ROM. However, this demonstration highlights a tool from the Windows 2000 Platform software development kit (SDK), ADSVW.EXE, which can also be used to examine object details. ADSVW.EXE is a powerful tool that provides the scriptwriter with a number of very useful features when used carefully.

▶ **To create a connection**

1. Run ADSVW.EXE from the folder *<install folder>*\Democode\Mod05.

2. Highlight **ObjectViewer**.

3. Click **OK**.

4. In the **Enter Ads Path** text box, type **LDAP://London**

5. Click to clear the check box for **Use OpenObject** and click **OK**.

   You should now see a binding to your domain. Notice the ADsPath that shows a connection to your server.

▶ **To view properties of directory objects**

1. Go to the **Users** container, and highlight the **Administrator** account.

2. Highlight and copy the **AdsPath** entry, and then paste it into a blank Microsoft Notepad document. This can save you time when writing your scripts.

3. Select the **Properties** box and scroll through the properties, highlighting those that apply to this user account.

4. Note that the names displayed are the ones that will be used in your scripts. They are not the same as the display names shown in the MMC-based management tools.

5. Select the **Domain Admins** group and show the **Members**.

6. Review the Description of the Members.

▶ **To view security entries**

1. Select the domain controller's OrganizationUnit.

2. Select the **nTSecurityDescriptor** for OrganizationUnit.

Highlight the **DACL** and **SACL** entries, and show the ACEs (Access Control Entries) in the DACL.

◆ Searching Active Directory

- **Searching Active Directory Using ADO**
- **Using a Single Connection for Multiple Searches**
- **Using a Single Connection for Each Search**

You will often need to search for specific objects located in Active Directory. This section describes how you can use Microsoft ActiveX® Data Objects (ADO) to perform efficient and powerful search routines.

In this section, you will learn how to use ADO connections and other ADO objects to perform Active Directory searches.

Searching Active Directory Using ADO

- **Using ADO for Active Directory Searches**
  - Connections
  - Commands
  - Recordsets
- **Building an LDAP Query String**

The ADO object model is one the most common approaches used in script to search for objects in Active Directory. ADO can perform queries against the directory based on the OLE DB support that is built into ADSI.

Using ADO for Active Directory Searches

ADO is a simple and efficient way to perform Active Directory searches. When performing a search, you will often use three ADO objects: **Connection**, **Command**, and **Recordset**.

- The **Connection** object is used to specify the provider name, alternate credentials (if applicable), and other flags.

- The **Command** object is used to specify search preferences and the query string.

   Note The **Connection** object must be associated with a **Command** object before the query is executed.

- The **Recordset** object is used to represent the result set.

Using these three objects to issue a query against Active Directory involves the following four basic steps:

1. Establish the connection to the data source by using the **Connection** object.
2. Execute a command by using the **Command** object.
3. Create a recordset by using the **Recordset** object.
4. Read the information in the recordset.

Note Although it is possible to use Microsoft SQL Server™ syntax for these queries, this technique is outside the scope of this course. For more information about this technique, visit http://www.microsoft.com/data/ado/

Building an LDAP Query String

To successfully search Active Directory by using ADO, you must first understand how the LDAP query strings are constructed. The following example shows the basic syntax for an LDAP query string:

Example

```
"<FQADsPath>;(Filter);Attributes;Scope"
```

In this example, "FQADsPath" is the fully qualified name of the starting point for your search. "Filter" is the list of elements to be included in or excluded from the search. These elements can be qualified by using the symbols shown in the following table.

Name	Symbol
Logical AND	&
Logical OR	|
Logical NOT	!
Equal to	=
Approx equal to	~=
Greater than	>=
Less than	<=

The following example shows how a symbol is used to qualify an element:

Example

```
LDAP://DC=NWTraders,DC=msft>;(&(objectCategory=Person) _
    (objectClass=user));name,telephonenumber;subTree
```

In this example, the logical AND symbol is used to ensure that the only value returned belongs to the object category "Person" and the object class "user".

You can also use wild card characters, such as asterisks, as shown in the following example:

Example

```
(ObjectClass=*)
```

Note The search string does not contain any spaces. If a space is included, the returned results will contain incorrectly formatted data.

The following list provides explanations for the different parts of the query string:

- *Attributes* are the required values that will be returned by the search. A comma separates each attribute. In the above example, these are the users' **name** and **telephonenumber** properties.

- *Scope* refers to the boundary of the search. After the start point has been declared, the scope determines where the search stops, based on the following choices:

  - Base

    Search the object itself.

  - OneLevel

    Extend the search to the immediate children of the object, but exclude the base object itself.

  - Subtree

    Extend the search down to multiple sublevels of the object, and include the base object.

    If no scope is specified, the search will default to a Subtree search.

Using a Single Connection for Multiple Searches

```
Set con = CreateObject("ADODB.Connection")
Set com = CreateObject("ADODB.Command")
con.Provider = "ADsDSOObject"
con.Open
Set Com.ActiveConnection = con
Com.CommandText = "<LDAP://DC=NWTraders,DC=msft>;" _
    & "(objectClass=user);name,telephonenumber;subTree"
Set rs = Com.Execute
Do Until rs.EOF
  sResultText = sResultText & rs.Fields("Name") & " , " _
      & rs.Fields("telephonenumber")& vbCrLf
  rs.MoveNext
Loop
WScript.Echo sResultText
```

The following script example echoes to the screen, telephone number, and name for all users in the NWTraders.msft domain.

The approach shown here is best used when you need to perform several searches consecutively, because only one connection is required. After the connection has been opened, any number of Recordsets can be generated. Notice that the third line specifies which ADO provider this connection will use for all Active Directory searches. The ADsDSOObject provider is used.

Example

```
'Create connection and command object
  Set con = CreateObject("ADODB.Connection")
  Set com = CreateObject("ADODB.Command")
'Open the connection with the ADSI-OLEDB provider name
  con.Provider = "ADsDSOObject"
  con.Open
'Assign the command object for this connection
  Com.ActiveConnection = con
'Create a search string
  Com.CommandText = "<LDAP://DC=NWTraders,DC=msft>;" _
      & "(objectClass=user);name,telephonenumber;subTree"
'Execute the query
  Set rs = Com.Execute()
'Navigate the record set
  Do Until rs.EOF
      'Build Result Text
      sResultText = sResultText & rs.Fields("Name") & " , " _
& rs.Fields("telephonenumber") & vbCrLf
      rs.MoveNext
  Loop
  WScript.Echo sResultText
```

Using a Single Connection for Each Search

- **Create the ADO Recordset object**
- **Open the recordset based on the arguments**
- **Build result text**

```
Set rs = CreateObject("ADODB.Recordset")
rs.Open "<LDAP://DC=nwtraders,DC=msft>;" _
        & "(objectClass=user);name,telephonenumber;subTree" _
        , "provider = ADsDSOObject"
Do Until rs.EOF
  sResultText = sResultText & rs.Fields("Name") & " , " _
  & rs.Fields("telephonenumber") & vbCRLF
  rs.MoveNext
Loop
WScript.Echo sResultText
```

This example of an ADO search of Active Directory can be scripted much more quickly than the previous example, because it simply creates an instance of an ADODB **Recordset** and then uses it to conduct a search based on a single line of script. The basic syntax for this search is very similar to the previous example, except that a comma and provider statement are added after the search string as shown in the following example:

Example

```
, "provider = ADsDSOObject"
```

This simple addition allows the query to function without the **Connection** or **Command** objects that were used in the previous example. The following is a complete example of how you can use this approach:

Example

```
' Create the ADO Recordset Object
    Set rs = CreateObject("ADODB.Recordset")
' Open the Record Set based on the arguments
    rs.Open "<LDAP://DC=nwtraders,DC=msft>;" _
      & "(objectClass=user);name,telephonenumber;subTree" _
      , "provider=ADsDSOObject"
    Do Until rs.EOF
' Build Result Text
      sResultText = sResultText & rs.Fields("Name") & " , " &
          rs.Fields("telephonenumber") & vbCrLf
      rs.MoveNext
    Loop
  WScript.Echo sResultText
```

The disadvantage of this example is that a new connection is created each time the query is executed. If multiple queries were run in the same script, the previous example would be more efficient than this one.

Lab 5.1: ADO Search

Objectives

After completing this lab you will be able to:

- Search through the WST organizational unit.

- Return a number of properties of the user objects by using the ADSI LDAP query syntax.

Scenario

In this lab, you will create scripts that perform searches by using ADSI and ADO.

Estimated time to complete this lab: 15 minutes

Exercise 1
Performing Searches with ADSI and ADO

In this exercise, you will write ADO code that performs searches by using an ADSI provider.

▶ **To create a new script**

1. Log on to your computer as **Administrator@nwtraders.msft** with a password of **password**.

2. Start **PrimalSCRIPT**.

3. On the **File** menu, click **New**.

4. In the **New** dialog box, select **Text**, and then click **OK**.

▶ **To declare ADO object variables**

1. Type the following line of code to force variable declaration:

```
Option Explicit
```

2. Type the following **Dim** statements to declare three variables that will be used to manipulate ADO objects:

```
Dim aCon, aCmd, aRst, sResultText
```

The first three variables will be used to instantiate and manipulate a **Connection** object, a **Command** object, and a **Recordset** object, respectively.

▶ **To instantiate and manipulate the Connection and Command objects**

1. Type the following lines of code to instantiate the objects:

```
Set aCon = CreateObject("ADODB.Connection")
Set aCmd = CreateObject("ADODB.Command")
```

2. Type the following lines of code to manipulate the objects:

```
aCon.Provider="ADsDSOObject"
aCon.Open
aCmd.ActiveConnection = aCon
aCmd.CommandText="<LDAP://OU=WST,DC=NWTraders,DC=msft>;" _
    & "(objectClass=user);name,SamAccountName,givenName," _
    & "sN,telephonenumber;subTree"
```

▶ **To open the RecordSet object and return the results to the user**

1. Type the following line of code to create the **Recordset** object:

```
Set aRst = aCmd.Execute()
```

2. Type the following lines of code to loop through the **Recordset** object and build a string from its contents:

```
Do While Not aRst.EOF
    sResultText = sResultText _
        & aRst.Fields("samaccountname") _
        & ", " & aRst.Fields("givenname") _
        & ", " & aRst.Fields("sN") _
        & ", " & aRst.Fields("telephonenumber") _
        & vbCRLF
    aRst.MoveNext
Loop
```

3. Complete the script by displaying the string to the user as follows:

```
WScript.Echo sResultText
```

4. On the **File** menu, click **Save As**.

5. In the **Save As** dialog box, move to <*install folder*>\Labs\Lab05\Lab5_1\Starter.

6. In the **File name** box, type **ADOSearch.vbs**.

7. Click **Save**.

8. On the **Script** menu, click **Run Script**.

9. Review the details that are displayed in the message box, and click **OK**.

◆ Creating New ADSI Objects

- **Creating New OUs**
- **Creating New Users**
- **Creating New Groups**

In addition to searching for information about objects in Active Directory, you can also write code that creates new objects.

In this section, you will learn how to create new Organizational Unit (OU) objects, new users, and new groups.

Creating New OUs

■ Creating an OU

```
Set oRootDSE = GetObject("LDAP://RootDSE")
Set oDom = GetObject _
  ("LDAP://" & oRootDSE.Get ("defaultNamingContext"))
Set oOU = oDom.Create("organizationalUnit", "OU=HQ")
oOU.Description = "Company Headquarters"
oOU.SetInfo
```

Creating a new OU is a simple task with ADSI.

Creating an OU

The following example script shows the process of creating a new OU object in Active Directory:

Example

```
Set oRootDSE = GetObject("LDAP://RootDSE")
Set oDom = GetObject
      ("LDAP://" & oRootDSE.Get ("defaultNamingContext"))
Set oOU = oDom.Create("organizationalUnit", "OU=HQ")
oOU.Description = "Company Headquarters"
oOU.SetInfo
```

The first line in this example creates an object called **oRootDSE** that returns a connection to the root object of the directory service.

Using the **Get** method of the **oRootDSE** object creates a new object called **oDom**. This object references the default-naming context for the domain.

Using the **oDom** object and the **Create** method creates a new organizational object called **oOU** with the name of "HQ". A name is a mandatory property.

It is important to remember that the object is not committed to Active Directory at this point. There is an ADSI object reference on the client that you can use to set or modify locally cached attributes, such as the **Description**. To save the object back to the directory service, the **SetInfo** method is called.

Creating New Users

Creating a New User

```
Set oOU = GetObject _
    ("LDAP://OU=HQ,DC=lab,DC=Microsoft,DC=com")
Set oUSR = oOU.Create("user", "CN=Kathie Flood")
oUSR.Put "samAccountName", "kathief"
oUSR.Put "userPrincipalName", _
        "Kathie@northwindtraders.com"
oUSR.SetInfo
oUSR.SetPassword "TempPassword"
oUSR.AccountDisabled = False
oUSR.SetInfo
```

After you have created an OU, it is easy to create new users in that OU.

Creating a New User

In the following example, a new user is created in the HQ organizational unit.

Example

```
Set oOU = GetObject ("LDAP://OU=HQ,DC=lab,DC=contentm,DC=com")
Set oUSR = oOU.Create("user", "CN=Alan Steiner")
oUSR.Put"samAccountName", "Alan"
oUSR.Put "userPrincipalName", "Alan@northwindtraders.com"
oUSR.SetInfo
oUSR.SetPassword "TempPassword"
oUSR.AccountDisabled = False
oUSR.SetInfo
```

To create a user, you need to provide two required properties: the common name (CN) and the down-level NetBIOS user name.

Note that, in this example, the object is committed back to the directory service twice. This is because the properties **SetPassword** and **AccountDisabled** can only be used against an object that already exists in the directory. The first instance of "SetInfo" commits the new user object to Active Directory, and the second instance sets the password and enables the account.

Note Setting the **userPrincipalName** property is optional when a script is used to create the user.

Creating New Groups

- **Group Types**
- **Security and Distribution**
- **Properties and Methods of Groups**
- **Creating Groups**

```
Set oOU = GetObject("LDAP://OU=WST,DC=NWTraders,DC=MSFT")
Set oGroup = oOU.Create("group", "CN=Script Users")
oGroup.Put "groupType" ADS_GROUP_TYPE_DOMAIN_LOCAL_GROUP _
    Or ADS_GROUP_TYPE_SECURITY_ENABLED
oGroup.Put "samAccountName", "Script Users"
oGroup.Put "name", "Script Users"
oGroup.Put "displayName", "Script Users"
oGroup.Put "description", "Script Users Security Group"
oGroup.SetInfo
```

- **Adding Users to Groups**

```
oGroup.Add("LDAP://cn=MyUser,ou=WST,dc=NWTraders,dc=msft")
```

- **Removing Users from Groups**

In addition to creating users with ADSI scripts, you can create new groups. However, note that there are several different types of groups supported by Active Directory.

Group Types

Windows 2000 has the following four basic group types:

- Universal groups

    Universal groups can contain accounts and groups, except for local and domain local groups, from any domain in the forest. Universal groups can also be added to local groups and other universal groups in any domain in the forest. These groups are only available when Active Directory is in native mode.

- Global groups

    Global groups can contain only accounts and other groups from its own domain. These groups can be added to global, local, and universal groups in all domains in the forest.

- Domain local groups

    Domain local groups can contain accounts and global and universal groups from any domain in the forest, as well as other domain local groups from the same domain. They can only be included in access-control lists of the same domain in which they were created, and can only be a member of other domain local groups in the same domain.

- Local groups

    Local groups exist only in the local computer's Security Access Manager (SAM). They can only be manipulated on that computer, and can contain users and groups from any domain in the forest. On domain controllers, this type of group maps straight onto the domain local group type.

Security and Distribution

Each of these group types can be defined as either security (can be used for assigning permissions) or distribution (equivalent to an e-mail distribution list). If no group type or security properties are specified when you write the script, a global security group will be created. However, if only the group type is defined, a distribution group of that type is created.

Properties and Methods of Groups

In addition to the standard properties and methods shown earlier in this module, groups expose the following specific properties and methods.

Property	Description
Description	Provides a place for a string comment about the group

Method	Description
Members	Returns a collection of the group's members
IsMember	Returns **True** if the given ADsPath is a member of the group
Add	Adds the given ADsPath to the group
Remove	Removes the given ADsPath from the group

Creating Groups

The following example shows how you can create groups using ADSI:

Example

```
' Setup Constants
Const ADS_GROUP_TYPE_GLOBAL_GROUP = &H2
Const ADS_GROUP_TYPE_DOMAIN_LOCAL_GROUP = &H4
Const ADS_GROUP_TYPE_LOCAL_GROUP = &H4
Const ADS_GROUP_TYPE_UNIVERSAL_GROUP = &H8
Const ADS_GROUP_TYPE_SECURITY_ENABLED = &H80000000

' Bind to OU
Set oOU = GetObject("LDAP://OU=WST,DC=NWTraders,DC=MSFT")
' Create new group
Set oGroup = oOU.Create("group", "CN=Script Users")
' Set the group type
oGroup.Put "groupType", ADS_GROUP_TYPE_DOMAIN_LOCAL_GROUP Or _
ADS_GROUP_TYPE_SECURITY_ENABLED
' Set the group properties
oGroup.Put "sAMAccountName", "Script Users"
oGroup.Put "name", "Script Users"
oGroup.Put "displayName", "Script Users"
oGroup.Put "description", "Script Users Security Group"
' Save back to the AD
oGroup.SetInfo
```

In this script, the ADSI constants are declared first. Next, the script binds to the Users container in the NWTraders.msft domain. Then, a new group called "Script Users" is created by using the **Create** method of the **oOU** object. The **Put** method is then used to add the following information to the new group:

- The group type
- The NetBIOS sAMAcountName
- The display name
- The description

Finally, the **SetInfo** method writes this information from the object's local cache back to Active Directory.

ADSI Constants

The constants (and their values) that are used in the group creation process are listed in the following table.

Constant	Value
ADS_GROUP_TYPE_GLOBAL_GROUP	&H2
ADS_GROUP_TYPE_DOMAIN_LOCAL_GROUP	&H4
ADS_GROUP_TYPE_LOCAL_GROUP	&H4
ADS_GROUP_TYPE_UNIVERSAL_GROUP	&H8
ADS_GROUP_TYPE_SECURITY_ENABLED	&H80000000

Adding Users to Groups

The **Add** method of the **Group** object is used to add a specific user account to that group. The following example adds a user to the group referenced by the oGroup variable.

Example

```
oGroup.Add ("LDAP://cn=MyUser,ou=WST,dc=NWTraders,dc=msft")
```

If you are adding multiple users, you can specify additional accounts as shown in the following:

Example

```
oGroup.Add ("LDAP://cn=MyUser,ou=WST,dc=NWTraders,dc=msft,
↪LDAP://cn=MyUser2,ou=WST,dc=NWTraders,dc=msft,
↪LDAP://cn=MyUser3,ou=WST,dc=NWTraders,dc=msft")
```

Removing Users from a Group

You can remove users from a group by using the **Remove** method of that **Group** object. The following example uses the WinNT provider and removes the user **MyUser** from the group referenced by the oGroup variable.

Example

```
oGroup.Remove ("WinNT://NWTraders/WST/MyUser")
```

Setting Security in Active Directory

- **Security Components**
- **Windows 2000 Platform Software Developer Kit**
- **Script vs. DSACLS.EXE**

After you create a new object in Active Directory, it is likely that the security permissions of the objects will need to be modified.

Security Components

Each object in Active Directory has a corresponding security descriptor that enables you to modify and propagate permissions on the object, perform auditing, and so on.

Each security descriptor has two Access Control Lists (ACL). The first is the Discretionary ACL (DACL) and the second is the System ACL (SACL). The DACL contains all administrator-assigned permissions for the object. The SACL is used to track changes to Active Directory in the security event log of the domain controller for audit purposes. Each ACL can contain Access Control Entries (ACE).

An ACE contains the following components:

- AccessMask
- AceType
- AceFlags
- Trustee
- Flags

Windows 2000 Platform Software Developers Kit.

Manipulating security by using ADSI involves an often complex set of tasks. Before you attempt to write code that manipulates Active Directory security, you should refer to the Windows 2000 Platform Software Developers Kit.

Script vs. DSACLS.EXE

Although you can script the manipulation of security in Active Directory, it is much easier to use the command-line tool Dsacls.exe, which is provided as part of the Windows 2000 support tools. Using this tool enables you to achieve all of the functionality of ADSI, but requires far less code.

For more information about this tool, see the Windows 2000 support tools Help file.

Managing Shares Using ADSI

- **Binding to the LanManServer Service**

```
Set objShare = GetObject("WinNT://MyComp/LANMANSERVER")
```

- **Properties:**
  - Name
  - CurrentUserCount
  - Description
  - HostComputer
  - MaxUserCount
  - Path

Managing shares by using ADSI is a simple process.

Binding to the LanManServer Service

The first step in using a script to create or modify a share is to bind to the LanManServer file service on the host computer. You do this by using the WinNT provider with the syntax shown in the following example:

Example

```
Set oLMServer = GetObject("WinNT://MyComputer/LanManServer")
```

This code creates an instance of the **LanManServer** object by binding to the LanManServer file service on the computer called MyComputer.

After this binding occurs, and the object is successfully created, the following methods and properties are available.

Property	Description
Name	The share name
CurrentUserCount	The number of users currently connected to the share (read-only)
Description	The friendly description for the file share
HostComputer	The ADsPath for the computer where this share resides
MaxUserCount	The maximum number of users that are allowed to connect to this share simultaneously
Path	The local file system path for the shared folder

The following example demonstrates how to enumerate all of the shares from a computer called MyComputer:

Example

```
Set oLMServer=GetObject("WinNT://MyComputer/LANMANSERVER")
    For Each share in oLMServer
        WScript.Echo share.Name & " = " & share.Path
    Next
```

The following example shows how to create a share on MyComputer ("MyComp") with the following properties:

- Name = DemoShare

- Path = C:\Temp

- Description = "This is a demo share"

- User Limit = 5

Example

```
Set oLMServer=GetObject("WinNT://MyComp/LANMANSERVER")
Set oNewShare = oLMServer.Create("fileshare", "DemoShare")
oNewShare.Path = "C:\Temp"
oNewShare.Description = "This is a demo share"
oNewShare.MaxUserCount = 5
oNewShare.SetInfo
```

Note   This object currently has no methods that allow you to set permissions that will apply to the share. One possible solution to this could be to use the Windows 2000 Resource Kit utility Permcopy. See the Resource Kit documentation for more details.

Controlling Services Using ADSI

- **Enumerating Services**
  - Testing service status
- **Starting a Service**
- **Stopping a Service**

ADSI provides several features for managing services on a Windows NT or Windows 2000 computer. These features enable you to determine what services are running on a computer and to start and stop these services.

Enumerating Services

The first step in managing services is to enumerate the existing services on a computer, as shown in the following example:

Example

```
Option Explicit
Dim objComputer, Service, strSvrList
Set objComputer = GetObject("WinNT://MyServer")
strSvrList = "The Services on " & objComputer.ADsPath _
  & " are " & vbCrLf
For Each Service in objComputer
    If Service.Class = "Service" Then
        strSvrList = strSvrList & Service.Name & vbCrLf
    End If
Next
WScript.Echo strSvrList
```

This example binds to the server MyServer and then creates a string variable, strSvrList, which is used to hold the list of services. A **For...Next** loop is then set up to loop through all of the elements in **objComputer**. For each of these elements, an **If...Then** statement tests if the **Class** of the element is of the type **Service**. If it is, it is added to the strSvrList variable. After all of the elements have been tested, the **For...Next** loop exits, and the strSvrList variable is echoed.

To return only the services that are currently running, you can add a test of the services' status. The following list of constants can be used when testing for the status of these services:

- ADS_SERVICE_STOPPED   = &H1
  ADS_SERVICE_START_PENDING   = &H2
  ADS_SERVICE_STOP_PENDING   = &H3
  ADS_SERVICE_RUNNING   = &H4
  ADS_SERVICE_CONTINUE_PENDING   = &H5
  ADS_SERVICE_PAUSE_PENDING   = &H6
  ADS_SERVICE_PAUSED   = &H7
  ADS_SERVICE_ERROR   = &H8

The following is an example of a script returning only the services that are running on the computer MyServer:

Example

```
Option Explicit
Const ADS_SERVICE_RUNNING = &H4

Dim objComputer, Service, strSvrList

Set objComputer = GetObject("WinNT://MyServer")
strSvrList = "The Services on " & objComputer.ADsPath _
  & " are: " & vbCrLf
For Each Service in objComputer
    If Service.Class = "Service" Then
        If Service.Status = ADS_SERVICE_RUNNING Then
            strSvrList = strSvrList & Service.Name & vbCRLF
        End If
    End If
Next
WScript.Echo strSvrList
```

This script works in the same way as the previous example script, but an extra **If...Then** statement has been added to test that the status of a service is equal to ADS_SERVICE_RUNNING before its name is appended to the strSvrList string.

Starting a Service

If the name of the required service is known, the process of starting the service is very simple, as the following example shows:

Example

```
Set oBrowser = GetObject("WinNT://MyServer/browser")
oBrowser.start
```

In this example, a **oBrowser** object is created that references the browser service on the computer MyServer. A call to the **Start** method starts the service.

Stopping a Service

Similarly, stopping a known service is very simple, as shown in the following example:

Example

```
Set oMessenger = GetObject("WinNT://MyServer/messenger")
oMessenger.stop
```

In this example, the object is called **oMessenger**, and the **Stop** method is used to stop the messenger service.

In real-world scripting, it is a good practice to also use the **Status** method to check that the service started or stopped correctly before terminating the script.

ADSI Resources

- **Platform SDK**
  - ADSI Resource Kit
- **Microsoft ADSI Web Site**
  - http://www.microsoft.com/adsi
- **MSDN Library**
  - http://msdn.microsoft.com/library/Default.asp
- **Microsoft Scripting Web Site**
  - http://www.microsoft.com/scripting
- **Microsoft Newsgroup**
  - news://microsoft.public.active.directory.interfaces

This module introduced the basics of how ADSI can be used in VBScript. If you require more advanced information, you will find additional material at the following locations.

The Platform SDK

This provides a comprehensive resource, primarily aimed at programmers. The ADSI Developers Guide that is part of the SDK is invaluable as a reference tool.

Microsoft ADSI Web Site

The Internet site http://www.microsoft.com/adsi is a public ADSI site. It provides links to many other useful resources and sites.

MSDN Library

The MSDN® Library site provides access to an online version of the Windows 2000 Platform SDK, as well as Knowledge Base and technical articles that can be very useful for providing script examples.

Microsoft Scripting Web Site

The MSDN Web site includes a script-specific area that provides online versions of the script Help documentation and many downloads and articles. You can find this site at http://msdn.microsoft.com/scripting

Microsoft Newsgroup

Microsoft maintains a moderated public newsgroup dedicated to ADSI issues at news://microsoft.public.active.directory.interfaces

Lab 5.2: Scripting Administrative Tasks Using ADSI

Objectives

After completing this lab, you will be able to:

- Create scripts that bind to the domain by using several different methods.
- Manipulate various objects by using the ADSI interface.

Scenario

In this lab, you will create scripts that bind to the domain by using several different methods. You will also create and manipulate various objects, such as users and groups, by using the ADSI interface. These are common tasks that will help you to administer your domains.

Lab Setup

To complete this lab, you need a student number. See the "Student Numbers" section of the lab for this information.

Student Numbers

The following table provides the computer name, IP address, and student number of each student computer in the fictitious domain nwtraders.msft.

Find the computer name or IP address assigned to you, and make a note of the student number.

Computer name	IP address	Student number
Vancouver	192.168.x.1	1
Denver	192.168.x.2	2
Perth	192.168.x.3	3
Brisbane	192.168.x.4	4
Lisbon	192.168.x.5	5
Bonn	192.168.x.6	6
Lima	192.168.x.7	7
Santiago	192.168.x.8	8
Bangalore	192.168.x.9	9
Singapore	192.168.x.10	10
Casablanca	192.168.x.11	11
Tunis	192.168.x.12	12
Acapulco	192.168.x.13	13
Miami	192.168.x.14	14
Auckland	192.168.x.15	15
Suva	192.168.x.16	16
Stockholm	192.168.x.17	17
Moscow	192.168.x.18	18
Caracas	192.168.x.19	19
Montevideo	192.168.x.20	20
Manila	192.168.x.21	21
Tokyo	192.168.x.22	22
Khartoum	192.168.x.23	23
Nairobi	192.168.x.24	24

Estimated time to complete this lab: 45 minutes

Exercise 1
Retrieving Properties Using ADSI

In this exercise, you will write code that interacts with ADSI.

▶ **To create a new script**

1. Log on to your computer as **Administrator@nwtraders.msft** with a password of **password**

2. Start **PrimalSCRIPT**.

3. On the **File** menu, click **New**.

4. In the **New** dialog box, click **Text**, and then click **OK**.

▶ **To declare ADSI object variables**

1. Type the following line of code to force variable declaration:

```
Option Explicit
```

2. Type the following statements to declare the variables that will be used to manipulate ADSI objects:

```
Const ADS_SECURE_AUTHENTICATION = &H1
Dim oMyDomain, oRootDSE, oMyDS, iCount, iLoop, sPropList,
↪sProp, sPropName
```

Tip   The line continuation character (↪) indicates that the subsequent code should be typed on the same line as the preceding code

---

▶ **To instantiate and manipulate ADSI objects**

1. Type the following lines of code to instantiate the objects and retrieve a count of the number of properties:

```
Set oRootDSE = GetObject("LDAP://RootDSE")
Set oMyDS = Getobject("LDAP:")
Set oMyDomain = oMyDS.OpenDSObject("LDAP://" _
    & oRootDSE.Get("defaultNamingContext"), _
    "administrator", "password", ADS_SECURE_AUTHENTICATION)
oMyDomain.GetInfo
iCount = oMyDomain.PropertyCount
sPropList = "There are " & iCount _
    & " values in the local property cache for Domain: " _
    & oMyDomain.ADSPath & vbCRLF
WScript.Echo sPropList
sPropList = ""
```

2. Type the following lines of code to display the property names and values in two message boxes:

```
On Error Resume Next
If iCount Mod 2 = 0 then
   For iLoop = 0 To (iCount/2)-1
      Set sProp = oMyDomain.Item(CInt(iLoop))
      sPropName = sProp.Name
      sPropList = sPropList & sPropName & ": " _
         & oMyDomain.Get(sPropName) & vbCrLf
      If err.number <> 0 then
         err.clear
         sPropList = sPropList & sPropName & ": " _
            & "<MultiValued>" & vbCrLf
      End If
   Next
   WScript.Echo sPropList
   sPropList=""
   For iLoop = (iCount/2) To iCount-1
      Set sProp = oMyDomain.Item(CInt(iLoop))
      sPropName = sProp.Name
      sPropList = sPropList & sPropName & ": " _
         & oMyDomain.Get(sPropName) & vbCrLf
      If err.number <> 0 then
         Err.Clear
         sPropList = sPropList & sPropName & ": " _
            & "<MultiValued>" & vbCrLf
      End If
   Next
   WScript.Echo sPropList
   sPropList=""
Else
   For iLoop = 0 To (iCount/2)-0.5
      Set sProp = oMyDomain.Item(CInt(iLoop))
      sPropName = sProp.Name
      sPropList = sPropList & sPropName & ": " _
         & oMyDomain.Get(sPropName) & vbCrLf
      If err.number <> 0 then
         Err.Clear
         sPropList = sPropList & sPropName & ": " _
            & "<MultiValued>" & vbCrLf
      End If
   Next
   WScript.Echo sPropList
   sPropList=""

' Code continued next page
```

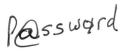

```
' Code continued from previous page

  For iLoop = (iCount/2)+0.5 To iCount-1
    Set sProp = oMyDomain.Item(CInt(iLoop))
    sPropName = sProp.Name
    sPropList = sPropList & sPropName & ": " _
      & oMyDomain.Get(sPropName) & vbCrLf
    If err.number <> 0 then
      Err.Clear
      sPropList = sPropList & sPropName & ": " _
        & "<MultiValued>" & vbCrLf
    End If
  Next
  WScript.Echo sPropList
  sPropList=""
End If
```

Although the loops may appear to be complex, their purpose is simply to make the size of the message boxes manageable and readable. The loops display half of the properties in one message box and half in another message box.

3. On the **File** menu, click **Save As**.

4. In the **Save As** dialog box, navigate to the folder
   <install folder>\Labs\Lab05\Lab5_2\Starter.

5. In the **File name** box, type **GetProperties.vbs**

6. Click **Save**.

7. On the **Script** menu, click **Run Script**.

8. Review the details that are displayed in the message boxes, and then click
   OK.

Exercise 2
Creating OUs, Users, and Groups Using ADSI

▶ **To create a new script**

1. On the **File** menu, click **New**.

2. In the **New** dialog box, click **Text**, and then click **OK**.

▶ **To declare ADSI object variables and constants**

1. Type the following line of code to force variable declaration:

```
Option Explicit
```

2. Type the following statements to declare the variables and constants that will be used to manipulate ADSI objects:

```
Const ADS_GROUP_TYPE_GLOBAL_GROUP = &H2
Const ADS_GROUP_TYPE_DOMAIN_LOCAL_GROUP = &H4
Const ADS_GROUP_TYPE_LOCAL_GROUP = &H4
Const ADS_GROUP_TYPE_UNIVERSAL_GROUP = &H8
Const ADS_GROUP_TYPE_SECURITY_ENABLED = &H80000000
Dim oMyDomain, oRootDSE, oOU, grp, oUSR, sDomainADSPath
```

▶ **To instantiate ADSI objects and create an OU object**

1. Type the following lines of code to instantiate the objects:

```
Set oRootDSE = GetObject("LDAP://RootDSE")
Set oMyDomain = GetObject("LDAP://" _
  & oRootDSE.Get ("defaultNamingContext"))
sDomainADSPath = oMyDomain.ADSPath
```

2. Type the following lines of code to create a new OU:

Important Remember to substitute your student number where you see "X". For example, StudentXOU becomes Student24OU if you are Student 24.

```
Set oOU = oMyDomain.Create _
  ("organizationalUnit", "OU=StudentXOU")
oOU.Description = "Student number X private OU"
On Error Resume Next
oOU.SetInfo
If err.Number = -2147019886 then
  WScript.Echo "The OU already exists, but can continue"
  Err.Clear
Set oOU = GetObject _
  ("LDAP://OU=StudentXOU,DC=NWTraders,DC=msft")
End If
```

▶ **To create a new group object and a new user object**

1. Type the following lines of code to create a new group object:

```
Set grp = oOU.Create("group", "CN=DeptAdmin")
grp.Put "samAccountName", "dptAd" 55
grp.Put "groupType", ADS_GROUP_TYPE_DOMAIN_LOCAL_GROUP Or
ADS_GROUP_TYPE_SECURITY_ENABLED
grp.SetInfo
```

2. Type the following lines of code to create a new user object:

```
Set oUSR = oOU.Create("user", "CN=Frank Lee")
oUSR.Put "samAccountName", "FrankL"
oUSR.Put "department", "MIS"
oUSR.Put "sn", "Lee"
oUSR.SetInfo
oUSR.SetPassword "TempPassword"
oUSR.AccountDisabled = False
oUSR.SetInfo
If Err.Number <> 0 then
  WScript.Echo "Errors occurred - make sure that the user
and group do not already exist..."
Else
  WScript.Echo "Finished"
end if
```

3. On the **File** menu, click **Save As**.

4. In the **Save As** dialog box, navigate to the
   <install folder>\Labs\Lab05\Lab5_2\Starter.

5. In the **File name** box, type **CreateNewObjects.vbs**

6. Click **Save**.

7. On the **Script** menu, click **Run Script**.

8. Review the information in the message box, and then click **OK**.

▶ **To create a new Active Directory Users and Computers console**

1. On the **Start** menu, click **Run**.

2. In the **Open** box, type **MMC**, and then press ENTER.

   An empty MMC console will open.

3. On the **Console** menu, click **Add/Remove Snap-in**.

4. In the **Add/Remove Snap-in** dialog box, click **Add**.

5. In the **Add Standalone Snap-in** dialog box, click **Active Directory Users and Computers**, and then click **Add**.

6. Click **Close**.

7. Click **OK**.

▶ **To verify that the objects have been created**

1. In the **Tree** pane, expand the **Active Directory Users and Computers** node.

2. Expand **nwtraders.msft**.

3. Click **Student*X*OU** (where *X* is your student number).

4. Verify that this OU contains a user named **Frank Lee** and a group named **DeptAdmin**.

5. Close the MMC console, and then click **Yes** in the **Save console settings to Console1?** dialog box.

6. Name the console **AD Users and Computers**, and then click **Save**.

Review

- ADSI Overview
- Binding with ADSI
- ADSI Objects
- Searching Active Directory
- Creating New ADSI Objects
- Setting Security in Active Directory
- Managing Shares Using ADSI
- Controlling Services Using ADSI
- ADSI Resources

1. What is the main directory service provider used for Windows 2000?

2. Before you can use ADSI to work with the objects in a directory, what action must your script perform with an ADSI provider?

3. What is the preferred method of binding?

4. When you work with the properties of an object, where are the updates being stored?

5. How are changes committed back to the directory from the local properties cache?

msdn training

Module 6: Creating Logon Scripts

Contents

Microsoft

Overview

- ■ **Verifying the WSH Environment**
- ■ **Common Logon Script Tasks**
- ■ **Managing Logon Scripts**
- ■ **Troubleshooting Logon Scripts**

To successfully deploy logon scripts throughout the enterprise network, you must understand the processes involved in creating and managing these scripts.

In this module, you will learn how to create and manage logon scripts.

At the end of this module, you will be able to:

- ■ Check that the correct version of Microsoft® Windows® Script Host (WSH) is installed.
- ■ Call logon scripts from batch files.
- ■ Accomplish common tasks in logon scripts.
- ■ Assign logon scripts to users.
- ■ Describe common issues with logon scripts.
- ■ Describe good practices for using logon scripts.

◆ Verifying the WSH Environment

- ■ **The Testing Process**
- ■ **Checking the WSH Installation**
- ■ **Checking the WSH Version**
- ■ **Automatically Installing WSH**
- ■ **Running the Logon Script**

To ensure that your logon scripts will run successfully, you must be able to test whether the correct version of WSH is installed on the user's computer.

In this section, you will learn how to verify whether the correct version of WSH is available to run your logon scripts. In addition, you will learn how to install WSH automatically if it is not installed.

The Testing Process

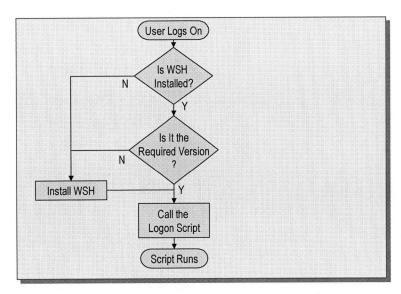

When a user logs on, you must verify whether your script can run successfully. This involves checking whether WSH is installed on the computer that the script is run on.

If WSH is installed, your script checks whether it is the correct version.

After these tests are passed, your script can continue. If a test fails, your logon script installs the correct version of WSH before it continues.

Checking the WSH Installation

- **Calling Scripts from a Batch File**
  - Test for error level
- **Testing for the Existence of Installed Files**
  - Example: CScript.exe, WScript.exe, VBScript.dll

Before a logon script runs, you can test whether WSH is installed on a user's computer. To test this, you can either run a script from a batch file, or use a batch file to locate the WSH files. If script files are used, and WSH is not installed, then the tests fail.

Calling Scripts from a Batch File

You can create a batch file that attempts to run a script by using CScript. The batch file determines whether an error level is returned. If no error is returned, WSH is installed. You can then test the version of WSH.

The following is an example of a batch file that performs this test. If an error level is returned, the batch file installs WSH.

Example

```
Rem Try and run wshver.vbs script
CScript //i //nologo WshVerTest.vbs
Rem If wshver fails install latest WSH in quiet mode
if errorlevel 1 Ste51en /q
```

Note For more information about installing WSH, see "Automatically Installing WSH" later in this module.

Testing for the Presence of Installed Files

Another method that tests for a WSH installation is to search for the files that are present when WSH is installed.

The following files are present:

- Core script files

  CScript.exe, WScript.exe, WScript.hlp

  ScrRun.dll, Wshom.ocx, Wshext.dll, Msvcrt.dll, Scrobvj.dll, Dispex.dll, Advpack.dll

- Script engines

  VBScript.dll, Jscript.dll

To test for these files, you can use the **If Exist...**statement, as shown in the following example:

Example

```
Rem Test places file is usually found
If exist C:\WINNTPRO\system32\wshom.ocx goto :FoundFile
If exist C:\WINNTPRO\wshom.ocx goto :FoundFile
If exist C:\WINNTPRO\system\wshom.ocx goto :FoundFile
Rem No file found install latest WSH in quite mode
Ste51en /q
:FoundFile
Rem The file was found a version of WSH is installed
Rem Now launch the WSH version testing script
CScript //I //nologo WshVerTest.vbs
```

Tip   To make the process of using batch files easier, you can use the **Start** command to launch the logon batch file in a minimized window, as shown below:

START /MIN LOGON.BAT

Checking the WSH Version

- ■ **Using Script**
  - ● WScript.Version property
  - ● Script engine test
    ScriptEngineMajorVersion
    ScriptEngineMinorVersion
- ■ **Using Script or Batch Files**
  - ● File size or file date

There are several versions of WSH that are available. If you want your logon script to run successfully, your script must first check that the required version of WSH is installed on the client machine.

It is important to understand that there are two major parts to the WSH environment. The first is the host, which calls the relevant script engines and enables them to run. The second is the script engines themselves, which are the most likely to change. The script engine that ships with Microsoft Windows 2000 is version 5.1. Version 5.5 is now available as part of Microsoft Internet Explorer 5.5, or as a download from the Microsoft Script Web site.

Using Script

You can check the version of WSH by using the properties of the WSH object model and the script engine. The following example tests for the version of WSH:

Example

```
nVer = WScript.Version
If nVer = 5.1 Then
    WScript.Echo "WSH Version is OK"
    WScript.Quit(0)
  Else      WScript.Echo "WSH needs updating"
    WScript.Quit (1)
End If
```

The following example checks the version of the Microsoft Visual Basic® Scripting Edition engine that processes the script:

Example

```
nVerMaj = ScriptEngineMajorVersion
nVerMin = ScriptEngineMinorVersion
If nVerMaj = 5 and nVerMin = 1 Then
    WScript.Echo "Script Engine version is OK"
    WScript.Quit(0)
Else
    WScript.Echo "Script Engine needs updating"
    WScript.Quit (1)
End If
```

Using Script or Batch Files

Another method for checking WSH and script engine versions is to test the size of the required files. This method has one possible advantage over the previous method: it can be conducted from within a batch file and in a script. The following example shows script that tests the size of the required files:

Example

```
Dim oFso, ofile
Set oFso = CreateObject("Scripting.FileSystemObject")
Set ofile = oFso.GetFile("C:\WINNTPRO\system32\wshom.ocx")
If ofile.size = 73776 Then
  WScript.Echo "Wshom.ocx File OK"
Else
  WScript.Echo "Wshom.ocx needs updating"
End If
```

By updating line 4 of this script, you can check the date that the file was originally created as follows:

Example

```
If ofile.DateCreated = "07/12/1999 12:00:00" Then
```

Note While this example works on all computers running Windows 2000 Professional it fails on all others, because the file date is the time that the original media image was compiled. Therefore, different times and dates are returned for all versions of Windows 2000 and for the down-level clients running the downloaded WSH update. You should modify this example accordingly if you encounter this issue.

Automatically Installing WSH

- **Installing WSH Using Batch Files**
  - Ste55en.exe for Win95, Win98, and WinNT
  - Scripten.exe for Win2000
- **Performing a Silent Installation**

If your tests fail to find the correct version of WSH installed, you can use the logon batch files to automatically install the correct version of WSH. This approach ensures that all clients have installed the required version of WSH.

Installing WSH Using Batch Files

Ste55en.exe installs WSH on Microsoft Windows 95, Microsoft Windows 98, and Microsoft Windows NT® version 4.0.

Because WSH is part of all versions of Windows 2000, a separate program called Scripten.exe is used to install WSH on that operating system. This program only installs version 5.5 of the script engines.

Both Ste55.exe and Scripten.exe are available from
http://www.microsoft.com/msdownload/vbscript/scripting.asp

Note Microsoft Windows Millennium Edition (Me) has version 5.1 of the hosts and version 5.5 of the script engines.

Performing a Silent Installation

You can use several command-line switches when you install WSH. The /Q switch performs a silent installation.

This switch installs WSH with no user interaction. It may however require you to restart the system.

Running the Logon Script

- **Calling the Script**
  - Directly: CScript //i //nologo LogonScript.vbs
  - With a .wsh file: CScript LogonScript.wsh
- **Determining the Script Path**
  - %LOGONSERVER%
  - %0\..\

After your batch files determine the presence of the correct version of WSH, they can call the logon script.

Calling the Script

Usually, your batch file calls the main script file. However, you can call a .wsh file that calls the logon script. Using this method gives you more control over how the script runs. The following examples illustrate both methods. You will only use one of these:

Example

```
CScript //I //nologo LogonScript.vbs
```

Example

```
CScript LogonScript.wsh
```

Determining the Script Path

To run the logon script, the batch file must determine the path to the script and how the script should be run. Windows NT and Windows 2000 make this information available in the %LOGONSERVER% system variable. You can use this variable to launch the script, as the following example illustrates:

Example

```
CScript \\%LOGONSERVER%\Netlogon\Scripts\Logon.vbs
```

For clients running Windows 95 or Windows 98, this is more complex. These clients do not make the %LOGONSERVER% variable available.

To solve this problem, you can use the %0 variable. This variable returns the full path of the script that is running. If you add \..\ to the path that is returned by the %0 variable, the batch process uses the folder that the file is being run from. As long as the script file is in the same folder as the running file, usually the logon server's NETLOGON share, this batch file can call a script file that works from any platform. The following example shows the use of these variables:

Example

```
CScript %0\..\LogonScript.vbs
```

◆ Common Logon Script Tasks

- **Sending Messages**
- **Getting User Input**
- **Creating Desktop Shortcuts**
- **Mapping Drives**
- **Mapping Printers**
- **Launching Utility Programs**

There are several commonly performed tasks that you will encounter when you develop logon scripts.

This section explains how to send messages to the user, retrieve input from the user, create shortcuts, map drives and printers, and launch other programs and utilities.

Sending Messages

- **WScript.Echo**
    - Echoes to command line in CScript.exe
- **MsgBox**
    - Opens a message box.
- **PopUp**
- **UserName**

You can include messages in logon scripts. The messages will be displayed to the user each time that the script runs. You can send messages to users to inform them of network events, or you can send a simple "Message of the Day" as part of a logon script. Messages can also display legal disclaimers and reminders.

There are several methods for displaying messages to users from your logon scripts.

WScript.Echo

If the host running the script is WScript.exe, the **WScript.Echo** method displays output in a dialog box. If the host running the script is **WScript.exe**, the Wscript.Echo method displays output in the command console.

MsgBox

You can use the **MsgBox** function in Visual Basic Scripting Edition if you want to display a message in a pop-up message box. This opens a message box in Windows when either script engine is used, even if the batch mode switch (//B) has been declared.

The **MsgBox** function also enables you to display various types of message boxes, with different button configurations and icon settings. For example, the **MsgBox** function can display any of the following icons in the message box:

- **Critical Message**
- **Warning Query**
- **Warning Message**
- **Information Message**

In addition, you can specify the buttons that you want to present in the message box. You can use the following combination of buttons:

- **OK** only
- **OK** and **Cancel**
- **Yes** and **No**
- **Yes**, **No**, and **Cancel**
- **Abort**, **Retry**, and **Ignore**
- **Retry** and **Cancel**

The **MsgBox** function accepts the **buttons** argument, which you can use to specify both the icons and the buttons for the message box.

The following table lists the possible values for the **buttons** argument. Note that you can use the intrinsic VBScript constants in place of the values to read and write the script more easily.

Constant	Value	Description
vbOKOnly	0	Display the **OK** button only.
vbOKCancel	1	Display the **OK** and **Cancel** buttons.
vbAbortRetryIgnore	2	Display the **Abort**, **Retry**, and **Ignore** buttons.
vbYesNoCancel	3	Display the **Yes**, **No**, and **Cancel** buttons.
VbYesNo	4	Display the **Yes** and **No** buttons.
vbRetryCancel	5	Display the **Retry** and **Cancel** buttons.
vbCritical	16	Display the **Critical Message** icon.
vbQuestion	32	Display the **Warning Query** icon.
vbExclamation	48	Display the **Warning Message** icon.
vbInformation	64	Display the **Information Message** icon.
vbDefaultButton1	0	The first button is the default.
vbDefaultButton2	256	The second button is the default.
vbDefaultButton3	512	The third button is the default.
vbDefaultButton4	768	The fourth button is the default.
vbApplicationModal	0	The user must respond to the message box before the script continues.
vbSystemModal	4096	On Windows 32-bit operating systems, this constant provides an application modal message box that always remains on top of any other programs running. On Windows 16-bit operating systems, applications are suspended until the user responds to the message box.

To specify both an icon and a set of buttons, you can add the numbers or constants together, as shown below:

Example

```
MsgBox "OK button and Info Icon", vbOKOnly + vbInformation
```

PopUp

The WSH object model provides a method that enables you to display a pop-up window. The **PopUp** method of the **WScript.Shell** object has features similar to the **MsgBox** function, but the **PopUp** method adds a time value that governs how long a message is displayed before it is dismissed automatically. The syntax is:

Syntax

```
oShell.Popup(Text, [Secs2Wait], [Title], [Type])
```

Text is the body of the message, *Secs2Wait* is the number of seconds that the message is displayed, *Title* is the title bar message, and *Type* is the type of buttons and icons displayed in the pop-up window.

Note   For more information about this method, see the WSH documentation.

UserName

If you want the script to output the name of the user that is logging on, you can use the **UserName** property of the **WScript.Network** object to display the user's logon name. This personalizes the messages to the user, as the following example shows:

Example

```
oNetwork = CreateObject("WScript.Network")
WScript.Echo "Welcome " & oNetwork.UserName
```

Getting User Input

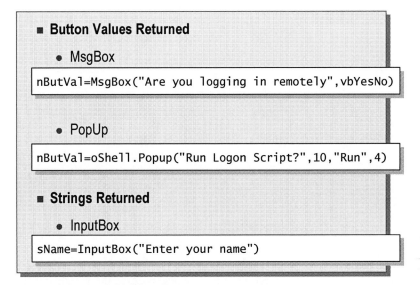

■ **Button Values Returned**

  ● MsgBox

```
nButVal=MsgBox("Are you logging in remotely",vbYesNo)
```

  ● PopUp

```
nButVal=oShell.Popup("Run Logon Script?",10,"Run",4)
```

■ **Strings Returned**

  ● InputBox

```
sName=InputBox("Enter your name")
```

Your scripts will often need to retrieve information from the user while it runs. You can use this data later in the script to adjust the way that the rest of the script runs based on the user. This information can be in the form of simple "Yes/No" answers or in message strings that are more complex.

Button Values Returned

Two functions collect information from a user while the logon script runs. Simple "Yes/No" questions collect integer values that correspond to the button that the user clicks.

MsgBox

As well as specify the buttons displayed in a message box, the **MsgBox** function returns a value to your script, indicating which button the user clicks. Because there are several different buttons available, each button returns a different number in the range 1 through 7. The following table documents the return values of the **MsgBox** function.

Button	Value	Intrinsic constant
OK	1	vbOK
Cancel	2	vbCancel
Abort	3	vbAbort
Retry	4	vbRetry
Ignore	5	vbIgnore
Yes	6	vbYes
No	7	vbNo

The following example displays a message asking the user if he or she has logged on by using Remote Access Service (RAS). When the user clicks a button, the corresponding value is stored in the variable vMyVal. If vMyVal is 6, the user clicked the **Yes** button. As a result, the first message is displayed. If vMyVal is not 6, the second message is displayed:

Example

```
vMyVal = MsgBox ("Logging on using RAS?", vbYesNo)
If vMyVal = 6 Then
  WScript.echo "User Logging in Remotely"
Else
  WScript.Echo "User Logging in on LAN"
End If
```

Note that you can use the intrinsic constant vbYes in place of the literal number 6.

PopUp

The **PopUp** method of the **WSHShell** object can also collect user feedback in a manner similar to the **MsgBox** function. The message box types, buttons, and return values are identical to the **MsgBox** function. However, as previously mentioned, you can configure this method to time out if no input is forthcoming.

If the **PopUp** method times out before the user clicks a button, it returns a value of -1. You must always check for this value in addition to the values that are returned by the user when he or she clicks a button.

Strings Returned

The **InputBox** function can return a text string typed by the user to your script. If this function is employed, error handling should be used to ensure that appropriate input is received from the user.

Input Box

This function has the following syntax:

Syntax

```
InputBox(prompt[, title][, default][, xpos][, ypos][,
↪helpfile, context])
```

The **prompt** and **title** arguments provide the message box text and title bar text, respectively, similar to the **MsgBox** and **PopUp** functions. The **default** argument specifies a default text value for the input box.

InputBox also gives you a high level of control over the position of the message box on the screen through the **xpos** and **ypos** arguments. The **helpfile** argument enables you to access a help file if you press the F1 key while the message box is displayed. The **context** argument specifies which page of the help file should be displayed.

An example of the **InputBox** function is shown below:

Example

```
Option Explicit
Dim vFirstName, vLastName, vFullName
vFirstName = InputBox ("Enter your first name", "First Name")
vLastName = InputBox ("Enter your last name", "Last Name")
vFullName = vFirstName & " " & vLastName
WScript.Echo vFullName
```

In this example, the first line prompts the user for his or her first name and assigns the answer to the variable vFirstName. The second line prompts for his or her last name and assigns it to the variable vLastName. These values are concatenated and stored in the variable vFullName, which is then echoed to the screen.

Creating Desktop Shortcuts

- **Two Shortcut Types**
  - Standard file (.lnk)
  - Universal resource locator file (.url)
- **Copying Files to the Desktop**
  - Using the SpecialFolders method
- **Using the WScript.Shell Object**

```
Set oIntraLnk=oShell.CreateShortcut("Path\Intranet.URL")
oIntraLnk.TargetPath = "http://Intra.nwtraders.msft"
oIntraLnk.Save
```

As an administrator, you may want to control user desktop environments. While Windows 2000 Group Policy makes this possible, scripts still provide useful functions with Windows 2000 clients and legacy Windows systems. For example, a script can provide desktop shortcuts to particular resources on the network, such as a shared group drive, a network printer, or a departmental intranet.

Two Shortcut Types

You can provide both standard file shortcuts (.lnk) and Universal Resource Locator (URL) file shortcuts (.url).

Copying Files to the Desktop

You can create these links in two separate ways.

You can copy an existing .lnk or .url file from the server to a shortcut folder, such as the desktop or programs folder. You can access these folders by using the **SpecialFolders** method of the **Shell** object; for example:

Example

```
DesktopPath = oShell.SpecialFolders("Desktop")
ProgramsPath = oShell.SpecialFolders("Programs")
```

Note The "Programs" special folder references the Programs folder on the **Start** menu, not the Program Files folder.

Using the WScript.Shell Object

Alternatively, you can use the **CreateShortcut** method of the **WScript.Shell** object, passing in the path and shortcut name. If you do not specify a path, the shortcut is created in the current working folder of the script file. You can then set the **TargetPath** string property with the path to the file or URL. Finally, you must save your changes. The shortcut is created on the user's desktop. The following examples show the creation of both types of shortcuts:

Example

```
Set oShell = CreateObject("WScript.Shell")
Set oShortCut = oShell.CreateShortcut("Mytext.lnk")
oShortCut.TargetPath = "C:\Mytext.txt"
oShortCut.Save
Set oUrlLink = oShell.CreateShortcut("MSWeb Site.URL")
oUrlLink.TargetPath = "http://www.microsoft.com"
oUrlLink.Save
```

Other properties of the shortcut can also be set, such as **IconLocation**, **Description**, and **WindowStyle**.

Mapping Drives

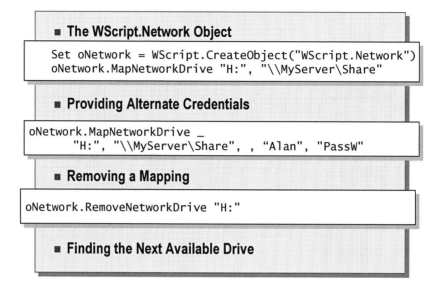

Mapping drives is another common task that you may want to perform during the logon process.

The WScript.Network Object

The **WScript.Network** object provides the functionality to map drives through the **MapNetworkDrive** method. The following syntax shows how the method can be used:

Syntax

```
Object.MapNetworkDrive strLocalName, strRemoteName,
↪[bUpdateProfile], [strUser], [strPassword]
```

In the previous syntax, **strLocalName** is the new drive letter that you want to map, **strRemoteName** is the share to map that you want to map to, **bUpdateProfile** is an optional Boolean value that indicates whether to save the new mapping in the user profile (the default is **false**), **strUser** is an optional alternative user identifier, and **strPassword** is the optional password for the alternative user.

The following example maps the H drive to a shared folder:

Example

```
Set oNetwork = WScript.CreateObject("WScript.Network")
ONetwork.MapNetworkDrive "H:", "\\MyServer\Share"
```

Note that the security credentials in this example are those of the user running the script.

Providing Alternative Credentials

You can supply alternative security credentials when mapping drives, if needed. The following example uses alternative credentials to map the H drive:

Example

```
ONetwork.MapNetworkDrive "H:", "\\MyServer\Share1",, _
  "Alan", "PassW"
```

Removing a Mapping

To remove a mapping, you can use the **RemoveNetworkDrive** method of the **Network** object. You must pass the drive letter as an argument. The following example removes the mapping for the H drive:

Example

```
Set oNetwork = WScript.CreateObject("WScript.Network")
oNetwork.RemoveNetworkDrive "H:"
```

Finding the Next Available Drive

To find the next available drive that you can map, there are two methods that you can use.

The **EnumNetworkDrives** method of the **WScript.Network** object returns a collection that stores the local drives as the first items, followed by any current share mappings. As the method name suggests, it lists only the currently mapped network drives. If no network drive is mapped, no values are returned. The following script is an example of the use of the **EnumNetworkDrives** method:

Example

```
Set oNetwork = CreateObject("WScript.Network")
For Each oDrive in oNetwork.EnumNetworkDrives
  WScript.Echo oDrive
Next
```

This produces an output similar to the following when running CScript.exe from a console window:

Example

```
E:
\\Myserver\data
F:
\\Myserver\copy
G:
\\Myserver\personal
```

The second method uses the **FileSystemObject** object from the Windows Script Runtime to view all the systems drives. This method is advantageous, because it returns information about local drives and network drive.

Example

```
Set oFS = CreateObject("Scripting.FileSystemObject")
For Each oDrive in oFS.Drives
  sFinalDrive = left(oDrive, 1)
Next
```

After the last drive letter has been found, the **ASC** and **CHR** functions in Visual Basic Scripting Edition can be used to calculate the next letter in the alphabet. This is useful when writing a script that maps a new drive while keeping all existing mappings in place.

The following example shows how to use this approach:

Example

```
Option Explicit
On Error Resume Next
Dim oNetwork, oFSO, Drive, sNextDrive, sFinalDrive
'Create Network and FSO objects
Set oNetwork = CreateObject("WScript.Network")
Set oFSO = CreateObject("Scripting.FileSystemObject")
'Loop Through all used drives
For Each Drive in oFSO.Drives
   'Take the first letter from the drive
   sFinalDrive = left(Drive, 1)
Next
'Convert final used drive to ASC, add 1 and return to
'character
sNextDrive = Chr(Asc(sFinalDrive) + 1) & ":"
'Map new drive
oNetwork.MapNetworkDrive sNextDrive, "\\MyServer\Share"
```

Mapping Printers

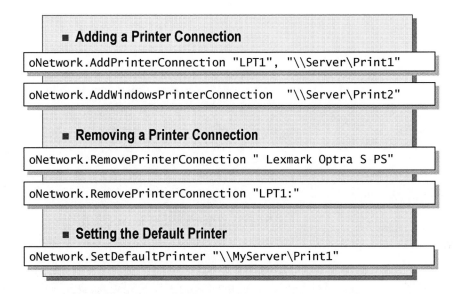

- **Adding a Printer Connection**

```
oNetwork.AddPrinterConnection "LPT1", "\\Server\Print1"
```

```
oNetwork.AddWindowsPrinterConnection  "\\Server\Print2"
```

- **Removing a Printer Connection**

```
oNetwork.RemovePrinterConnection " Lexmark Optra S PS"
```

```
oNetwork.RemovePrinterConnection "LPT1:"
```

- **Setting the Default Printer**

```
oNetwork.SetDefaultPrinter "\\MyServer\Print1"
```

Adding a printer object in a script is similar to adding a drive object.

Adding a Printer Connection

The **AddPrinterConnection** method of the **WScript.Network** object uses syntax similar to the **MapNetworkDrive** method.

Syntax

```
object.AddPrinterConnection strLocalName,
↪strRemoteName[,bUpdateProfile][,strUser][,strPassword]
```

In the above syntax, **strLocalName** refers to a local port, and **strRemoteName** refers to a shared printer. This method is limited to the number of line printer (LPT) ports on the system.

The following example maps LPT1 to a shared printer:

Example

```
oNetwork.AddPrinterConnection "LPT1", "\\Server\Print1"
```

You can avoid the limitation of only being able to use the number of LPT ports on the system, by using the **AddWindowsPrinterConnection** method with Windows client computers. The syntax for this method is as follows:

Syntax

```
object.AddWindowsPrinterConnection(strPrinterPath,
↪strDriverName[,strPort])
```

In this syntax, **strPrinterPath** is the full Universal Naming Convention (UNC) printer path. This is the only required argument if the computer using the script is running Windows 2000 or Windows NT. The next arguments are only used if the computer is running Windows 95, Windows 98, or Windows Millennium Edition (Me). For these operating systems, **strDriverName** is the name of the Windows printer driver. The **strPort** argument specifies the printer port that you use for the mapping.

> **Note** If the printer driver name is used in the **AddWindowsPrinterConnection** statement, the name must be identical to the description shown in the properties of the printer under the **Model:** heading, including spaces.

You can enumerate printers like drive mappings. The **EnumPrinterConnections** method is used in the same way as the **EnumNetworkDrives** method; for example:

Example

```
Set oNetwork = CreateObject("WScript.Network")
For Each oDrive in oNetwork.EnumPrinterConnections
  WScript.Echo oDrive
Next
```

Removing a Printer Connection

Removing a mapping to a printer is a simple task. The **RemovePrinterConnection** method has only one required argument, which is the local name of the printer, such as LPT1, or the remote name if no local name exists. Two optional arguments allow you to remove the printer, even if it is in use, and update the user's profile.

Example

```
object.RemovePrinterConnection strName, [bForce],
↪[bUpdateProfile]
```

Setting the Default Printer

You can set a printer as the default printer by using the **SetDefaultPrinter** method and passing the remote printer name as an argument as shown below:

Example

```
oNetwork.SetDefaultPrinter "\\MyServer\Print1"
```

> **Note** There is a dynamic-link library (DLL) that is provided with the Windows 2000 Resource Kit called PrnAdmin.dll. This DLL provides many properties and methods that you can use to manage printers. For more information, see the Windows 2000 Resource Kit Tools help file.
>
> If a local printer exists, you can publish it in Active Directory™ by using a script that is installed as part of the WSH environment. The script is in the system folder and is called Pubprn.vbs. For more information about this script, see the Knowledge Base article Q234619.

Launching Utility Programs

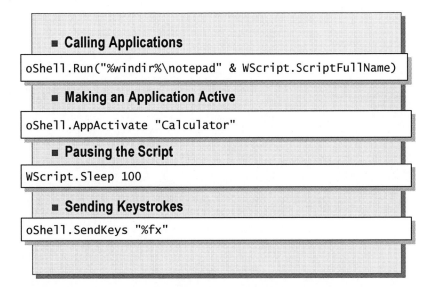

- **Calling Applications**

  `oShell.Run("%windir%\notepad" & WScript.ScriptFullName)`

- **Making an Application Active**

  `oShell.AppActivate "Calculator"`

- **Pausing the Script**

  `WScript.Sleep 100`

- **Sending Keystrokes**

  `oShell.SendKeys "%fx"`

Your logon scripts may need to launch other programs to perform certain tasks, such as virus scanning, disk checking or other maintenance utilities. The simplest way to launch another program is to use the **Run** method of the **WScript.Shell** object as follows:

Syntax

`object.Run (strCommand, [intWindowStyle], [bWaitOnReturn])`

In the above syntax, **strCommand** is the command to run, **intWindowStyle** is the window style for the new program, such as minimized or maximized, and **bWaitOnReturn** allows the script to continue to run without waiting for the new program to end (default) or forces the script to wait until the program ends.

Calling Applications

The following example shows how to run Notepad from a script. As well as starting Notepad, it also passes the name of the file that you want to open:

Example

`oShell.Run "%windir%\notepad.exe " & WScript.ScriptFullName`

Making an Application Active

You can change the active program by using the **AppActivate** method of the **WScript.Shell** object. In this method, you specify the title of the window that you want to activate.

Pausing the Script

You can call the **Sleep** method of the **WScript** object if you want to pause the script. You specify the length of time delay in milliseconds.

Sending Keystrokes

You can send keystrokes to another program by first calling the **AppActivate** method and then calling the **SendKeys** method of the **WScript.Shell** object. The effect of this is like a user entering keystrokes manually. With this method, you can run menu items and shortcut keys, such as %fx, which is like a user pressing ALT + F and then X. This closes the program through the **File** menu.

A complete listing of various control keys is included here for reference.

Key	Code
BACKSPACE	{BACKSPACE}, {BS}, or {BKSP}
BREAK	{BREAK}
CAPS LOCK	{CAPSLOCK}
DEL or DELETE	{DELETE} or {DEL}
DOWN ARROW	{DOWN}
END	{END}
ENTER	{ENTER}or ~
ESC	{ESC}
HELP	{HELP}
HOME	{HOME}
INS or INSERT	{INSERT} or {INS}
LEFT ARROW	{LEFT}
NUM LOCK	{NUMLOCK}
PAGE DOWN	{PGDN}
PAGE UP	{PGUP}
PRINT SCREEN	{PRTSC}
RIGHT ARROW	{RIGHT}
SCROLL LOCK	{SCROLLLOCK}
TAB	{TAB}
UP ARROW	{UP}
F1	{F1}
F2	{F2}
F3	{F3}
F4	{F4}
F5	{F5}
F6	{F6}
F7	{F7}
F8	{F8}
F9	{F9}

(continued)

Key	Code
F10	{F10}
F11	{F11}
F12	{F12}
F13	{F13}
F14	{F14}
F15	{F15}
F16	{F16}

To specify keys combined with any combination of the SHIFT, CTRL, or ALT keys, precede the key code with one or more of the following codes.

Key	Code
SHIFT	+
CTRL	^
ALT	%

Caution   While using the **SendKeys** method can be very useful, it is important to understand its limitations. It is easy for a user to change the focus of a window while the script is running. This causes the script to fail. **SendKeys** is not a robust method and should be used when there is no other way to control an application.

Lab 6.1: Creating Logon Scripts

Objectives

After completing this lab, you will be able to create a logon script that performs administration tasks such as mapping drives and printers and creating desktop shortcuts.

Scenario

In this lab, you will write a logon script that maps drives and printers. In addition, it will create a desktop shortcut to a text file.

After you create and test the script, you will assign it to a user. You will then test that it runs as expected during the logon process.

Estimated time to complete this lab: 45 minutes

Exercise 1
Mapping Drives and Printers

In this exercise, you will create logon scripts that map drives and printers for the users in the Northwind Traders domain.

▶ **To create a new script file**

1. Log on to your machine as **Administrator@nwtraders.msft** with a password of **password**

2. Click **Start**, point to **Programs**, point to **SAPIEN Technologies, Inc**, and then click **PrimalSCRIPT 2.0**.

3. On the **File** menu, click **New**.

4. In the **New** dialog box, click **Text**, and then click **OK**.

▶ **To map drives**

1. Type the following lines of code to force variable declaration and declare variables that will be used in this script:

```
Option Explicit
On Error Resume Next
Dim oNetwork, oDrives, oFSO, Drive
Dim sFinalDrive, iChar, sNewDrive
```

2. Type the following lines of code to instantiate a **WScript.Network** object and use it to map a specific drive letter to a share on the Instructor's computer:

```
Set oNetwork = CreateObject("WScript.Network")
oNetwork.MapNetworkDrive "H:", "\\London\LabShare"
```

3. Type the following lines of code to instantiate a **Scripting.FileSystemObject** object and use it to obtain the next available drive letter that you can use to map to a share:

```
Set oFSO = CreateObject("Scripting.FileSystemObject")
For Each Drive in oFSO.Drives
    sFinalDrive = left(Drive, 1)
Next
iChar = Asc(sFinalDrive)
sNewDrive = Chr(iChar + 1)
```

4. Type the following lines of code to map the drive letter that is determined above to a share on the instructor's computer:

```
oNetwork.MapNetworkDrive sNewDrive & ":", _
    "\\London\LabShare"
```

▶ **To map printers**

1. Type the following lines of code to map to a printer:

   ```
   oNetwork.AddWindowsPrinterConnection "\\London\ClassPrn"
   ```

2. Type the following line of code to set the printer as the default printer:

   ```
   oNetwork.SetDefaultPrinter "\\London\ClassPrn"
   ```

3. On the **File** menu, click **Save As**.

4. In the **Save As** dialog box, go to the *install_folder*\Labs\Lab06\Lab6_1\Starter folder.

5. In the **File Name** box, type **Logon*x*.vbs** (where *x* is your student number), and then click **Save**.

   Leave the script open, because you will use it in the next exercise.

Exercise 2
Creating Shortcuts

In this exercise, you will create shortcuts to a text file by using Visual Basic Scripting Edition.

▶ **To create a shortcut to a text file**

1. Using Windows Explorer, navigate to the root of the C drive, and then click it.

2. On the **File** menu, click **New**, and then click **Text Document**, type **Readme.txt** as the file's name, and then press ENTER.

3. Switch to PrimalSCRIPT.

4. After the code that you have already written, type the following code to create a shortcut to the Readme.txt file that you have just created:

```
Dim oShell, oShortCut, sDesktop, sLnkPath
Set oShell = CreateObject("WScript.shell")
sDesktop = oShell.SpecialFolders("Desktop")
Set oShortCut = oShell.CreateShortcut _
    (sDesktop & "\readme.lnk")
oShortCut.TargetPath = "C:\Readme.txt"
oShortCut.Save
WScript.Echo "Logon Script Complete"
```

▶ **To test your script**

1. On the **File** menu, click **Save**.

2. On the **Script** menu, click **Run Script**.

3. Click **OK** when you receive the message "Logon Script Complete."

4. On your desktop, double-click **My Computer**.

5. Verify that you now have a drive mapped to the LabShare on the London computer.

6. On the **Start** menu, click **Settings**, and then click **Printers**.

7. Verify that you have a connection to the printer on the London computer.

   You have now created and tested your logon script.

Exercise 3
Assigning Logon Scripts to a User

In this exercise, you will assign the logon script that you have just created to a user. You will then test that it runs as expected when the user logs on to the domain.

▶ **To assign your script to a user**

1. Switch to PrimalSCRIPT.

2. On the **File** menu, click **Save As**.

3. In the **File name** box type:
   \\London\Admin$\SYSVOL\sysvol\NWTraders.msft\scripts \Logon*x*.vbs (where *x* is your student number).

4. On the **Start** menu, click **Run**.

5. In the **Open** box, type **MMC** and then press ENTER.

6. On the **Console** menu, click **1 ADUsers and Computers**.

7. In the **Tree** pane, click **WST**.

8. In the details pane, click **Admin*x*** (where *x* is your student number).

9. On the **Action** menu, click **Properties**, and then click the **Profile** tab.

10. In the **Logon script** box, type **Logon*x*.vbs** (where *x* is your student number), and then click **OK**.

▶ **To verify that your script runs correctly during the logon process**

1. Close all open windows and programs.

2. Log off from Windows.

3. Log on to the NWTraders.msft domain as **Admin*x*** (where *x* is your student number).

4. Click **OK** when prompted that the logon script has finished.

5. Verify that you have a shortcut to Readme.txt on your desktop.

6. Double-click **My Computer**.

7. Verify that the drives have been mapped as expected.

8. On the **Start** menu, click **Settings**, and then click **Printers**.

9. Verify that you have a connection to the printer on the London computer.

You have now successfully created, assigned, and tested a logon script written in VBScript.

Frank 155

◆ Managing Logon Scripts

- **Assigning Logon Scripts**
- **Script Time Windows**
- **Securing WSH**
- **Protecting Logon Scripts**

In addition to performing the common tasks outlined so far in this module, you will also need to successfully manage the logon scripts in your enterprise network.

This section describes assigning logon scripts, script time windows, securing the WSH environment, protecting logon scripts, and troubleshooting logon scripts. It also outlines good practices for managing your logon scripts.

Assigning Logon Scripts

- **Using Active Directory**
  - Assign logon scripts on a *per user basis*
- **Using Group Policy**
  - Logon/logoff scripts
  - Startups/shutdown scripts

Windows 2000 provides two mechanisms for assigning a logon script to a user account. You can do this through the user properties in Active Directory or through Group Policy.

Using Active Directory

In the Active Directory Users and Computers snap-in, you can specify a logon script as part of the user properties, on a per-user basis. This approach enables you to assign logon scripts to individual user accounts.

Using Group Policy to Assign Logon Scripts

Group Policy is a Windows 2000 technology that provides centralized control over the configuration of computer and user environments. This includes the assignment of logon scripts to users, groups of users, and computers.

To assign logon scripts to groups, it is recommended that you use Group Policy Objects (GPOs). Group Policy gives you access to the user's logon/logoff script windows and to the computer's Startup/Shutdown windows. With this method, you can also assign multiple logon scripts to a collection of users.

When assigning scripts in this way, you have greater control over how the script runs.

Using Group Policy to assign logon scripts requires the following settings:

- Run logon scripts synchronously

  This setting directs the system to wait for the logon scripts to end before starting Microsoft Windows Explorer. The default is for the scripts and Windows Explorer to run asynchronously, so that scripts are still running when Windows Explorer is starting.

  Note that the computer version of this setting takes precedence over this setting.

- Run legacy logon scripts hidden

  This hides the running of batch files that were written for logon scripts in Windows NT. By default, these batch files are displayed.

- Run logon scripts visible

  This processes the logon script as a visible process, thereby displaying each instruction in the script. By default, these instruction are hidden.

- Run logoff script visible

  This assigns the same setting as "Run logon scripts visible," but for logoff scripts.

Important If you use Group Policy to deploy your logon/logoff scripts, be sure that a large number of scripts do not run synchronously. The overall script execution time can cause an unacceptable delay in the logon time for users. Always test the scripts to make sure that the execution time is acceptable before assigning the logon script in the production environment.

For computers, using Group Policy to assign logon scripts requires the following settings:

- Run logon scripts synchronously

  This setting directs the system to wait for the logon scripts to end before starting Windows Explorer. The default is for the scripts and Windows Explorer to run asynchronously, so that scripts are still running when Windows Explorer is starting.

  Note that this setting takes precedence over the user version of this setting.

- Run startup scripts asynchronously

  This enables startup scripts to run simultaneously. The default is for each script to end before the next script runs.

- Run startup scripts visible

  This processes the startup script written in Visual Basic Scripting Edition as a visible process, thereby displaying each instruction in the script. By default, these instructions are hidden.

- Run shutdown script visible

  This assigns the same setting as "Run startup scripts visible," but for shutdown scripts.

- Maximum wait time for Group Policy scripts

  This setting governs how long the system waits to process startup or shutdown scripts. If this time-out is reached, script processing is forcibly stopped, and an error is reported in the system event log.

  This setting can be very important, because many scripts require some sort of user interaction. For example, you may write a startup script to connect to a domain resource. If the account password changes, a dialog box is displayed that prompts the user to type the correct password.

However, in a startup script, this dialog box will not be displayed, because the startup script is not interactive. As a result, the system appears to be hung. In this situation, the "Maximum wait time for Group Policy scripts" setting governs how long the machine stays in this state before the script is forcibly stopped. By default, the system waits for 600 seconds (ten minutes).

Script Time Windows

- **Execution Order:**
    1. System Startup
    2. User Logon
    3. User Logoff
    4. System Shutdown

Windows 2000 extends the functionality of logon scripts by providing additional script time-windows for you to execute them in. As well as the logon script window that is provided when the user logs on to the system, Windows 2000 provides three additional script time-windows: User Logoff, System Startup, and System Shutdown.

The order of execution for these script time-windows is as follows:

1. System Startup

   This runs when the computer is powered up and the operating system is booted.

2. User Logon

   This runs after the user has been successfully authenticated.

3. User Logoff

   When the user has chosen to log off or shut down the computer, this script runs.

4. System Shutdown

   The shutdown script is only run when the computer shuts down. If a user has a logoff script, this script runs before the shutdown script runs.

Securing WSH

■ **VBScript-Based Viruses**
  - Remove WSH
  - Change default action on .vbs .vbe .js .jse .wsf

■ **Restrict Access to Host**
  - NTFS file system permissions
  - CScript.exe and WScript.exe

It is important that you understand how to secure the WSH environment to prevent the proliferation of VBScript-based viruses in your enterprise network.

VBScript-Based Viruses

VBScript-based viruses show that creators of viruses can use script. You can take several steps to minimize the risk of these viruses using the WSH environment.

One way is to remove the WSH environment. Another way to prevent script viruses is to change the default application handler for script files.

The following procedure changes the application that opens vbs, .vbe, .js, .jse, or .wsf files. If those files open, it opens with Notepad.exe and not with the application handler.

1. Double-click **My Computer**.
2. On the **Tools** menu, click **Folder Options**.
3. Click the **File Types** tab, and then scroll down to the first item in the list above .jse, which is a Microsoft JScript® encoded file.
4. Click the .jse file, and then click **Edit**.
5. In the Action window, click **Open**, and then click **Edit**.
6. Change the following line from:

    `C:\WINNT\System32\WScript.exe "%1" %*`

    To:

    `C:\WINNT\System32\Notepad.exe "%1" %*`

7. Click **OK**, and then click **Close**.

Repeat these steps for each of the other file types listed previously.

Note Many administrators and users reconfigure the default method of files with a .vbs or .js extension on their systems so that they open rather than run when invoked. This is an effective counter-measure that you can use to prevent the spread of script viruses.

On systems with this configuration, startup and shutdown scripts run correctly. Logon and logoff scripts fail, because they use the default method. As a result, instead of having the logon script run, users see the script in an editor (such as Notepad) when the user logs on and logs off. Users can work around this by calling the login script directly from within a batch file.

Restricting Access to the Host

It is also possible to further restrict the WSH environment by using NTFS file system permissions to control how users run scripts. This is best achieved by concentrating on the host executables, because they are the simplest files to set permissions on. For WSH, the host files are CScript.exe and WScript.exe. By setting appropriate NTFS file system permissions on these files, you can restrict someone's ability to run scripts.

Note For more information about this subject, go to:

http://www.microsoft.com/technet/security/default.asp

You can also find information in the Knowledge Base article Q263568, "Information on Preventing Certain Types of Software from Running Automatically."

Protecting Logon Scripts

- **Scripting Encoder**
  - Basic script protection
  - Seamless to the user
  - Suffix must be .vbe or .jse
- **Script Encoder Syntax**
- **Examples**

You may want to hide the contents of your scripts from the users that run them to protect sensitive data, such as passwords, and prevent users from changing the contents of the file.

Script Encoder

The Script Encoder (Screnc.exe) is a command-line tool that protects the contents of a script from unauthorized viewing, copying, or modification, while still enabling the script to run. The script file is passed to the Script Encoder, which then performs an encoding routine against the file and creates a new file with a .vbe (or .jse for Jscript) extension.

This file, if viewed in a text editor, contains what appear to be random command characters. Changing any part of the file renders it inoperable. This ensures the integrity of the encoded script, while enabling it to be decoded and executed by WSH.

Important   This encoding only protects the script from a casual attempt at viewing and modifying script. It does not protect the script from a determined attempt to crack the encoding mechanism.

The Script Encoder is available from the Microsoft Script Web site at:

http://msdn.microsoft.com/scripting/default.htm?/scripting/vbscript/download/vbsdown.htm

It is important to note that this script encoder was written primarily for the encoding of Web-based scripts such as Active Server Pages (ASP). As a result, many of the switches and examples given as part of the documentation should not be used for encoding WSH files.

Script Encoder Syntax

The following shows the syntax for the Script Encoder:

Syntax

```
screnc [/?] [/s] <source> <destination>
```

The arguments are described in the following table.

Argument	Description
/?	Help.
/s	Silent. Display no messages.
source	The file to encode. It can include wildcard characters.
destination	The destination file.

Note This is a simplified list of the syntax for Screnc.exe. It shows the switches that are important to the encoding of standard WSH files. For a more detailed explanation of all of the switches, see the Script Encoder documentation.

Examples

The following are some examples of how the Script Encoder can be used:

Example

```
screnc Demo.vbs EncodedDemo.vbe
```

This encodes Demo.vbs into EncodedDemo.vbe.

Example

```
screnc Demo.vbs /s c:\testscripts\EncodedDemo.vbe
```

This encodes Demo.vbs into c:\testscript\EncodedDemo.vbe, without generating any messages.

Troubleshooting Logon Scripts

- **Replicating Logon Scripts**

- **Setting Time-Outs**

- **Preventing Premature Execution of Logon Scripts in Windows 95 and Windows 98**

- **Network Bandwidth**

  - At server and client

- **Testing for Required Files**

Before distributing logon scripts to the enterprise network, there are several issues that you must understand and plan for.

Replicating Logon Scripts

Windows 2000 can use the File Replication Service (FRS) to replicate logon scripts between servers in the enterprise network. Windows NT uses the Directory Replicator (LMRepl) in a similar way. By default, logon scripts are stored in the SysVol folder, at \...\SYSVOL\SysVol\MyDomain\Scripts.

This folder is in the NETLOGON share that is used by the client computers for running logon scripts. Placing the logon script in this folder ensures that it is available on all domain controllers, because the contents of the SysVol folder automatically replicate throughout the domain. Replication is performed by FRS on all domain controllers.

In a mixed-mode environment, logon scripts must be available in the Netlogon share of all Windows NT and Windows 2000 domain controllers. The replication of logon scripts is slightly more complex, because there is no support for down-level replication in Windows 2000.

To bridge the replication process between the two operating systems, you can use Lbridge.cmd from the Windows 2000 Resource Kit.

Note   For more information, see Knowledge Base article Q248358, "Windows 2000 Does Not Support Windows 4.0 Directory Replication."

Setting Time-Outs

Setting time-outs can help prevent a hung script from degrading the logon experience for users.

Setting the script time-out can be achieved by changing either the settings for the script host or the setting in a .wsh file. However, you can also set a time-out by using the **Script Parameters** option when the startup/shutdown or logon/logoff scripts are assigned in Group Policy. This setting accepts any of the standard command-line switches for the script engines. For example, the following switch sets the maximum run-time for the script to 30 seconds:

Example

```
//T:30
```

Preventing Premature Execution of Logon Scripts in Windows 95 and Windows 98

Windows 95 and Windows 98 can run a user's logon script before the user account is authenticated. This can cause problems in a logon script if the user's credentials are required when the script runs. To fix this, add a test to the logon script that waits for the **UserName** property to be populated. By doing so, the script proves that the user has been authenticated fully. An example of a loop that you can use to do this is shown below:

Example

```
Username = ""
Do
   Username = oNetwork.UserName
Loop Until Username <> ""
```

Network Bandwidth

There are two areas to consider when using scripts over a network:

- Server bottlenecks

  Bottlenecks may be the result of multiple simultaneous logon attempts at peak times. Domain controllers are responsible for authenticating users and accepting incoming connections from the client computers to retrieve computer startup scripts and user logon scripts. Servicing all of these requests may have a negative impact upon the performance of domain controllers.

- Connectivity bottlenecks

  The speed of physical links, such as Wide Area Network (WAN) links for remote sites or RAS links for mobile users, is a factor when assigning scripts to users and computers. Before any of the scripts run, they must be copied over the link to the local computer. This can significantly increase the time it takes for a script to run.

To address these bottlenecks, consider the following:

- Ensure that there are enough domain controllers to authenticate users. By using Domain Naming Service (DNS) Records, Windows 2000 clients load balance across multiple domain controllers. The authenticating domain controller for each user has a copy of the scripts that are assigned to that user in the Netlogon share.

- Distribute the processing across multiple member servers. The user's logon script in the Netlogon share of the domain controller can be a pointer to the main script. The client can then connect to a share on a member server to retrieve this script.

Testing for Required Files

It is always a good practice to ensure that scripts run without generating unnecessary errors. As a result, a script should test for the possibility of an error. If possible, a script should correct the error, or at least exit gracefully with a helpful message. A logon script should check that the files required for it to run successfully are present and that the files are the required version.

Best Practices

- **Test All Changes to Production Logon Scripts**

- **Implement Error Handling**

- **Document Scripts**

- **Be Aware of Network Bandwidth Issues**

- **Protect Scripts with Encoding**

- **Create a "Script Fix" and "Test User" Logon**

You should adhere to good practices when developing logon scripts.

Test All Changes to Production Logon Scripts

Do not make any changes to a production logon script without first testing the script thoroughly in all environments that the script is likely to run. Consider using a product like Microsoft Visual SourceSafe™ to keep track of versions of your scripts. By doing so, you can retrieve older versions of scripts if the changes implemented are problematic.

Implement Error Handling

Error handling is as essential for scripts as it is for compiled programs. If you fail to test for errors, your script may not complete all of the functions that you intended.

Document Scripts

Comments help scriptwriters and administrators to understand a script written by someone else, or even a script that they wrote themselves a few months previously. Comments make maintaining scripts easier.

Be Aware of Network Bandwidth Issues

Do not forget about network bandwidth issues. Assess whether scripts have unnecessary functionalities; for example, they copy items over the network that can be stored on the local computer.

Protect Scripts with Encoding

If you do not want users to be able to view the contents of your logon scripts, consider encoding them with the Windows Script Encoder.

Create a "Script Fix" and "Test User" Logon

Having a user account specifically for fixing problems with logon scripts can be a benefit if something goes wrong with a script. Make sure that no scripts are assigned to this user. Then, you can logon anywhere without any scripts running.

It may also be useful to create a test user for the logon script. This test user has the first account to have a new or modified logon script assigned to it. This account should have the same level of permissions as the users that the script will be assigned to.

Lab 6.2: Assigning Logon Scripts

Objectives

After completing this lab, you will be able to understand the script time windows available in Windows 2000 and how you can use them to run script.

Scenario

You are the administrator for the Northwind Traders domain. To ensure that all of the computers and users in your domain have the appropriate settings, you must write startup, logon, logoff, and shutdown scripts. You want to use Group Policy settings to achieve this.

Estimated time to complete this lab: 45 minutes

Exercise 1
Configuring Scripts with Group Policies

In this exercise, you will write scripts and manage them by using Group Policy settings.

▶ **To create the script folder**

1. Using Windows Explorer, go to the root of your C drive.

2. On the **File** menu, point to **New**, click **Folder**, type **ScriptWindows** as the folder name, and then press ENTER.

▶ **To create the scripts**

1. Click **Start**, point to **Programs**, point to **SAPIEN Technologies, Inc**, and then click **PrimalSCRIPT 2.0.**

2. On the **File** menu, click **New**.

3. In the **New** dialog box, click **Text**, and then click **OK**.

4. Type the following line of code:

   ```
   MsgBox "Starting Up!"
   ```

5. On the **File** menu, click **Save As**.

6. In the **Save As** box, navigate to the C:\ScriptWindows folder.

7. In the **File name** box, type **Startup.vbs** and then click **Save**.

8. Repeat steps 2 through 7, to create the following files and message boxes:

   - Logon.vbs

     ```
     MsgBox "Logging on!"
     ```

   - Logoff.vbs

     ```
     MsgBox "Logging off!"
     ```

   - Shutdown.vbs

     ```
     MsgBox "Shutting Down!"
     ```

9. Close PrimalSCRIPT.

▶ **To open the Group Policy Microsoft Management Console (MMC)**

1. Click **Start**, and then click **Run...**

2. In the **Open** box, type **MMC** and then click **OK**.

3. On the **Console** menu, click **Add/Remove Snap-in**.

4. In the **Add/Remove Snap-in** dialog box, click **Add**.

5. In the **Available Standalone Snap-ins** list, click **Group Policy**, and then click **Add**.

6. In the **Select Group Policy Object** dialog box, click **Finish**.

7. In the **Add Standalone Snap-in** dialog box, click **Close**.

8. In the **Add/Remove Snap-in** dialog box, click **OK**.

▶ **To assign the startup script**

1. In the **Tree** pane, expand **Local Computer Policy**, **Computer Configuration**, and **Window Settings**.

2. In the details pane, double-click **Scripts (Startup/Shutdown)**.

3. Click **Startup**.

4. On the **Action** menu, click **Properties**.

5. In the **Startup Properties** dialog box, click **Add**.

6. In the **Add a Script** dialog box, click **Browse**.

7. Go to the C:\ScriptWindows folder, click **Startup.vbs**, and then click **Open**.

8. In the **Add a Script** dialog box, click **OK**.

9. In the **Startup Properties** dialog box, click **OK**.

▶ **To assign the shutdown script**

1. In the detail pane, click **Shutdown**.

2. On the **Action** menu, click **Properties**.

3. In the **Shutdown Properties** dialog box, click **Add**.

4. In the **Add a Script** dialog box, click **Browse**.

5. Go to the C:\ScriptWindows folder, click **Shutdown.vbs**, and then click **Open**.

6. In the **Add a Script** dialog box, click **OK**.

7. In the **Shutdown Properties** dialog box, click **OK**.

▶ **To assign the logon script**

1. In the **Tree** pane, under User Configuration, expand **Windows Settings**.

2. In the **Details** pane, double-click **Scripts (Logon/Logoff)**.

3. Click **Logon**.

4. On the **Action** menu, click **Properties**.

5. In the **Logon Properties** dialog box, click **Add**.

6. In the **Add a Script** dialog box, click **Browse**.

7. Go to the C:\ScriptWindows folder, click **Logon.vbs**, and then click **Open**.

8. In the **Add a Script** dialog box, click **OK**.

9. In the **Logon Properties** dialog box, click **OK**.

▶ **To assign the logoff script**

1. In the detail pane, click **Logoff**.

2. On the **Action** menu, click **Properties**.

3. In the **Logoff Properties** dialog box, click **Add**.

4. In the **Add a Script** dialog box, click **Browse**.

5. Go to the C:\ScriptWindows folder, click **Logoff.vbs**, and then click **Open**.

6. In the **Add a Script** dialog box, click **OK**.

7. In the **Logoff Properties** dialog box, click **OK**.

8. You have now assigned a script to each of the script time windows that are provided by Windows 2000.

▶ **To save the MMC**

1. On the **Console** menu, click **Save As**.

2. In the **Save As** dialog box, in the **File name** box, type **GrpPol** and then click **Save**.

3. Close the MMC console.

▶ **To test the script time windows scripts**

1. Click **Start**, and then click **Shut Down**.

2. In the **Shut Down Windows** dialog box, click **Restart**, and then click **OK**.

3. In the **Logging Off!** message box, click **OK**.

4. In the **Shutting Down!** message box, click **OK**.

   Windows restarts.

5. In the **Starting Up!** message box, click **OK**.

6. Log on to the Northwind Traders domain as **Admin**x (where x is your student number).

7. In the **Logging On!** message box, click **OK**.

   Note that your logon script, assigned in the previous lab, also runs.

8. Click **OK**.

You have now successfully written scripts that run in the script time windows that are provided by Windows 2000.

Review

- **Verifying the WSH Environment**
- **Common Logon Script Tasks**
- **Managing Logon Scripts**
- **Troubleshooting Logon Scripts**

1. What object exposes the **MapNetworkDrive** method?

2. What can you assign a logon script to?

3. What are the four script time-windows that are provided by Windows 2000?

4. What does the command-line variable %0 return?

msdn training

Module 7:
Administrative Scripts

Contents

Microsoft

Overview

- **Script Arguments**
- **Working with Event Logs**
- **Generating E-Mail Messages**
- **Managing the Registry**
- **Working with Drives, Folders, and Files**
- **Setting Folder-Level and File-Level Security**
- **Scheduling Scripts**

Using script to perform administrative functions offers many advantages. In this module, you will learn how to use script to perform typical administrative tasks by using the various scripting models that are available through Microsoft® Windows® Script Host (WSH) and Microsoft Visual Basic® Script (VBScript).

After completing this module, you will be able to:

- Manage arguments in scripts.
- Add entries to Microsoft Windows 2000 event logs.
- Use Collaborative Data Objects (CDO) to generate e-mail messages.
- Use script to manage the registry.
- Work with drives, folders, and files by using script.
- Schedule scripts.

Script Arguments

- **WScript Object**

  - Arguments Collection

  ```
  For i = 0 to WScript.Arguments.Count - 1
    MsgBox "Argument " & i+1 & " is " & WScript.Arguments.Item(i)
  Next
  ```

- **Using the Drag-and-Drop Operation**

  - File name passed as an argument

  - If script does not check for arguments, they are ignored

As with most command line utilities, you can send arguments to a script. This is especially useful for administrative scripts. To avoid changing your script files every time they need to perform a series of slightly different tasks, you can develop the scripts so that they accept arguments. You can then supply these arguments at run time to modify the tasks being performed.

WScript Object

The **WScript** object has an Arguments collection that gives your code access to all of the values that are passed in to the script as arguments. The following script example shows how you can loop through the Arguments collection and process each argument individually:

Example

```
For i = 0 to WScript.Arguments.Count - 1
  MsgBox "Argument " & i+1 & " is " _
      & WScript.Arguments.Item(i)
Next
```

When you invoke a script, you can provide multiple arguments by separating them with spaces. If you need to pass in values that themselves contain spaces, you can enclose the values in double quotes (" "). The following is an example of a command line that provides two arguments to a script. Note that one of the arguments contains spaces:

Example

```
Cscript.exe Args.vbs kathief@Microsoft.com "Kathie Flood"
```

Using the Drag-and-Drop Operation

If you drag a file onto a script, the full path and file name are passed to that script as an argument. If the script has no argument-handling routine, the arguments will be ignored, and the script will run as if no arguments were passed in.

Working with Event Logs

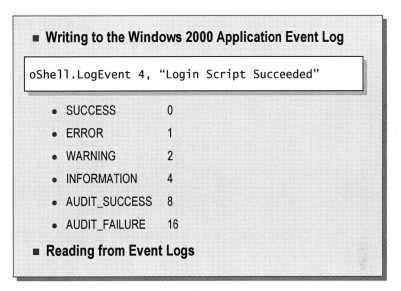

When a script is being executed, it can log events to the Windows 2000 Application Event Log.

Writing to the Windows 2000 Application Event Log

You can use the **LogEvent** method of the **Shell** object to log events. The source of the log message is shown in Event Viewer as "WSH." The syntax for this command is shown in the following example:

Example

```
object.LogEvent (intType, strMessage [,strTarget])
```

The **intType** argument is an integer value that represents the type of event to log.

You can choose from the integer values in the following table.

IntType Value	Meaning
0	SUCCESS
1	ERROR
2	WARNING
4	INFORMATION
8	AUDIT_SUCCESS
16	AUDIT_FAILURE

Note that "strMessage" is the text entry of the event, and "strTarget" is the target system where the event should be logged. The default target is the local system.

If the script is run on a Microsoft Windows 95 or a Microsoft Windows 98 machine, the events are logged in a text file called WSH.log in the Windows folder.

An example of code to log an event is shown in the following example:

Example

```
oShell.LogEvent 4, "Logon Script Succeeded"
```

Reading from Event Logs

You cannot use the WSH objects to read information from system event logs. However, you can achieve this by using the following alternative solutions:

- Use the Dumpel.exe utility from the Windows 2000 Resource Kit. This utility creates a tab-separated text file that can be manipulated by using the FileSystemObject.

  Use the Microsoft Windows Management Instrumentation (WMI) object model. WMI has a Microsoft Windows NT® Event Log Provider that provides access to data and event notifications from the Windows 2000 Event Log.

- Use some of the available third-party COM components that provide read and write access to the system event logs. For examples of Web sites that provide such components, see Module 8, "Beyond the Basics."

Generating E-Mail Messages

> - **Generating E-Mail Messages**
>   - CDO Object Model
> - **Sending an E-Mail Message**
>
> ```
> Set oMyMail = CreateObject("CDO.Message")
>  oMyMail.To = "Someone@Microsoft.com"
>  oMyMail.Subject = "Test Mail from Script"
>  oMyMail.TextBody = "Please Ignore"
>  oMyMail.Send
> ```
>
> - **Configuration Changes**
>   - Inherits either IIS or default identity of Outlook Express

The Collaborative Data Objects (CDO) libraries can be used to programmatically access messaging functionality. This is especially useful for tasks such as sending administrative alerts by e-mail.

Generating E-Mail Messages

There are four different versions of CDO libraries that provide e-mail functionality. This example concentrates on CDO for Windows 2000 because it is the standard on all computers running Windows 2000. In order to function, this library must reside on a computer that has either local or network access to a Simple Mail Transfer Protocol (SMTP) or Network News Transfer Protocol (NNTP) service.

Note If Microsoft Exchange 2000 is installed on your Windows 2000 server, the CDO library for Exchange 2000 replaces the CDO library for Windows 2000. The Windows 2000 library is a subset of the Exchange 2000 library, so any programs written for the first library will continue to function if the new library is installed.

Sending an E-Mail Message

The CDO library **Message** object provides the functionality that enables you to send e-mail messages as part of your scripts.

The following example shows how easy it is to add messaging features to your scripts:

Example

```
Set oMyMail = CreateObject("CDO.Message")
oMyMail.To = "Someone@microsoft.com"
oMyMail.Subject = "Test Mail from Script"
oMyMail.TextBody = "Please Ignore"
oMyMail.AddAttachment "C:\ErrorLog.txt"
oMyMail.MIMEFormatted = False
oMyMail.Send
WScript.Echo "Message Sent From : " & oMyMail.From
Wscript.Echo "              To   : " & oMyMail.To
```

The properties and methods of the **Message** object are self-explanatory, such as **To** (comma separators for multiple addresses), **Subject**, and **From**. **AddAttachment** is a method that can be called multiple times to add several attachments to a message.

Configuration Changes

You can also configure many settings, such as language, time zone, proxy, and connection-timeout values, by using the **CDO.Configuration** object.

If these settings are not changed, default values are loaded from either Microsoft Internet Information Services (IIS) or the identity of the default MAPI profile used by your mail client (such as Microsoft Outlook®). Therefore, it is advisable to use configuration objects if there is a possibility that the default configuration settings may be inappropriate. If a local SMTP or NNTP service is found on the computer, the default submittal method for messages is through the associated pickup directory.

For more information about configuration, see "Configuring the Message Object" in the *CDO for Windows 2000 Platform SDK*.

Lab 7.1: Administrative Scripts

Objectives

In this lab, you will use the drag-and-drop operation to pass arguments to a script. You will also write an entry into the Windows 2000 Application Event Log.

Scenario

As the administrator responsible for writing scripts, you want to make your scripts as reusable as possible. One way to achieve this is to allow arguments to be passed to the scripts when they are run. In this lab, you will learn how to write scripts that accept arguments.

Estimated time to complete this lab: 30 minutes

Exercise 1
Passing Arguments to Scripts

In this exercise, you will create a script that accepts a file name as an argument and displays a message box that contains the script's full path and file name.

▶ **To create a script that accepts file names as arguments**

1. Start **PrimalSCRIPT** if it is not already running.

2. On the **File** menu, click **New**.

3. In the **New** dialog box, click **Text**, and then click **OK**.

4. Type the following code, which uses an **If...Then** block to check for arguments passed to the script. The code also stores the value of each argument in an array (for later use in the lab):

```
Option Explicit
Dim vArg, aArgs(), iCount
If WScript.Arguments.Count = 0 then
    MsgBox "No Arguments Supplied"
    WScript.Quit
Else
    ReDim aArgs(WScript.Arguments.Count - 1)
    For iCount = 0 to WScript.Arguments.Count - 1
        aArgs(iCount) = WScript.Arguments(iCount)
        MsgBox aArgs(iCount)
    Next
End If
```

5. On the **File** menu, click **Save As**.

6. In the **Save As** dialog box, go to the folder
   <install folder>\Labs\Lab07\Lab7_1\Starter.

7. In the **File name** box, type **VBArg.vbs**

8. Click **Save**.

▶ **To create files to be used as arguments for your script**

1. In Windows Explorer, move to the folder
   <install folder>\Labs\Lab07\Lab7_1\Starter.

2. On the **File** menu, click **New**.

3. Click **Text Document**.

4. Type **Text1.txt** as the new file name, and press ENTER.

5. Repeat steps 2 through 4 to create two more text documents named
   Text2.txt and **Text3.txt**, respectively.

▶ **To run the script that accepts file names as arguments**

1. Drag **Text1.txt** and drop it onto the **VBArgs.vbs** script file.

2. In the message box that appears, click **OK**.

3. Select **Text1.txt**, **Text2.txt**, and **Text3.txt**.

4. Drag **Text1.txt**, **Text2.txt**, and **Text3.txt** onto the **VBArgs.vbs** script file.

    Note that three message boxes appear, one for each file.

5. Double-click the **VBArgs.vbs** script to run it directly without any arguments.

    Note the message box that appears.

Exercise 2
Writing an Event into the Application Event Log

In this exercise, you will add a new section to the previous script that writes a new entry into the Windows 2000 Application Event Log to indicate which files were passed as arguments.

▶ **To write events to the Application Event Log**

1. Switch to **PrimalSCRIPT**.

2. Add the following lines of code to the end of the script to write entries to the Application Event Log:

```
Dim oShell, sLogEntry
Set oShell = CreateObject("WScript.Shell")
sLogEntry = "Script was run with :"
For iCount = 0 to UBound(aArgs)
    sLogEntry = sLogEntry & vbCrLf & aArgs(iCount)
Next
oShell.LogEvent 4, sLogEntry
```

3. On the **File** menu, click **Save**.

4. Switch to Windows Explorer.

5. Select **Text1.txt, Text2.txt,** and **Text3.txt**.

6. Drag **Text1.txt, Text2.txt,** and **Text3.txt** onto the **VBArgs.vbs** script file.

7. Click **OK** for each of the message boxes.

▶ **To review the events in the Application Event Log**

1. On the **Start** menu, point to **Programs**, point to **Administrative Tools**, and then click **Event Viewer**.

2. In the **Tree** pane, click **Application Log**.

3. In the right pane, double-click and review the entry at the top of the list.

Tip   The **Source** columns will specify **WSH** for the entry generated by your script.

---

4. Click **OK**.

5. Close Event Viewer.

You have now written a script that accepts arguments and writes entries to the Windows 2000 Application Event Log.

Managing the Registry

■ **Reading from the Registry**

```
sValue = oShell.RegRead ("HKLM\System\Current...")
```

■ **Writing to the Registry**

```
oShell.RegWrite "HKLM\..\Current...", "New value"
```

■ **Deleting from the Registry**

```
oShell.RegDelete "HKLM\System\Current..."
```

The registry is one of the most important storage locations in the Microsoft Windows environment. Administrators often need to access information stored in the registry and manipulate key configuration settings to reconfigure systems. You can accomplish this by using script. The **WScript.Shell** object allows access to the registry to read, write, and delete keys and values.

Reading from the Registry

To read data in the registry, you can create a **WScript.Shell** object and use the **RegRead** method, as shown in the following example:

Example

```
Set oShell = CreateObject("WScript.Shell")
MsgBox oShell.RegRead("HKLM\Software\Microsoft\
↪Windows NT\CurrentVersion\CurrentVersion")
```

This method returns different data types, depending on the key value that is set in the registry. This may cause problems, but the majority of values returned are strings, integers, or binaries.

Tip Use the VBScript **Join** function to read from a value registry entry of REG_MULTI_SZ.

For more information about the **Join** function, see the VBScript documentation.

If your script attempts to read a key that does not exist, an error will occur. You can trap the error by using the **On Error Resume Next** statement and checking for an Err.Number value that is not 0 (zero). In this way, you can verify the existence of a key by attempting to read from it.

This is demonstrated in the script below, which tests for the existence of a registry key for Microsoft SQL Server™.

Example

```
Dim oShell, sSQLServ
On Error Resume Next
Set oShell = WScript.CreateObject("WScript.Shell")
sSQLServ = oShell.RegRead( _
   "HKLM\SOFTWARE\Microsoft\MSSQLServer\MSSQLServer\" _
   & "CurrentVersion\CurrentVersion")
If Err.Number = 0 Then
   WScript.Echo "SQL Server Version is: " & sSQLServ
Else
   WScript.Echo "SQL Server Version not found"
End If
```

Writing to the Registry

Writing to the registry is more restrictive than reading registry values. You can only write strings, integers, and binary values to the registry by using script. You cannot write REG_MULTI_SZ (array) values by using script.

You can use the **RegWrite** method to write to the registry. In the following example, a new string value will be created in a registry key:

Example

```
oShell.RegWrite "HKLM\Software\Newvalue", "My new value"
```

If the last character of the key name is a backslash (\ ), a new key is created instead of a value. A third optional string argument tells the function what type of value to write: REG_SZ (string), REG_DWORD (integer), or REG_BINARY (binary). If no value type is specified, the decision is made by analyzing the second argument to see if it is a string or an integer.

Deleting from the Registry

A key or a value can easily be deleted from the registry by using the **RegDelete** function, as shown in the following example:

Example

```
oShell.RegDelete "HKCU\ScriptEngine\Val" 'Delete value "Val"
oShell.RegDelete "HKCU\ScriptEngine\Key\" 'Delete key "Key"
```

Caution   Use extreme care when deleting or modifying the registry by using a script. Modifying or deleting certain values or keys may make the operating system unstable or even unusable.

◆ Working with Drives, Folders, and Files

- ■ **Accessing Drives, Folders, and Files**
- ■ **Working with Folders**
- ■ **Working with Files**

Scripting gives you a high level of control over drives, files, and folders. WSH exposes a variety of methods that you can use to manage file system resources. You can use these methods to create, delete, write, and extract information from local and remote drives, files, and folders. You can also record this information for later reference.

In this section, you will learn how to manage file system resources by using script.

Accessing Drives, Folders, and Files

- **The FileSystemObject**

```
Set oFS = CreateObject("Scripting.FileSystemObject")
```

- **Drive Access**
  - **Drives** collection or **GetDrive** method of FileSystemObject
- **Folder Access**
  - **GetFolder** method of FSO
  - **RootFolder** property of a drive
  - **SubFolders** collection of folder
- **File Access**
  - **GetFile** method of FSO
  - **Files** collection of folder

The Scripting Object Model (Scrrun.dll) provides useful objects that you can use to manage drives, folders, and files. The root of these objects is the **FileSystemObject**. All other objects are created or retrieved from the **FileSystemObject**.

The FileSystemObject

This main object allows creation, copying, deletion, and information retrieval from folders, files, and drives. You must create this object before any other objects in the Scripting Object Model can be instantiated or used. You use the following line of script to create an instance of the **FileSystemObject** object:

Example

```
Set oFSO = CreateObject("Scripting.FileSystemObject")
```

Drive Access

Disk drives are accessed through the **Drives** collection property of the **FileSystemObject** object or by calling the **GetDrive** method. The following example shows how to loop through available drives and display some of the drive properties. Note the use of the **IsReady** property to check the availability of a drive. This is useful when you access removable media such as floppy disks. Also note the use of the **With** statement, which enables you to perform a series of actions on a specified object without having to retype the name of the object for each action.

Example

```
Dim oFS, oDrive, sOutput
Set oFS = CreateObject("Scripting.FileSystemObject")
For Each oDrive In oFS.Drives
  With oDrive
    If .IsReady Then
        sOutput = "Drive:" & .DriveLetter & vbCRLF
        sOutput = sOutput & "  Type:" &  .FileSystem _
        & vbCRLF
        sOutput = sOutput & "  Serial:" & .SerialNumber _
        & vbCRLF
        sOutput = sOutput & "  Label:" & .VolumeName _
        & vbCRLF
        sOutput = sOutput & "  Size:" & _
        Round((.TotalSize / 1073741824), 2) & "GB" _
        & vbCRLF
        sOutput = SOutput & "  Avail:" & _
        Round((.AvailableSpace / 1073741824), 2) & "GB" _
        & vbCRLF
        WScript.Echo sOutput
    else
        WScript.Echo "Drive:" & .DriveLetter & " not ready"
    End If
  End With
Next
```

Folder Access

You can access folders by using the **GetFolder** method of the
FileSystemObject object or by using the **RootFolder** property of the **Drive**
object to gain access to the SubFolders collection.

The following example loops through the SubFolders collection of the C drive:

Example

```
Set oDrive = oFS.GetDrive("C")
For Each oFolder In oDrive.RootFolder.SubFolders
    WScript.Echo  oFolder.name
Next
```

Because each folder also has the **SubFolders** collection property, it is possible
to loop through all of the child folders of a particular item.

File Access

You can use the Files collection of the **Folder** object to access file objects on
the hard drive. File properties, including **Name**, **Path**, **Size**, **Type**, and so on,
are available to your script. The following example loops through the Files
collection of a folder and displays each file name and type:

Example

```
For Each oFile In oFolder.Files
    Wscript.Echo  "  " & oFile.Name & " " & oFile.Type
Next
```

Caution Use caution when using script to manipulate the file system because it is easy to delete every file and folder from a hard drive when using these powerful objects and methods. Be sure to test your scripts thoroughly before releasing them into a production environment.

Working with Folders

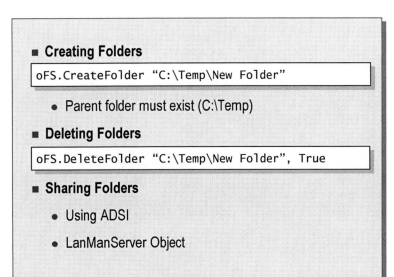

■ **Creating Folders**

```
oFS.CreateFolder "C:\Temp\New Folder"
```

- Parent folder must exist (C:\Temp)

■ **Deleting Folders**

```
oFS.DeleteFolder "C:\Temp\New Folder", True
```

■ **Sharing Folders**

- Using ADSI

- LanManServer Object

The **FileSystemObject** object provides methods that you can use to create or delete folders.

Creating Folders

To create a folder, call the **CreateFolder** method of the **FileSystemObject** object as shown in the following example:

Example

```
oFS.CreateFolder strFolderName
```

When you create a folder with this object, the parent of the folder must exist before the new child folder is created or an error will occur.

Deleting Folders

You can use two methods to delete a folder. One is the **DeleteFolder** method of the **FileSystemObject** object. The syntax for this method is shown in the following example:

Syntax

```
oFS.DeleteFolder folderSpec [, force]
```

The first argument "*folderSpec,*" is the folder name and can include wildcard characters. The optional second argument, "force," is a Boolean value that forces folder deletion, even on read-only folders. The default value of this argument is **false**. The **DeleteFolder** method also deletes any files or subfolders in the chosen folder.

Alternatively, you can delete a folder by calling the **Delete** method of the **Folder** object itself.

Caution These methods will delete the folders and the files that they contain completely. The folders and files are not sent to the Recycle Bin.

Sharing Folders

You cannot share a folder by using the Scripting Runtime library. To do this, you must use the Microsoft Active Directory™ Service Interface (ADSI) **LanManServer** object. For more information about ADSI and the **LanManServer** object, see Module 5, "Understanding ADSI."

Working with Files

- **Creating a Text File**

```
Set oFile = oFS.OpenTextFile("c:\Users.txt", 1, )
```

- **Reading from a Text File**
  - OpenTextStream
  - Read, ReadLine, ReadAll
- **Writing to a Text File**
  - CreateTextFile
  - OpenTextFile
  - Write, WriteLine, WriteBlankLines

The **FileSystemObject** library enables you to create, read, and write to text files. If you want to create, read, or write to other file types, such as Microsoft Office documents, you must use the appropriate library to provide this functionality. Microsoft Office exposes objects and methods to allow you to do this.

Creating a Text File

The main way to create a file is by using the **CreateTextFile** method of the **FileSystemObject** or **Folder** objects. This method creates a new file and returns the **TextStream** object from the file, allowing you to write to the file. The syntax for creating a file is shown in the following example:

Syntax

```
object.CreateTextFile(filename[, overwrite[, unicode]])
```

The optional second argument is a Boolean value that indicates whether you want to overwrite an existing file. The default value for this argument is **false**. The optional third argument specifies the type of file to create, either ASCII (the default in Windows 2000) or UNICODE.

Reading from a Text File

You can use the following methods of the **TextStream** object to read data from a text file.

Method	Task
Read	Read a specified number of characters from a file.
ReadLine	Read an entire line.
ReadAll	Read the entire contents of a text file.

The **Skip** and **SkipLine** methods allow data to be skipped if required. The text string returned by these methods can be displayed, parsed by string functions (such as **Left**, **Right**, and **Mid**), concatenated with other data, and so on. The following VBScript example demonstrates how to open a file, and then read the first line from it:

Example

```
Dim oFso, oFile
Set oFso = CreateObject("Scripting.FileSystemObject")
Set oFile = oFso.OpenTextFile("c:\Users.txt", 1)
ReadTextFileTest =  oFso.ReadLine
```

Writing to a Text File

The **TextStream** object provides write access to a text file. You can open a **TextStream** object by using the **CreateTextFile** method of the **FileSystemObject** or **Folder** object, the **OpenTextStream** method of **FileSystemObject**, or the **OpenAsTextStream** method of a **File** object.

The following example shows the OpenTextFile syntax:

Syntax

```
object.OpenTextFile(filename[, iomode[, create[, format]]])
```

The *filename* argument is the path and filename of the file to be opened.

The "*iomode*" switch allows you to specify whether the file is to be opened as read-only, write-only, or appended to. You cannot open a file with the intention of reading some lines and then writing others; you must open the file as read-only, then close the file, and then reopen it as append or write. The following table shows the constant values that are use to specify the mode in which the method opens the file.

OpenTextFile Constants

Constant	Value	Description
ForReading	1	Open a file for reading only. You cannot write to this file.
ForWriting	2	Open a file for writing only. You cannot read from this file.
ForAppending	8	Open a file and write to the end of the file.

The **Create** argument allows the method to create a new file if the requested file does not exist. The value should be set to **True** if you are creating a new file or to **False** if this is not required. The default for this value is **False**.

The **Format** argument enables you to specify that the file should be opened as ASCII, UNICODE, or as the system default. You do this by using the values shown in the following table.

Format Constants

Constant	Value	Description
TristateUseDefault	-2	Opens the file by using the system default.
TristateTrue	-1	Opens the file as UNICODE
TristateFalse	0	Opens the file as ASCII.

Setting Folder-Level and File-Level Security

- **ADSI**
  - Part of ADSI SDK
  - Extension components required:
    ADsSecurity
    ADsSid
- **XCACLS**
  - Part of Windows 2000 Resource Kit
  - Parameters
- **/G in Detail**
- **Examples**

FileSystemObject does not have any methods for setting folder-level or file-level security permissions. If you want to set or change permissions by using script, you can use either the ADSI interface or the Windows 2000 Resource Kit utility XCACLS.EXE.

ADSI

Before you can use this interface to set security permissions, you need COM extensions to enable ADSI to access NT file system (NTFS) permissions. These extensions provide a consistent security interface for file permissions, but are currently only available from the ADSI Resource Kit.

For this reason, each machine that attempts to set permissions by using these extensions must have them installed, or the script will fail. The process is very similar to the process of setting permissions on objects in Active Directory. For more information about setting permissions on objects in Active Directory, see Module 5, "Understanding ADSI."

XCACLS

An alternative method of setting security permissions is to use the Extended Change Access Control List (XCACLS) tool from the Windows 2000 Resource Kit. Xcacls.exe enables you to set all Microsoft Windows Explorer file-system security options from the command line.

The following example, from C:\Labfiles\Mod6\Mod6xcaclsdemo.vbs, achieves the same result as the preceding ADSI example:

Example

```
Set oShell = CreateObject("WScript.shell")
oShell.Run "XCACLS F:\ADSIPerms /G NWTraders\FrankL:R /E
➥/Y", 2, TRUE
```

In this script, an instance of the **WScript.Shell** object is created, and its **Run** method is used to execute the **XCACLS** command. This command adds the permission for the user "FrankL" to have read-access to the F:\ADSIPerms folder. This approach requires much less code than using ADSI.

Parameters

Running XCACLS without any parameters displays the following syntax for the utility:

Syntax

```
XCACLS filename [/T] [/E] [/C] [/G user:perm;spec] [/R user
↳[...]][/P user:perm;spec [...]] [/D user [...]] [/Y]
```

This command allows the use of wildcard characters, multiple users in a single command, and the combination of multiple access rights.

The following table describes these parameters.

Parameter	Description
Filename	This is the name of the file or directory with which CACLS will work.
/T	Causes XCACLS to walk recursively through the current directory and all of its subdirectories.
/E	Edits the ACL instead of replacing it. The default is to replace the ACL.
/C	Causes XCACLS to continue if an "access denied" error occurs. If /C is not specified, XCACLS stops on this error.
/G *user:perm;spec*	Grants user access to the matching file or directory. See below for more details.
/R *user*	Revokes all access rights for the specified user.
/P *user:perm;spec*	Replaces access rights for the user. The rules for specifying perm and spec are the same as for the /G option. Some examples are given below in this documentation.
/D *user*	Denies user access to the file or directory.
/Y	Turns off the default confirmation when replacing user access rights.

/G in Detail

The /G switch is the most complex part of the XCACLS utility. It consists of the following three parameters.

User

This is the name of the account on which the permissions are being set. Acceptable name formats are:

UserName or DomainName\UserName

GroupName or DomainName\GroupName

Perm

Perm represents the special file-access-right mask for directories, which applies permissions to the files. Perm can be one of the following values:

- R (Read)
- C (Change)
- F (Full control)
- P (Change Permissions)
- O (Take Ownership)
- X (Execute)
- E (Read)
- W (Write)
- D (Delete)

Spec

Spec applies settings to folders only. It is possible to set an Access Control Entry (ACE) for the folder itself without specifying an ACE that is automatically applied to new files created in that folder. You accomplish this by using the specifier, T, following the semicolon. All access rights specified between the semicolon and the T are ignored. At least one access specifier must follow the T. This means that only an ACE for the folder will be created.

All other options, which can also be set in Windows Explorer, are subsets of the possible combinations of the basic access rights. Therefore, there are no special options for directory access rights, such as List or Read.

Spec can be the same as Perm, and is only applied to a directory. In this case, Perm will be used for file inheritance in this directory.

Examples

Example

```
XCACLS *.* /G administrator:RW /Y
```

This command replaces the access control list (ACL) of all files and folders found in the current folder without scanning any subfolders and without confirmation.

Example

```
XCACLS *.* /G MyUser:RWED;RW /E
```

This command edits the ACL of a file or a folder, but its effect on a folder is different. The ACE that is added to the folder is also an inherited ACE for new files created in this folder. In this example, "MyUser" is granted read, write, execute, and delete rights for all new files created in this folder, but only read and write permissions for the folder itself.

Example

```
XCACLS *.* /G MyUser:R;TRW /E
```

This command grants read and write permissions for a folder without creating an inherit entry for new files. Therefore, in the previous example, new files created in this folder do not get an ACE for MyUser.

Scheduling Scripts

- **The AT Scheduler**
- **Scheduling Service**
  - Scheduled Task Wizard
- **Error Log if Task Fails**
  - SchedLog.txt

Scripting certain tasks eases the administrative load on an organization. Some of these tasks, such as running and controlling maintenance or utility programs, can be run after normal office hours. If you can script a process, you do not have to be in the office to run the script. Instead, you can schedule scripts to be executed at appropriate times.

The AT Scheduler

The AT command line utility for scheduling, or AT Scheduler, is available in all Windows 2000 operating systems. You can use this utility to schedule the running of scripts from the command line.

In Windows 2000, you will see tasks created by the **AT** command in the Scheduled Tasks folder of the Control Panel.

Scheduling Service

The Scheduled Tasks folder in the Control Panel contains a wizard that helps you to add any application or script file to a schedule. The schedule can be set for daily, weekly, monthly, and other frequencies, and requires a user name and a password with sufficient security permissions to run the program or execute the script. In addition to these basic features, you can set advanced properties to control the schedule, including the ability to run the application or script only when the machine is in an idle state.

Error Log if Task Fails

If an error occurs during a scheduled task, the scheduling service appends an error log to Schedlog.txt in the Windows directory.

An example of using script to control a scheduled application is the Microsoft Management Console (MMC) Disk Defragmenter tool. If the AT Scheduler calls C:\Winnt\System32\dfrg.msc, the Disk Defragmenter will run, but the AT Scheduler has no way to control what the application does after it is launched. However, rather than scheduling the Disk Defragmenter to run, you can schedule a script. This script starts the Disk Defragmenter, and you can use the **SendKeys** method to control what the Disk Defragmenter does when it is running.

Tip   Scheduled tasks are stored as .job files in the Windows\Tasks folder. Because these tasks can be copied in the same way as any file, you can create your job on one machine, and then copy the file as part of a logon script to make distribution easier.

Best Practices

- Build Error Handling into the Scripts

- Test All Administrative Scripts Extensively

- Be Careful When Using the FileSystemObject for Deletions

- Back Up the Registry Before Testing Scripts

Consider the following practices when working with administrative scripts.

Build Error Handling into the Scripts

Administrative scripts should include built-in error handling. It is very important that you are aware of any script failures.

Test All Administrative Scripts Extensively

Always test administrative scripts in a test environment before releasing them on a production system. Try testing scripts in varied scenarios to ensure that they will function correctly.

Be Careful when Using the FileSystemObject for Deletions

FileSystemObject can remove every file and folder from a hard drive without a single prompt, if instructed to do so. Make sure that your script gives adequate warning if it is about to delete files or folders from a user's hard drive, and build in a routine to allow the user to cancel the script if it was run in error.

Back Up the Registry Before Testing Scripts

If you are writing scripts to modify the registry of any systems, ensure that you have backups that can be restored if the script damages the integrity of the system.

Lab 7.2: Working with the FileSystemObject

Objectives

After completing this lab, you will be able to use the **FileSystemObject** to create and write to files, and extract information about the folders on each of the drives on your computer.

Scenario

As an administrator, you often need to audit the contents of your users' computers. This can be a time-consuming and tedious task. You have decided that scripting the audit and recording the contents of the computer drives in a text file would suit your needs. In this lab, you will write a script that documents all of the folders on all of the drives of a computer. It will record the details in a text file.

Estimated time to complete this lab: 30 minutes

Exercise 1
Documenting your Computer Drives and Folders

In this exercise, you will use the **FileSystemObject** to create and write to a file that contains information about the folders and hard drives on your computer.

▶ **To create a script that documents the drives on your computer**

1. Start **PrimalSCRIPT**, if it is not already running.

2. On the **File** menu, click **New**.

3. In the **New** dialog box, click **Text**, and then click **OK**.

4. Type the following code to loop through the drives collection. Note that this code uses a call to a function named **GetDriveString** and a subprocedure named **WriteFolder**. You will create these procedures later in this exercise.

```
Dim oFS, oDrive, oFileTS, sOutPut
Set oFS = CreateObject("Scripting.FileSystemObject")
Set oFileTS = oFS.CreateTextFile("c:\driveData.txt")
For Each oDrive In oFS.Drives
    With oDrive
        sOutput = "Drive:" & .DriveLetter
        sOutput = sOutput & " Type:" _
            & GetDriveString(.DriveType)
        If .IsReady Then
        sOutput = sOutput & "  Format:" & .FileSystem
        sOutput = sOutput & "  Label:" & .VolumeName
        If .DriveType <>3 Then
            oFileTS.WriteLine sOutput
            WriteFolder oDrive.RootFolder, " "
        End If
    Else
        oFileTS.WriteLine sOutput & " not ready"
        End If
    End With
Next
WScript.Echo "All Done!!"
oFileTS.Close
WScript.Quit
```

5. Write the **GetDriveString** function at the end of the script by typing the following code:

```
Function GetDriveString(iDriveType)
Const CDRom = 4
Const Fixed = 2
Const RamDisk = 5
Const Remote = 3
Const Removable = 1
Const Unknown = 0
Const CDRomString = "CDROM"
Const FixedString = "Fixed"
Const RamDiskString = "RamDisk"
Const RemoteString = "Remote"
Const RemovableString = "Removable"
Const UnknownString = "Unknown"
Select Case iDriveType
Case CDROM
    GetDriveString = CDRomString
Case Fixed
    GetDriveString = FixedString
Case RamDisk
    GetDriveString = RamDiskString
Case Remote
    GetDriveString = RemoteString
Case Removable
    GetDriveString = RemovableString
Case Else
    GetDriveString = UnknownString
    End Select
End Function
```

6. Write the **WriteFolder** subprocedure at the end of the script by typing the following code:

```
Sub WriteFolder(ByRef oFol, ByVal sSpaces)
Dim oFolder
On Error Resume Next
For Each oFolder in oFol.SubFolders
    sOutPut = sSpaces & "-" & oFolder.Name
    If Err.Number = 0 Then oFileTS.WriteLine sOutput
    Err.Clear
    WriteFolder oFolder, sSpaces & " "
Next
End Sub
```

▶ **To save the script that documents the drives on your computer**

1. On the **File** menu, click **Save As**.

2. In the **Save As** dialog box, navigate to the *<install folder>*\Labs\Lab07\Lab7_2\Starter folder.

3. In the **File name** box, type **Drives.vbs**

4. Click **Save**.

▶ **To run the script that documents the drives on your computer**

1. On the **Script** menu, click **Run Script**.

2. When the **All Done** message appears, click **OK**.

Note   The script may take a few seconds to run because it retrieves information about all of the folders on all of your drives.

---

3. Using Windows Explorer, browse to the root of the C drive.

4. Double-click the file **DriveData.txt** to open it.

5. Review the file contents, and then close the DriveData.txt file.

You have now successfully documented all of the folders for all of the drives on your computer.

Review

- Script Arguments
- Working with Event Logs
- Generating E-Mail Messages
- Managing the Registry
- Working with Drives, Folders, and Files
- Setting Folder-Level and File-Level Security
- Scheduling Scripts

1. To which event log can you write by using the **LogEvent** method of the **Shell** object?

2. If no configuration information is set in a script when sending an e-mail message by means of CDO, where does the script get this information?

3. What VBScript function can you use to help manage REG_MULTI_SZ values in the registry?

4. Which object model exposes the **FileSystemObject**?

msdn training

Module 8: Beyond the Basics

Contents

Overview

- ■ Windows Script Files
- ■ Using COM Components
- ■ WMI
- ■ Scripting Microsoft Office
- ■ ASP Pages

You can relate the information that you have encountered already in this course to other products and scenarios. You can use the skills that you have gained when you work in other areas and with other programs.

In this module, you will learn about the application of script in scenarios other than system administration. This module provides an introduction to new topics. Further reading is required to develop skills in these areas.

At the end of this module, you will be able to:

- ■ Describe Microsoft® Windows® script (.wsf) files.
- ■ Describe how Component Object Model (COM) components enhance the power of your scripts.
- ■ Describe Windows Management Instrumentation (WMI).
- ■ Begin scripting applications in Microsoft Office.
- ■ Describe Active Server Pages (ASP).

◆ Windows Script Files

- ■ **Benefits of Windows Script Files**
- ■ **Practice: Using Windows Script Files**

Windows script files add functionality to your scripts.

In this section, you will learn about .wsf files and where to get more information about .wsf files.

Benefits of Windows Script Files

- ■ **XML Format Script File**
- ■ **Support for Multiple Script Engines**
- ■ **Multiple Jobs in a Single Script**
- ■ **Support for Including Other Script Files**
- ■ **Type Library Reference**

Windows script files were introduced with Windows Script Host (WSH) version 2.0.

XML Format Script File

A .wsf file is a text document containing Extensible Markup Language (XML) code. This code uses tags similar to those in Hypertext Markup Language (HTML) but incorporates several features that offer more scripting flexibility.

Note Before the release of WSH 2.0, the .ws extension was used for XML format script files and is still referred to by many reference books.

Support for Multiple Script Engines

WSH 2.0 enables you to use multiple languages in a single .wsf file through the XML format of a .wsf file.

The following example shows a .wsf file that includes script written in Microsoft Visual Basic® Scripting Edition (VBScript) and Microsoft JScript®:

Example

```
<job id="WSFDemo">
<script language="VBScript">
  WScript.Echo "This came from VBScript"
</script>
<script language="JScript">
  var strTxt1;
  var strTxt2;
  strTxt1 = "This came from JScript";
  strTxt2 = "XML is very Powerful! ";
  WScript.Echo (strTxt1 + "\n" + strTxt2);
</Script>
</Job>
```

WSH is extensible due to third party Microsoft ActiveX® scripting engines. As a result, .wsf files are not restricted to VBScript or Microsoft JScript®. You can use other script languages, such as PerlScript.

Multiple Jobs in a Single Script

Rather than keep related scripts in separate files, you can incorporate multiple files into a single .wsf file. Enclosing each script in an XML tag defines the scripts in a file as a collection of jobs, as follows:

Example

```
<Job id="JobName">
'Your Script Goes Here
<Job>
```

You must identify each job by using a unique job identifier. To run that portion of script, you can then reference these identifiers by using a command similar to the following:

Example

```
CScript //Job:JobName Allmyscripts.wsf
```

In this example, **JobName** is the name, or identifier, of the job contained in the Allmyscripts.wsf file.

Support for Including Other Script Files

If an existing script already provides a function that is required, a .wsf file enables you to use it without duplicating the script. This approach is similar to using **include** statements found in other environments, such as Microsoft Visual C++® and ASP.

A .wsf file encapsulates a library of functions that multiple .wsf files can use. The following example shows the contents of a .wsf file that includes a JScript file (fso.js). It also includes a VBScript function that calls the **GetFreeSpace** function in the included file, as follows:

Example

```
<Job id="IncludeExample">
<script language="JScript" src="FSO.JS"/>
<script language="VBScript"> ' Get the free space for drive C.
s = GetFreeSpace("c:")
WScript.Echo s
</Script>
</Job>
```

The contents of fso.js is as follows:

Example

```
function GetFreeSpace(drvPath) {
  var fs, d, s;
  fs = new ActiveXObject("Scripting.FileSystemObject");
  d = fs.GetDrive(fs.GetDriveName(drvPath));
  s = "Drive " + drvPath + " - " ;
  s += d.VolumeName;
  s += " Free Space: " + d.FreeSpace/1024 + " Kbytes";
  return s;
}
```

Type Library Reference

Although type libraries expose constants, WSH is unable to use them directly. Instead, it treats the constant name like an undeclared variable unless you specifically declare the constant and its value in your script. To address this issue, you can create a reference to a type library in a .wsf file so that you can use the constant directly. This is particularly useful when working with a type library that exposes many constants, such as ActiveX Data Objects (ADO).

In the following example, the script uses the ADO constant adOpenDynamic directly. The type library is contained in the ADO type library.

Example

```
<Job id="TypeLibExample">
<Reference Object = "ADODB.RecordSet"/>
<Script language="VBScript">
  Option Explicit
  Dim aCon, aRst
  Set aCon = CreateObject("ADODB.Connection")
  aCon.ConnectionString="Provider=SQLOLEDB.1;" _
    & "User ID=sa;Initial Catalog=Northwind;" _
    & "Data Source=(Local)"
  aCon.Open
  Set aRst = CreateObject("ADODB.RecordSet")
  aRST.Open "Select * From Employees",aCon,adOpenDynamic
  WScript.Echo aRst("LastName")
</Script>
</Job>
```

Practice: Using Windows Script Files

In this practice, you will use a .wsf file. This practice demonstrates some of the features of the XML format inside a .wsf file.

▶ **To use WSF files**

1. Using Microsoft Windows Explorer, go to the *install folder*\Practices folder.

2. Double-click **Mod8WSFInAction.wsf**.

   Note the name of the job that runs.

3. Using the command prompt, go to the *install folder*\Practices folder.

4. Type the following command at the command prompt, and then press ENTER:

   ```
   Cscript Mod8WSFInAction.wsf //Job:Job2
   ```

   Notice that a different script runs.

5. Repeat steps 4 and 5, but run Job4.

   Two scripts run in the same job.

6. Repeat steps 4 and 5, but run Job3.

   This script echoes the value of some of the Active Directory™ Services Interface (ADSI) constants used in group creation.

7. Open Mod8WSFInAction.wsf in Notepad, and then review the script. Close Notepad.

Using COM Components

- **Registering Components**
  - RegSvr32
- **Calling COM Components**

You can use the features of any COM component from within a script as long as the script can call the COM component.

For scripts to use COM components, the COM components must support automation and correctly handle the script data types. There are many Web sites that offer third party COM components to help you increase the functionality of scripts.

Registering COM Components

COM components must be registered on the computer that you will use them on. You can do this by using the installation routine of the component itself or by manually using the RegSvr32 utility. To use this utility, click **Start**, click **Run**, and then type **Regsvr32 COMComponentName**

The registration process adds the component to the **HKEY_CLASSES_ROOT** key of the registry. This is where the Component Services class registration database is stored. These registry entries are required for the component to be referenced and used.

Calling COM Components

After registration is complete, the documentation that comes with the COM component explains the object model that it exposes. You can call the component from a script by using this object model, as shown in the following example:

Example

```
Set oMyComp = WScript.CreateObject("MyComp.MyNewObj")
Wscript.Echo oMyComp.Name
```

In this example, a new object is created by using a hypothetical component. A property of this object, called **Name**, is then echoed to the screen.

Note   You have already used COM components in this course, such as the **Connection**, **Command**, and **Recordset** ADO objects.

◆ WMI

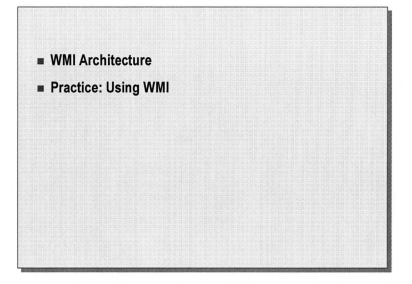

Windows Management Instrumentation (WMI) interfaces increase the functionality of your administrative scripts.

In this section, you will learn how to use WMI in your scripts.

WMI Architecture

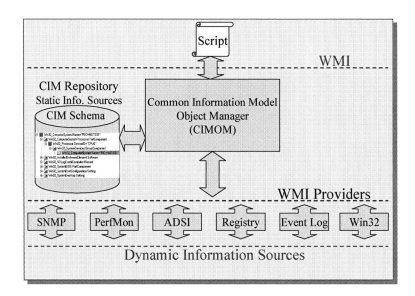

WMI is made up of several components that work together to enable WMI clients, such as management programs or scripts, to query, recover, and change information from the hardware, software, or operating system.

The basic components of WMI are:

- Common Information Model Object Manager (CIMOM)

  CIMOM manages any calls a WMI client makes to WMI. It determines whether the request involves static data stored in the Common Information Model (CIM) repository or dynamic data supplied by a provider. These WMI providers specialize in providing specific features to WMI for a specific data source, such as the Windows registry. When a provider finishes processing a request, it returns the results back to CIMOM. CIMOM forwards the result back to the WMI client.

- CIM repository

  The CIM repository is a central storage area managed by CIMOM. It stores the class definitions for static classes and stores static instances. If the data is regularly updated or dynamic, the WMI providers manage the updates.

- WMI providers

  WMI providers are COM objects that are interpreters for WMI. They enable WMI to communicate with specific objects in a manageable and scalable manner. Providers available as part of Microsoft Windows 2000 include:

  - Win32.

  - Registry.

  - ADSI (Active Directory Services Interface).

  - Event Viewer logs.

  - Performance Monitor (PerfMon).

  - Simple Network Management Protocol (SNMP).

  WMI is extensible. If a third-party developer wants to expose management information about his or her program, the developer can write a WMI provider and publish information about the provider's capabilities to WMI. Once published, WMI clients can also access this management information.

Practice: Using WMI

The demonstration script file, Mod8WMIInAction.vbs, shows how WMI can read information from a computer. It then uses WSH objects to create a text file and writes an event in the application log of the computer to help track the execution of the script.

▶ **To retrieve machine data using WMI**

1. Using Windows Explorer, go to the i*nstall folder*\Practices folder.

2. Double-click **Mod8WMIInAction.vbs**.

3. Using Windows Explorer, go to the root of drive C.

4. Open the *computer_name*.txt file in Notepad (where *computer_name* is your computer's name).

5. Review its contents.

6. Close Notepad.

7. Using Windows Explorer, go to the i*nstall folder*\Practices folder.

8. Open Mod8WMIInAction.vbs in Notepad.

9. Review its contents.

10. Close Notepad.

◆ Scripting Microsoft Office

- **Introduction to Scripting Microsoft Office**
- **Practice: Controlling Microsoft Office**

Because Microsoft Office programs expose automation objects, you can control them with your scripts.

In this section, you will learn more about writing scripts that control Microsoft Office programs.

Introduction to Scripting Microsoft Office

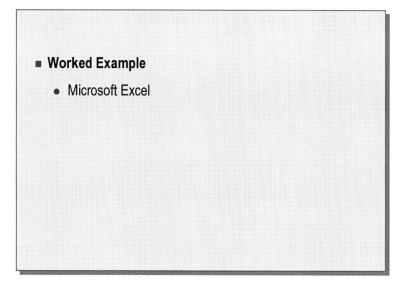

Microsoft Office programs provide automation interfaces that enable you to use script to manipulate the program and its data. These programs provide detailed programmable object models that enable you to access all of the functions available to an interactive user through script.

The following example uses Microsoft Excel as an example of what can be achieved by controlling Microsoft Office programs with script. Although the objects in the example are specific to Microsoft Excel, a similar approach can be employed to control any of the Microsoft Office programs.

Microsoft Excel has an extensive object model with many different classes. However, you can perform many administrative tasks with just a few objects. The Excel **Application** object is required to access Excel's automation functionality. To create an instance of the **Application** object, use the **CreateObject** function, as shown in the following example:

Example

```
Set oExcelApp = CreateObject("Excel.Application")
```

This opens a new instance of Excel, which is not visible by default. You can make the Excel instance visible by setting the **Visible** property of the **Application** object.

After you create the **Application** object, you use the **Workbooks** collection to perform tasks such as opening a file or creating a new file. Collections contain one or more objects of the same type, in this case, the **Workbook** objects. An example of how to open a **Workbook** object and store a reference, or variable, to it is shown below:

Example

```
Set oWorkbook = oExcelApp.Workbooks.Open("C:\Users.xls")
```

Most of the work that you want to do with Microsoft Excel can be done with **Worksheet** objects. This type of object gives you access to other objects, such as **Ranges**. There are various ways to navigate to a **Worksheet** object. The simplest approach is to specify the ordinal number or the name of the **Worksheet** object that you require in the **Workbook** object's **Worksheets** collection.

It is also useful to automate Excel for logging or reporting purposes. You can use the **Cells** property to write and read information.

You can also chart data by using the **Chart** object. You create a chart by using the **Add** method of the **Workbook** object's **Charts** collection.

The easiest way to create a chart is to programmatically select the data that you want to chart, and then use the following method:

Example

```
Set oChart = oWorkbook.Charts.Add
```

The following script manipulates the most commonly used Excel objects. The script:

- Creates an **Application** object.
- Creates a new **Workbook** object
- Populates a **Worksheet** with data.
- Selects the data.
- Creates a chart.
- Manipulates the chart.
- Saves the **Workbook** object.
- Quits Microsoft Excel.

Example

```
Dim xlApp, xlBook, xlChart, xlWks, xlRange
Dim iRows, iCols, iRotate
Const xl3DColumn = -4100
Set xlApp = CreateObject("Excel.Application")
Set xlBook = xlApp.Workbooks.Add
Set xlWks = xlBook.Worksheets(1)
Set xlRange = xlWks.Range("A1:C10")
For iRows = 1 To 10
  For iCols = 1 To 3
      xlRange.Cells(iRows,iCols).Value = iRows * iCols
  Next
Next
xlApp.Visible = True
xlWks.Activate
xlRange.Select
set xlChart = xlBook.Charts.Add
With xlChart
  .Activate
  .Type=xl3DColumn
  For iRotate = 0 to 360 Step 20
      xlChart.Rotation = iRotate
  Next
  xlChart.Rotation = 20
End With
xlBook.SaveAs "C:\AutomatingExcel.xls"
xlApp.Quit
Set xlRange= Nothing
Set xlChart= Nothing
Set xlWks= Nothing
Set xlBook= Nothing
Set xlApp = Nothing
```

Practice: Controlling Microsoft Office

The script in this practice automates Microsoft Excel.

▶ **To automate Microsoft Excel**

1. Logon as *Administrator@nwtraders.msft* with a password of **password**.

2. Using Windows Explorer, go to the *install folder*\Practices folder.

3. Double-click **User.xls**.

4. Review the contents of the file and modify the user account information to ensure that the accounts are unique in the enterprise network.

5. Close User.xls.

6. Open Mod8adduser.vbs in Notepad.

7. Modify the target organizational unit (OU) to that of your own Student OU that was created earlier in this course.

8. Close Notepad.

9. Double-click **Mod8adduser.vbs**.

10. In Microsoft Management Console (MMC), under **Active Directory Users and Computers**, check that the new user accounts were created.

11. Close MMC.

◆ ASP Pages

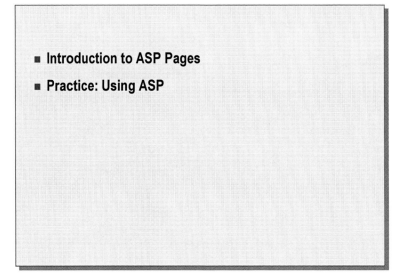

- **Introduction to ASP Pages**
- **Practice: Using ASP**

Active Server Pages (ASP) are the foundation for many Web applications. The most common language used to develop ASP pages is VBScript.

In this section, you will be introduced to ASP pages.

Introduction to ASP Pages

- ■ **Interactive Script**
- ■ **Client Versus Server**
- ■ **Advantages of Server-Side Scripting**
  - ● Easy maintenance
  - ● Lower bandwidth
  - ● Browser-independent
  - ● Full access to server-side object models

ASP pages were introduced in Microsoft Internet Information Server (IIS) version 3.0. They have been improved in each new release of IIS. ASP pages make it quick and easy to write simple Web applications. ASP pages are also easy to maintain, because they are composed of a simple scripting language.

Interactive Script

ASP pages combine the power of Visual Basic Scripting Edition with the display and interactivity of HTML. ASP pages are a simple platform on which you can develop rich and powerful Web applications. You can build intuitive administrative interfaces for Windows 2000 by using ASP pages.

Client Versus Server

When you use script for Web programming, there are two main techniques: client-side scripting and server-side scripting. Both methods are similar, because they mix standard HTML with script.

Advantages of Server-Side Scripting

Server-side scripting has the following unique advantages over client-side scripting:

- ■ The script runs on the server, so it is browser-independent.
- ■ Code runs on the server, which reduces data transfer to the client.
- ■ The script has full access to the object models on the server.

ASP is a large subject that is beyond the scope of this course. However, if you start programming with ASP pages, you will find that many of the concepts involved are easy for you to understand, because you use VBScript in ASP pages to achieve your goals.

Practice: Using ASP

This practice is designed to highlight some of the possibilities of an ASP page when used to access ADSI and Active Directory.

▶ **To run an ASP page**

1. Start Internet Explorer.

2. In the address bar, type **http://london/aspdemo**

3. Browse the Web site to see some of the information that you can use ASP pages and ADSI to expose.

Note   This demonstration is a slightly modified version of the DS Info Web site from the Microsoft Press book, "Building Enterprise Active Directory™ Services: Notes from the Field."

Review

- **Windows Script Files**
- **Using COM Components**
- **WMI**
- **Scripting Microsoft Office**
- **ASP Pages**

1. What command-line utility is used to register COM components?

2. List five WMI providers that ship with Windows 2000.

3. What is the name of the highest-level object that must be used to control Microsoft Excel in your scripts?

4. Does ASP code run on the Web browser or on the Web server?

Appendix A: VBScript Runtime and Parsing Error Reference

' Runtime errors:

```
Const VBSERR_None                = 0    'No error
Const VBSERR_IllegalFuncCall     = 5    'Invalid procedure call or argument
Const VBSERR_Overflow            = 6    'Overflow
Const VBSERR_OutOfMemory         = 7    'Out of memory
Const VBSERR_OutOfBounds         = 9    'Subscript out of range
Const VBSERR_ArrayLocked         = 10   'This array is fixed or temporarily
locked
Const VBSERR_DivByZero           = 11   'Division by zero
Const VBSERR_TypeMismatch        = 13   'Type mismatch
Const VBSERR_OutOfStrSpace       = 14   'Out of string space
Const VBSERR_CantContinue        = 17   'Can't perform requested operation
Const VBSERR_OutOfStack          = 28   'Out of stack space
Const VBSERR_UndefinedProc       = 35   'Sub or Function not defined
Const VBSERR_DLLLoadErr          = 48   'Error in loading DLL
Const VBSERR_InternalError       = 51   'Internal error
Const VBSERR_BadFileNameOrNumber = 52   'Bad file name or number
Const VBSERR_FileNotFound        = 53   'File not found
Const VBSERR_BadFileMode         = 54   'Bad file mode
Const VBSERR_FileAlreadyOpen     = 55   'File already open
Const VBSERR_IOError             = 57   'Device I/O error
Const VBSERR_FileAlreadyExists   = 58   'File already exists
Const VBSERR_DiskFull            = 61   'Disk full
Const VBSERR_EndOfFile           = 62   'Input past end of file
Const VBSERR_TooManyFiles        = 67   'Too many files
Const VBSERR_DevUnavailable      = 68   'Device unavailable
Const VBSERR_PermissionDenied    = 70   'Permission denied
Const VBSERR_DiskNotReady        = 71   'Disk not ready
Const VBSERR_DifferentDrive      = 74   'Can't rename with different drive
Const VBSERR_PathFileAccess      = 75   'Path/File access error
Const VBSERR_PathNotFound        = 76   'Path not found
Const VBSERR_ObjNotSet           = 91   'Object variable not set
Const VBSERR_IllegalFor          = 92   'For loop not initialized
Const VBSERR_CantUseNull         = 94   'Invalid use of Null
Const VBSERR_CantCreateTmpFile   = 322  'Can't create necessary temporary file
Const VBSERR_NotObject           = 424  'Object required
Const VBSERR_CantCreateObject    = 429  'ActiveX component can't create object
Const VBSERR_OLENotSupported     = 430  'Class doesn't support Automation
Const VBSERR_OLEFileNotFound     = 432  'File name or class name not found
during Automation operation
Const VBSERR_OLENoPropOrMethod   = 438  'Object doesn't support this property
or method
```

```
Const VBSERR_OLEAutomationError          = 440   'Automation error
Const VBSERR_ActionNotSupported              = 445   'Object doesn't support this
action
Const VBSERR_NamedArgsNotSupported           = 446   'Object doesn't support named
arguments
Const VBSERR_LocaleSettingNotSupported       = 447   'Object doesn't support current
locale setting
Const VBSERR_NamedParamNotFound              = 448   'Named argument not found
Const VBSERR_ParameterNotOptional            = 449   'Argument not optional
Const VBSERR_FuncArityMismatch               = 450   'Wrong number of arguments or
invalid property assignment
Const VBSERR_NotEnum                         = 451   'Object not a collection
Const VBSERR_InvalidDllFunctionName          = 453   'Specified DLL function not found
Const VBSERR_CodeResourceLockError           = 455   'Code resource lock error
Const VBSERR_DuplicateKey                    = 457   'This key is already associated
with an element of this collection
Const VBSERR_InvalidTypeLibVariable          = 458   'Variable uses an Automation type
not supported in VBScript
Const VBSERR_ServerNotFound                  = 462   'The remote server machine does
not exist or is unavailable
Const VBSERR_InvalidPicture                  = 481   'Invalid picture
Const VBSERR_UndefVariable                   = 500   'Variable is undefined
Const VBSERR_CantAssignTo                    = 501   'Illegal assignment
Const VBSERR_NotSafeForScripting             = 502   'Object not safe for scripting
Const VBSERR_NotSafeForInitializing          = 503   'Object not safe for initializing
Const VBSERR_NotSafeForCreating              = 504   'Object not safe for creating
Const VBSERR_InvalidReference                = 505   'Invalid or unqualified reference
Const VBSERR_ClassNotDefined                 = 506   'Class not defined
Const VBSERR_ComponentException              = 507   'An exception occurred
Const VBSERR_ElementNotFound                 = 32811 'Element not found
Const VBSERR_NeedRegExp                      = 5016  'Regular Expression object
expected
Const VBSERR_RegExpSyntax                    = 5017  'Syntax error in regular
expression
Const VBSERR_RegExpBadQuant                  = 5018  'Unexpected quantifier
Const VBSERR_RegExpNoBracket                 = 5019  'Expected ']' in regular
expression
Const VBSERR_RegExpNoParen                   = 5020  'Expected ')' in regular
expression
Const VBSERR_RegExpBadRange                  = 5021  'Invalid range in character set
```

```
' Parse errors

Const VBSERR_noMemory      = 1001    ' Out of memory
Const VBSERR_syntax        = 1002    ' Syntax error
Const VBSERR_noColon       = 1003    ' Expected ':'
Const VBSERR_noLparen      = 1005    ' Expected '('
Const VBSERR_noRparen      = 1006    ' Expected ')'
Const VBSERR_noRbrack      = 1007    ' Expected ']'
Const VBSERR_noIdent       = 1010    ' Expected identifier
Const VBSERR_noEq          = 1011    ' Expected '='
Const VBSERR_noIf          = 1012    ' Expected 'If'
Const VBSERR_noTo          = 1013    ' Expected 'To'
Const VBSERR_noEnd         = 1014    ' Expected 'End'
Const VBSERR_noFnc         = 1015    ' Expected 'Function'
Const VBSERR_noSub         = 1016    ' Expected 'Sub'
Const VBSERR_noThen        = 1017    ' Expected 'Then'
Const VBSERR_noWend        = 1018    ' Expected 'Wend'
Const VBSERR_noLoop        = 1019    ' Expected 'Loop'
Const VBSERR_noNext        = 1020    ' Expected 'Next'
Const VBSERR_noCase        = 1021    ' Expected 'Case'
Const VBSERR_noSelect      = 1022    ' Expected 'Select'
Const VBSERR_noExpr        = 1023    ' Expected expression
Const VBSERR_noStmt        = 1024    ' Epected statement
Const VBSERR_noEOS         = 1025    ' Expected end of statement
Const VBSERR_noIntCns      = 1026    ' Expected integer constant
Const VBSERR_noWhUn        = 1027    ' Expected 'While' or 'Until'
Const VBSERR_noWhUnEOS     = 1028    ' 'Until' or end of statement)
Const VBSERR_noWith        = 1029    ' Expected 'With'
Const VBSERR_idTooLong     = 1030    ' Identifier too long
Const VBSERR_badNumber     = 1031    ' Invalid number
Const VBSERR_illegalChar   = 1032    ' Invalid character
Const VBSERR_noStrEnd      = 1033    ' Unterminated string constant
Const VBSERR_noCmtEnd      = 1034    ' Unterminated comment
Const VBSERR_badMeUse      = 1037    ' Invalid use of 'Me' keyword
Const VBSERR_noDo          = 1038    ' 'loop' without 'do'
Const VBSERR_badExit       = 1039    ' Invalid 'exit' statement
Const VBSERR_badForVar     = 1040    ' Invalid 'for' loop control variable
Const VBSERR_redefName     = 1041    ' Name redefined
Const VBSERR_not1stOnLine  = 1042    ' Must be first statement on the line
Const VBSERR_asgByRef      = 1043    ' Cannot assign to non-ByVal argument
Const VBSERR_badParens     = 1044    ' Cannot use parentheses when calling a Sub
Const VBSERR_notConst      = 1045    ' Expected literal constant
Const VBSERR_noIn          = 1046    ' Expected 'In'
Const VBSERR_noClass       = 1047    ' Expected 'Class'
Const VBSERR_inClass       = 1048    ' Must be defined inside a Class
Const VBSERR_noPropSpec    = 1049    ' Expected Let or Set or Get in property
declaration
Const VBSERR_noProp        = 1050    ' Expected 'Property'
Const VBSERR_wrongArgsNum  = 1051    ' Number of arguments must be consistent
across properties specification
Const VBSERR_redefDefault  = 1052    ' Cannot have multiple default
property/method in a Class
```

```
Const VBSERR_noArgs        = 1053    ' Class initialize or terminate do not have
arguments
Const VBSERR_doArg         = 1054    ' Property set or let must have at least one
argument
Const VBSERR_badNext       = 1055    ' Unexpected 'Next'
Const VBSERR_badDefault    = 1056    ' 'Default' can be specified only on
'Property' or 'Function' or 'Sub'
Const VBSERR_illegalDefault= 1057    ' 'Default' specification must also specify
'Public'
Const VBSERR_defaultOnGet  = 1058    ' 'Default' specification can only be on
Property Get
```

Appendix B: Reference Error Codes for ADSI 2.5

ADSI Error Code	LDAP message	Win32 message	Description
0L	LDAP_SUCCESS	NO_ERROR	Operation succeeded.
0x80070005L	LDAP_INSUFFICIENT_RIGHTS	ERROR_ACCESS_DENIED	The user has insufficient access right.
0x80070008L	LDAP_NO_MEMORY	ERROR_NOT_ENOUGH_MEMORY	The system is out of memory.
0x8007001fL	LDAP_OTHER	ERROR_GEN_FAILURE	Unknown error occurred.
0x800700eaL	LDAP_PARTIAL_RESULTS	ERROR_MORE_DATA	Partial results and referrals received.
0x800700eaL	LDAP_MORE_RESULTS_TO_RETURN	ERROR_MORE_DATA	More results are to be returned.
0x800704c7L	LDAP_USER_CANCELLED	ERROR_CANCELLED	The user has cancelled the operation.
0x800704c9L	LDAP_CONNECT_ERROR	ERROR_CONNECTION_REFUSED	Cannot establish the connection.
0x8007052eL	LDAP_INVALID_CREDENTIALS	ERROR_LOGON_FAILURE	The supplied credential is invalid.
0x800705b4L	LDAP_TIMEOUT	ERROR_TIMEOUT	The search was timed out.
0x80071392L	LDAP_ALREADY_EXISTS	ERROR_OBJECT_ALREADY_EXISTS	The object already exists.
0x8007200aL	LDAP_NO_SUCH_ATTRIBUTE	ERROR_DS_NO_ATTRIBUTE_OR_VALUE	Requested attribute does not exist.
0x8007200bL	LDAP_INVALID_SYNTAX	ERROR_DS_INVALID_ATTRIBUTE_SYNTAX	The syntax is invalid.
0x8007200cL	LDAP_UNDEFINED_TYPE	ERROR_DS_ATTRIBUTE_TYPE_UNDEFINED	Type is not defined.
0x8007200dL	LDAP_ATTRIBUTE_OR_VALUE_EXISTS	ERROR_DS_ATTRIBUTE_OR_VALUE_EXISTS	The attribute exists or the value has been assigned.
0x8007200eL	LDAP_BUSY	ERROR_DS_BUSY	The server is busy.
0x8007200fL	LDAP_UNAVAILABLE	ERROR_DS_UNAVAILABLE	The server is not available.
0x80072014L	LDAP_OBJECT_CLASS_VIOLATION	ERROR_DS_OBJ_CLASS_VIOLATION	There was an object class violation.
0x80072015L	LDAP_NOT_ALLOWED_ON_NONLEAF	ERROR_DS_CANT_ON_NON_LEAF	Operation is not allowed on a non leaf object.
0x80072016L	LDAP_NOT_ALLOWED_ON_RDN	ERROR_DS_CANT_ON_RDN	Operation is not allowed on RDN.
0x80072017L	LDAP_NO_OBJECT_CLASS_MODS	ERROR_DS_CANT_MOD_OBJ_CLASS	Cannot modify object class.

ADSI Error Code	LDAP message	Win32 message	Description
0x80072020L	LDAP_OPERATIONS_ERROR	ERROR_DS_OPERATIONS_ERROR	Operations error occurred.
0x80072021L	LDAP_PROTOCOL_ERROR	ERROR_DS_PROTOCOL_ERROR	Protocol error occurred.
0x80072022L	LDAP_TIMELIMIT_EXCEEDED	ERROR_DS_TIMELIMIT_EXCEEDED	Time limit has exceeded
0x80072023L	LDAP_SIZELIMIT_EXCEEDED	ERROR_DS_SIZELIMIT_EXCEEDED	Size limit has exceeded
0x80072024L	LDAP_ADMIN_LIMIT_EXCEEDED	ERROR_DS_ADMIN_LIMIT_EXCEEDED	Administration limit on the server has exceeded.
0x80072025L	LDAP_COMPARE_FALSE	ERROR_DS_COMPARE_FALSE	Compare yielded FALSE.
0x80072026L	LDAP_COMPARE_TRUE	ERROR_DS_COMPARE_TRUE	Compare yielded TRUE.
0x80072027L	LDAP_AUTH_METHOD_NOT_SUPPORTED	ERROR_DS_AUTH_METHOD_NOT_SUPPORTED	The authentication method is not supported.
0x80072028L	LDAP_STRONG_AUTH_REQUIRED	ERROR_DS_STRONG_AUTH_REQUIRED	Strong authentication is required.
0x80072029L	LDAP_INAPPROPRIATE_AUTH	ERROR_DS_INAPPROPRIATE_AUTH	Authentication is inappropriate.
0x8007202aL	LDAP_AUTH_UNKNOWN	ERROR_DS_AUTH_UNKNOWN	Unknown authentication error occurred.
0x8007202bL	LDAP_REFERRAL	ERROR_DS_REFERRAL	Referral
0x8007202cL	LDAP_UNAVAILABLE_CRIT_EXTENSION	ERROR_DS_UNAVAILABLE_CRIT_EXTENSION	Critical extension is unavailable.
0x8007202dL	LDAP_CONFIDENTIALITY_REQUIRED	ERROR_DS_CONFIDENTIALITY_REQUIRED	Confidentiality is required.
0x8007202eL	LDAP_INAPPROPRIATE_MATCHING	ERROR_DS_INAPPROPRIATE_MATCHING	There was an inappropriate matching.
0x8007202fL	LDAP_CONSTRAINT_VIOLATION	ERROR_DS_CONSTRAINT_VIOLATION	There was a constrain violation.
0x80072030L	LDAP_NO_SUCH_OBJECT	ERROR_DS_NO_SUCH_OBJECT	Object does not exist.
0x80072031L	LDAP_ALIAS_PROBLEM	ERROR_DS_ALIAS_PROBLEM	The alias is invalid.
0x80072032L	LDAP_INVALID_DN_SYNTAX	ERROR_DS_INVALID_DN_SYNTAX	The distinguished name has an invalid syntax.
0x80072033L	LDAP_IS_LEAF	ERROR_DS_IS_LEAF	The object is a leaf.
0x80072034L	LDAP_ALIAS_DEREF_PROBLEM	ERROR_DS_ALIAS_DEREF_PROBLEM	Can not dereference the alias.
0x80072035L	LDAP_UNWILLING_TO_PERFORM	ERROR_DS_UNWILLING_TO_PERFORM	The server is unwilling to perform.
0x80072036L	LDAP_LOOP_DETECT	ERROR_DS_LOOP_DETECT	Loop was detected.
0x80072037L	LDAP_NAMING_VIOLATION	ERROR_DS_NAMING_VIOLATION	There was a naming violation.
0x80072038L	LDAP_RESULTS_TOO_LARGE	ERROR_DS_OBJECT_RESULTS_TOO_LARGE	Results returned are too large.
0x80072039L	LDAP_AFFECTS_MULTIPLE_DSAS	ERROR_DS_AFFECTS_MULTIPLE_DSAS	Multiple directory service agents are affected.
0x8007203aL	LDAP_SERVER_DOWN	ERROR_DS_SERVER_DOWN	Cannot contact the LDAP server.
0x8007203bL	LDAP_LOCAL_ERROR	ERROR_DS_LOCAL_ERROR	Local error occurred.

ADSI Error Code	LDAP message	Win32 message	Description
0x8007203cL	LDAP_ENCODING_ERROR	ERROR_DS_ENCODING_ERROR	Encoding error occurred.
0x8007203dL	LDAP_DECODING_ERROR	ERROR_DS_DECODING_ERROR	Decoding error occurred.
0x8007203eL	LDAP_FILTER_ERROR	ERROR_DS_FILTER_UNKNOWN	The search filter is bad.
0x8007203fL	LDAP_PARAM_ERROR	ERROR_DS_PARAM_ERROR	A bad parameter was passed to a routine.
0x80072040L	LDAP_NOT_SUPPORTED	ERROR_DS_NOT_SUPPORTED	The feature is not supported.
0x80072041L	LDAP_NO_RESULTS_RETURNED	ERROR_DS_NO_RESULTS_RETURNED	Results are not returned.
0x80072042L	LDAP_CONTROL_NOT_FOUND	ERROR_DS_CONTROL_NOT_FOUND	The control was not found.
0x80072043L	LDAP_CLIENT_LOOP	ERROR_DS_CLIENT_LOOP	Client loop was detected.
0x80072044L	LDAP_REFERRAL_LIMIT_EXCEEDED	ERROR_DS_REFERRAL_LIMIT_EXCEEDED	The referral limit has exceeded

Notes

Notes

Notes

Notes

Notes

Notes